Mr. Ramsey,

Listen carefully! We are a group of individuals that represent a small foreign fraction. We ~~do~~ respect your bussiness but not the country that it serves. At this time we have your daughter in our posession. She is safe and unharmed and if you want her to see 1997, you must follow our instructions to the letter.

You will withdraw $118,000.00 from your account. $100,000 will be in $100 bills and the remaining $18,000 in $20 bills. Make sure that you bring an adequate size attache to the bank. When you get home you will put the money in a brown paper bag. I will call you between 8 and 10 am tomorrow to instruct you on delivery. The delivery will be exhausting so I advise you to be rested. If we monitor you getting the money early, we might call you early to arrange an earlier delivery of the

money and handed earlier
~~delivery~~ pick-up of your daughter.
Any deviation of my instructions
will result in the immediate
execution of your daughter. You
will also be denied her remains
for proper burial. The two
gentlemen watching over your daughter
do particularly like you so I
advise you not to provoke them.
Speaking to anyone about your
situation, such as Police, F.B.I., etc.,
will result in your daughter being
beheaded. If we catch you talking
to a stray dog, she dies. If you
alert bank authorities, she dies.
If the money is in any way
marked or tampered with, she
dies. You will be scanned for
electronic devices and if any are
found, she dies. You can try to
deceive us but be warned that
we are familiar with law enforcement
countermeasures and tactics. You
stand a 99% chance of killing
your daughter if you try to out
smart us. Follow our instructions

and you stand a 100% chance
of getting her back. You and
your family are under constant
scrutiny as well as the authorities.
Don't try to grow a brain
John. You are not the only
fat cat around so don't think
that killing will be difficult
Don't underestimate us John.
Use that good southern common
sense of yours. It is up to
you now John!

Victory!

S.B.T.C

A Mother Gone Bad

A Mother Gone Bad

*The Hidden Confession
of JonBenét's Killer*

Andrew G. Hodges, M.D.

VILLAGE HOUSE PUBLISHERS
P.O. BOX 530312
BIRMINGHAM, ALABAMA 35253

Library of Congress Cataloging-in-Publication Data

Hodges, Andrew G.
A Mother Gone Bad
Summary: An analysis of the JonBenét Ramsey murder

1. True Crime 2. Psychology (Subconscious Mind) 3. Criminology 4. Psycholinguistics

Cover Photo: National Enquirer (Judith Phillips)

ISBN 0-9617255-1-6

Village House Publishers

Editorial (205) 328-4364
Sales & Marketing (800) 734-8188
For Consumer orders only: (888) 265-2732
Visit the author's website: http://www.aghodges.com

2nd Edition

Printed and bound in the USA

To my brother Greg
always generous, always encouraging

Table of Contents

ACKNOWLEDGMENTS

Writing a book is a process, and every step of the way there was someone who lightened my burden. Thanks to Joyce Farrell who saw the same light I did, and gave me a good push towards getting started and other ones along the way. Dale Short did, too, and added his fine editorial skills as did Norma McKittrick who took time she didn't have. Carolyn Marchant helped in so many ways, and was her usual generous self. With her administrative skills, Jane Sandford constantly gave me the time I needed to complete this book. Steve Pincus came along at the end to provide guidance and a steady hand. As always, I can never say enough about my wife Dorothy.

I owe a special debt of gratitude to Frank Coffman, Boulder resident and reporter, who knows the case as well as anyone outside of the law enforcement.

Thanks to you all.

Introduction

The day the investigation of the JonBenét Ramsey murder case changed hands—December 5, 1997—I found myself talking on the phone to Commander Mark Beckner of the Boulder Police Department, the new lead investigator.

My field is psychiatry, not criminal justice. But being the good detective that he is, Beckner had called in search of any clue that would help nail the murderer in this bizarre high-visibility case that continues to fascinate Americans and so many others around the world.

Beckner had learned of my work through a recently retired FBI agent. I had spoken to the agent about the psychological profile of the killer I had derived from studying the infamous "ransom" note found with JonBenét's body. As I told him, "I have decoded the confession hidden in the note—I know who the killer is."

The FBI agent had been more than a little skeptical of my claims before reading my profile, but he came away convinced—so convinced that he immediately called Beckner.

My fascination with the case stems from my work in psychiatry, which deals with the subliminal mind and its amazing ability to deeply observe reality and its "hidden" communications that tell what it sees. A recent scientific breakthrough reveals that the subliminal or "deeper" mind is far more complex and powerful than we ever suspected, and that through our speech, writing, and actions, the deeper mind insists on telling its unconscious truth, albeit in disguised *(encoded)* ways, particularly at times of fear and other great emotional stress.

I'm NOT referring to accidental literal confessions or to simply catching someone in a lie, but rather to a dual, between-the-lines message that can be decoded with amazing accuracy by anyone who has learned how to consistently break the "code" of the deeper mind.

I have used this new way of listening and decoding with patients every day for the last twenty-five years in my clinical practice. Patients send me one message—the conscious, or superficial, truth—while their more observant deeper mind is often saying the exact opposite. Inevitably the patient's deeper mind is far more perceptive and can be used to obtain valuable information of which the patient's conscious mind is not aware.

Now we can apply this recent clinical breakthrough to the subliminal mind to what FBI specialists refer to as "psycholinguistics"—reading communication between the lines for psychological clues. Thus, we now have a new and better way of doing psycholinguistics.

During the O.J. Simpson trial, I used this decoding technique to analyze Simpson's written and spoken communications. I was overwhelmed by the detail in which he revealed a secret story. In hidden but unmistakable ways, he confessed to his crimes.

I eagerly applied the same technique to the so-called ransom note left at the scene of JonBenét's murder. Unlike the Simpson case, this time I had the advantage of knowing that the note was obviously a communication from someone who was involved in the murder. Again, I was not disappointed. I still remember distinctly the rush of wonder and emotion I experienced the day the killer's identity leaped out of the words and brought the entire scenario into crystal-clear focus.

♦ ♦ ♦

Beckner and I had played several days of phone tag before we hooked up for a late-afternoon conference call. I didn't waste any time with preliminaries but went straight to the heart of my findings.

I took Beckner to the climax of the note and then worked my way back, explaining how I had arrived at my conclusions. The detective was a good listener: patient, polite, and seemingly open-minded. For nearly an hour he let me do virtually all the talking.

It was clear to me that Beckner had never heard anything like the decoding process. I was not surprised because I had seen comments from FBI profilers and other investigators that revealed they were missing crucial segments of the killer's deeper message hidden in the ransom note.

Beckner, as I expected, remained noncommittal for the most part, but thanked me for my time and asked to see my written report.

I have continued to study the ransom note as well as other documents such as the Ramsey family Christmas letters from 1995, 1996, and 1997—all of which Patsy wrote. I continue to decode clues that reinforce the confession I discovered in the ransom note, the confession of a mother gone bad.

In the following chapters, I will help you read between the lines of the ransom note and decode the hidden confession word by word. You will read what the killer's deeper mind is saying. You will hear the killer's confession in her own words.

FOREWORD

Let me say it as strongly as I can: I'm convinced that the following chapters are not just another conventional psychological profile of a suspected killer, but rather the most advanced and accurate one that we can possibly have because it comes entirely from the killer's own words. I'm only the reporter: an interpreter repeating what one part of the killer's mind is saying to the other—and to anyone who will listen.

To my knowledge, this is the first time that one of the most major advances in the history of psychology has been applied to studying criminal behavior and communication. I believe that it gives a foretaste of the way criminal investigations will be done in the 21st century.

Mr. Ramsey,

Listen carefully! We are a group of individuals that represent a small foreign faction. We ~~do~~ respect your bussiness but not the country that it serves. At this time we have your daughter in our posession. She and if you want you must fol the letter.

You wi From your ac in $130 bill $18,000 in that you attache get home in a bri call you tomorr The deli I advise we ma early arrange

money and hence d earlier ~~delivery~~ pick-up of your daughter. my deviation of my instructions will result in the immediate execution of your daughter. You will also be dénied her remains for proper burial. The two gon-tlemen watching over your daughter do particularly like you So I advise you not t Speakin situatio will n beheadd to a sy dert If the marked dies. electronic found, she deceive u we are f countermeas stand a your daught smart us

and you stand a 100% chance of getting her back. You and your family are under constant scrutiny as well as the authorities. Don't try to grow a brain John. You are not the only fat cat around so don't think that killing will be difficult Don't underestimate us John. Use that good southern common sense of yours. It is up to you now John!

Victory!
S.B.T.C

Chapter One
Opportunity: JonBenét's Killer Leaves Two Letters

W hen the alleged ransom note was first published nine months after JonBenét's murder, I began studying it as a hobby. Intrigued by the awesome ability of the human mind, I knew there would be some clues in the note, and I wanted to see how far my expertise in reading between the lines would take me.

As usual, insight unfolded slowly. But bit by bit, another story began to emerge within the note. A story within the story—actually several stories within *the story*. I had begun to develop a picture of JonBenét's murderer, but the puzzle was a long way from being completed until the day I came across the key "story." It was exactly like finding the center piece in a jigsaw puzzle that immediately causes all the other pieces to fall in place.

From that moment on, everything came together. I could look back at the parts of the note I had already "decoded"—the old pieces of the puzzle—and see them in a much deeper way, see how they all tied together. Of course the parts of the note I hadn't yet spent time on—the new pieces—were much easier to decipher because now I had an anchor.

Another fascinating thing about the human mind is that one idea can have multiple messages, just as you can see something new in a picture every time you really look at it. This means that even though I could see who JonBenét's killer is and why she had killed, I still continued to learn something new every time I looked at the note. I knew the killer's mind was phenomenally more capable than she realized and more capable than even the experts working on the note realize. Only recently have we learned that the human mind has at least a thousand times more ability than anyone, even most professionals, have ever imagined.[1]

First, I began to see that the note itself pointed toward a woman killer. Gradually I saw that this woman had certain personality traits. Eventually, the note pointed specifically toward one woman—Patsy Ramsey. Finally the note told me why Patsy did it—pointing to one central motive but making plain there were other secondary motives.

The note reveals how many people were involved in JonBenét's murder, strongly hints at specifically what happened the night of the murder, tells what kind of cover-up to expect, and even predicts what the final outcome will be.

The note also enables us to look at Patsy's communications before

---

[1] With his radical breakthrough to subliminal perception and communication, New York psychiatrist Robert Langs has developed a new and deeper way of understanding human communication. Langs's work takes psychoanalysis to an entirely new level.

and after the murder in a new light, to examine them for deeper messages. Her 1997 "Ramsey Christmas message" fits hand in glove with the ransom note. The Ramsey Christmas letters for the two years *prior* to the murder contain striking similarities. In all of these documents, Patsy Ramsey left invaluable secret messages that continue to reveal her guilt.

UNBELIEVABLY FRESH EVIDENCE

A great deal of despair currently surrounds the JonBenét murder case: a bungled investigation, contaminated evidence, and political underpinnings, to mention only a few of the complications. Investigators worry that there's no possibility of turning up new evidence at this late date, more than a year after the murder, and as a result the case is already lost.

Yet there's great cause for hope that the killer will be identified—and convicted—because the ransom note contains *the one piece of evidence completely uncontaminated by the police. It provides the freshest evidence possible*—overlooked but incredibly revealing messages, a hidden confession straight from the mind of the killer, words spoken by the killer's deeper mind, the part that always tells the truth.

Renowned ex-FBI profiler Robert Ressler has reminded us that the single most valuable evidence we have in the JonBenét case is the ransom note. We have found the Rosetta stone the police are looking for. We must simply go back and mine the note for the gold it contains.

OUR FANTASTIC MIND

We have all heard about the deeper mind: intuition, the untapped potential of "the other 90 percent of our mind," dreaming about solutions to problems, subliminal advertising, police hypnotizing witnesses to obtain more information, Freudian slips, and psychoanalysis. Add to these a superficial understanding of "right and left brain" communication, and we will be prepared to read the ransom note in a new way, to read between the lines, to read the killer's confession.

We think of left-brain messages as conscious, literal, straightforward communications. Right-brain messages are disguised and symbolic, based on intuition. The human mind can and often does communicate two messages at the same time—one obvious, the other hidden. Each part of the mind—in my model the conscious/left brain and the subliminal/right brain—tells what it sees from its perspective. Our deeper mind is a thousand times quicker and more perceptive, and it picks up on things that our conscious mind misses. (This means that unbeknownst to her, Patsy Ramsey's subliminal mind was observing the entire murder, and the events that led up to it and after it, with far more accuracy and in more detail than her conscious mind.)

The deeper mind creates its own language and can send incredibly clear messages even though they are disguised. If this sounds strange, think about *body language*. The idea is that the deeper mind actually guides the body to convey certain messages. Think also about *lie detector tests*. No matter how much someone wants to get away with lying, something deep inside them outside of their conscious control causes their pulse rate, their breathing rate, etc., to change. *Voice detectors* work in similar ways.

Our mind works on two levels at the very same time, and what we have learned in the recent breakthrough studies with the subliminal mind is that this deeper mind, which secretly guides our thoughts and body, is brilliant beyond belief. We have discovered what I call the deeper intelligence that sees everything—and tells us about it. The following example from everyday life illustrates how the deeper intelligence works.

A mother dreamed that she was walking through a forest of poison ivy with her teenage son. When she woke up, she asked herself what poison ivy could possibly mean to her. Suddenly she thought of how poison ivy reminded her of marijuana plants, and then she realized that her deeper mind was picking up that her son was involved in drugs *(which indeed was the case)*. Her deeper intelligence enabled her to get help for her son. This is an example of two-level communication. On one level the dream was about poison ivy, on another it was about drugs.

The mind works the same way in every day waking life, and so we will find two messages in the ransom note. The killer using her left brain writes a note designed to cover up the murder, but her right brain tells the truth. The killer's deeper intelligence is secretly guiding her every thought—even when she is trying to lie to us. *Without realizing it, the killer is profiling herself at the exact moment of the crime. If we decode the killer's right-brain message hidden in the ransom note, we will hear a confession/profile from the killer's own lips.*

STUDYING THE EVIDENCE

The byword of criminal profilers is to study the crime scene— because the killer will leave clues. *In the JonBenét Ramsey case, we have a rare occurrence—the killer left her actual thoughts that occurred immediately after the murder. She left behind two types of thoughts: Her superficial thoughts designed to conceal, and her deeper thoughts that reveal her personal feelings about the murder.* Of course these deeper thoughts are disguised in the ransom note, but if we read between the lines we will clearly see a deeper train of thought. In essence, we have not one, but two notes.

When I have verbatim communication, which is at the heart of this case, I am in my element. As an expert in reading between the lines, I am no different from a detective who enters a crime scene and says, "Don't move a thing. Don't touch anything." His first function is to observe as much as humanly possible about the scene, gleaning every possible clue, even those so seemingly ordinary or minuscule that an untrained person might overlook them altogether. That's how I read the ransom note: I try not to miss anything. I look at every letter of the handwriting, every misspelling, every correction, and most of all at every word in the context of what we know about the deeper mind— something far beyond typical handwriting analysis.

I look at each word for two messages, not one. It's the second message, the encoded message, that reveals Patsy Ramsey's deeper intelligence and tells the real story.

Decoding the ransom note reveals that it is clearly a ploy to throw the police off the trail, but the ploy backfires and reveals the mind of the killer. Patsy Ramsey's encoded message also points to John Ramsey's involvement in the murder.

Why would two people as successful and fortunate as Patsy and John Ramsey carry out such a murder? The answer will become clear when we look closely at the note and at their lives. We will get an up-close look at the human heart: its capacity for good or evil and for hiding pain. We will see how good parents can go bad, an idea reflected in one of the great ironies of the JonBenét case: Patsy Ramsey played on a woman's softball team called "**Moms Gone Bad**."

THE HIDDEN CONFESSION IN THE
RANSOM NOTE REVEALS:

- the killer accidentally left two ransom notes.

- the second ransom note is hidden in the first.

- the hidden note is the key to solving the crime.

- the killer is a woman.

- the woman has certain personality traits.

- the woman is Patsy Ramsey.

- John Ramsey participated in the murder.

Chapter Two
The Ransom Note: Reading Between the Lines

"Mr. Ramsey,
*   Listen carefully! We are a group of individuals that repre-*
sent a small foreign faction."

When *Newsweek* magazine reprinted the ransom note, it head-lined one part of the article "Ransom note, or Red Herring?" But they overlooked another possibility: "Ransom note, or Confession?" The killer or killers had just taken the life of a young girl, a very special one. A human being—even a psychopath—however deviant or cold-hearted simply cannot kill someone without feeling significant guilt deep down. Accordingly, we find in the note guilt and, eventually, two of the coldest hearts we could ever imagine. We also find several different confessions.

Newsweek printed the note in full along with an article titled "A Case Forever Unraveling." The writer and layout editor were asking for help in salvaging this case by printing the note verbatim. Consciously, and even more so deep down, they knew that this note contained invaluable clues. Some law enforcement officials initially resisted the publication of the note, but it has turned out to be to their advantage.

In the note *the killer herself is secretly speaking to law enforcement* and provides invaluable counsel on how to apprehend her—just as serial killers leave clues in order to be stopped.

Reading between the lines of the note, we find a disguised story telling us who wrote the ransom note and who the killer is. *Ultimately, just as tributaries become one river, everything builds to one central part of the note that has Patsy Ramsey's unmistakable signature on it.* Everything in her life and in the note uniquely fits with this central story, so much so that the note cannot be anyone's but hers. This is where she supplies the primary motive behind her horrible deed, although there are other strong hints throughout the note.

It is helpful to know a few background facts in order to fully appreciate the note. First, John Ramsey found JonBenét's body in a basement room in his own home after the police failed to find it. He immediately moved the body upstairs.

The police noticed a broken window downstairs at the time of the investigation; John said he had broken the window months earlier. The window was repaired a few days later after the police left the house, but

John apparently broke it again before an interview with Diane Sawyer to make it appear on camera that the old broken window hadn't been fixed. All of this indicates that when John Ramsey is pressured he may resort to deception.

Second, it was Patsy who found the ransom note. Later that morning, a "practice note" was found in the back of the same notepad (Patsy's) on which the ransom note was written. It is not clear whether the police discovered the practice note on their own or if John inadvertently gave it to them when they asked for a sample of Patsy's handwriting. Either way, it was a hidden confession by both Patsy and John. In summary, the father found the body, the mother found the note.

Oddly the note is addressed to *Mr.* Ramsey, not to Mr. and Mrs. Ramsey. The killer never appeals to the mother, someone who logically would pressure her husband to get the demanded money quickly. Furthermore in the whole note there's *no reference whatsoever* to the mother—no warning to her not to call the police, no threats warning her not to act impulsively.

If the killer knew even the most elemental facts about John and Patsy Ramsey, it would have been clear that *Patsy* was the more impulsive, emotional parent, the one most prone to panic, while John was the rational, coolheaded one who stayed in control. But there's not a single sentence warning John to keep his wife under control if they wanted to see their daughter alive again.

I think it's plain that the killer was trying to steer attention away from Patsy. *(The practice ransom note—addressed to both "Mr. and Mrs. Ramsey"—confirms this.)* At the same time, by leaving out "Mrs. Ramsey," the killer could be saying that a big part of the problem is Patsy's feeling that she is left out of important matters.

Communication from the right brain can have several meanings at any one time. *(Later, we will see one more important meaning to leaving out "Mrs. Ramsey" that links to the central story we're waiting on.)* In the very first line of the note, in the simple greeting, in this initial brief glimpse into the mind of the killer, we see her left brain (conscious mind) attempting to conceal her identity and her right brain (subliminal mind) attempting to reveal it.

VALUABLE CLUES FROM THE BEGINNING

Following the greeting, the first sentence—arranged neatly and indented in an orderly fashion—is **"Listen carefully!"** This shows the killer's need for order and neatness, and it is evidence of an exceptionally controlling nature. This demanding tone is repeated throughout the note, and it covers up an inordinate fear of not having control.

"Listen carefully" also tells us to pay particular attention to the note—to look for the deeper meaning behind the words and between the lines. Throughout the ransom note (and other letters written by both Patsy and John) we will see that *key words such as "listen" or "school" or "hence" (meaning conclusion)—all of which convey the idea of learning and communication—are* **"message markers"** *from the deeper mind, tip-offs telling us to pay particular attention to what immediately follows. The fact that the killer does this at the very beginning of the ransom note is a major clue, again from the killer's subliminal mind, that the entire note contains powerful hidden messages.*

The first sentence ends with an exclamation point. This punctuation mark occurs three times—once at the very beginning of the note and twice at the very end.

What comes next is "We are a group of individuals that represent a small foreign faction." This simple sentence is extremely revealing and contains one of the most vivid descriptions (a small foreign faction) in the entire note. "We" established that more than one person is involved in the murder. Just five words into the note, the killer cannot contain herself: The guilt is so great she must share it.

The use of the phrase "a group of individuals" may be a tip-off that if the group is ever caught, some individuals might be more inclined to confess than others. It might mean that, because they are individuals, one might be more guilt-ridden or have different culpability.

Major Clue: A Small Foreign Faction

"... *that represent a small foreign faction.*" The calculated *(left-brain)* aspect of the message is designed to disguise the identity of the killers, making them appear to be part of some established terrorist organization—a common ruse in ransom notes. But at the same time, the killer's right brain takes another opportunity to tell us more about who's really behind this crime: *a small foreign faction.*

First, the killer says that the group is small, and then she describes the group as a *foreign* faction, indicating that a hidden secret part of both parents killed JonBenét *(a "small foreign—French" entity herself).*

Even the way the handwriting forms the word *faction* reflects this "foreignness" in the killer, the failure to understand a part of herself. The word is difficult to read. It's compressed with a very small "c" in faction, as though the "c" is small and difficult to comprehend, just like the "secret" part of the killers. (The way the word is written offers impressive evidence for this deeper intelligence, which not only controls our thoughts but also our motor skills.)

"A foreign faction" is a beautifully symbolic description of what drove Patsy and John Ramsey to do what they did—*a foreign part of themselves* that appeared small but eventually erupted into a horrible catastrophic act, exactly like a terrorist group erupting within what appears to be a civilized country.

With the emotional metaphor "foreign faction," the killer is telling us that she and her accomplice are in over their heads and very frightened of the outcome. It certainly doesn't excuse their actions, but it helps us appreciate how Patsy and John Ramsey really are controlled by forces in themselves they haven't yet understood. *(One of the central and most innate drives of the deeper intelligence is to help us understand ourselves—and as perverse as it might seem, this whole ransom letter represents for the killer an effort to gain that self-understanding.)*

The killer is trying to establish a revenge motive by a group of terrorists. Ignore the cover-up but stay with the idea of revenge—revenge was one of Patsy Ramsey's major motives for several different reasons.

TWO OF SEVEN IMPORTANT SLIPS OF THE PEN

"We (don't) respect your bussiness [sic] but not the country that it serves."

Now we come to a very significant slip of the pen, and we need to pay special attention because it's one of seven times in the note where the killer's deeper, right brain, mind, most visibly overrides the left brain's cover-up plan.

"We *(don't)* respect your *bussiness* but not the country that it serves." Actually this sentence contains two slips—the word "don't," which is crossed out, and the misspelling of the word "business." The first slip is obvious: For some reason the killer doesn't respect John Ramsey's business and is confessing to the fact. *The killer is eager to maintain an image of someone who's not attacking John Ramsey, but she can't help herself.* Patsy may be saying that deep down she feels left out—specifically in comparison to her husband who has had such remarkable success in business.

THE KILLER IS A WOMAN

Shift to the word "bussiness" and ask yourself what it reminds you of. A quick word association leads to "buss ... bustle ... bust."

A "buss" is a kiss. The writer has changed John Ramsey's beloved successful business and career into "kissiness," which changes him from an aggressive male to a soft feminine character. This is consistent with the earlier slip-up in the same sentence that in essence said, "We don't respect your business."

The same idea continues with "bustle." The dictionary defines bustle as "a pad or frame formerly worn to swell out the fullness at the back of a woman's skirt." Women don't wear bustles anymore, but clearly it's a feminine image. The closest thing to it is a Las Vegas showgirl who wears a feather boa attached to her backside, similar to a Playboy Bunny wearing a bunny tail, although far more prominent.

A woman who wore a bustle might be saying, "I want to stand out and be noticed." She might also be saying, "Look—I feel vulnerable as a woman, and I need to find some way of making myself stronger, some way of bolstering my femininity." In other words, she is creating a sort of "masculine femininity" since masculinity is traditionally equated in her mind with power.

If we had any questions about the meaning of the slip-up "bussiness", the last option "bust" removes all doubts. Like buss and bustle, bust is a very feminine word. And is not a prominent bust similar to the idea of a bustle—often used for power, to get certain women where they want to go? Many times it has nothing to do with sex. Bust, whether used to refer to a woman or a statue, contains the same idea—prominence and power.

Some commentators have surmised that the killer misspelled "business," to appear uneducated. If that was the case, the killer's deeper motive would still be the same as she could have misspelled it in other ways. But I doubt she intentionally misspelled it because *natural slips are so characteristic of Patsy Ramsey.*

A Picture Worth a Thousand Words

Two photographs cut to the heart of the Ramsey family story. First is a picture of a young Patsy Ramsey in 1977 wearing a seductive, Las Vegas-showgirl outfit with a "bustle" in the back—a huge, floor-length feather boa coming off her backside. The second is the May 1996 photograph of her daughter JonBenét at the age of six—in an identical showgirl outfit, "bustle" and all.

Those two pictures make it clear that Patsy Ramsey was merging with her daughter, living out her sexual fantasies through her daughter. But don't mistake the motive: Such merging is not about sex or intimacy—it is secretly about *power*, which is so often the case when sex is used in an inappropriate way.

At the core of Patsy Ramsey's view of sex, and her beauty-pageant mentality, is a search for power. It is a subconscious attempt to be male-like since she believed (and was taught) men had the power. In actuality, Patsy was indifferent about sex. Clearly she used her sexuality for other purposes.

The photographs of Patsy in her showgirl costume show obvious phallic symbols—the huge boa, the massive headdress, and a white dove, prominently displayed with wings outspread on her left wrist as she holds her left arm straight out. We begin to get a sense of what fueled her obsession with winning beauty contests—and later her obsession with JonBenét's winning them at an early age. When Patsy could no longer be a beauty queen, she found a way to compete vicariously—through JonBenét.

JonBenét, pageant costume, 1996 (Zuma)

Patsy Ramsey, circa 1977 (The Globe)

"But not the country it serves."

Once again the killer elaborates on the terrorists' motives—and at the same time elaborates on the real motives. "The country it serves" refers to John's business connection to Lockheed-Martin, which served the military. Supposedly the foreign faction has something against the United States but the idea of the military and serving your country has a soldierly masculine ring to it. Some people think the same idea is repeated in the closing of the letter (S.B.T.C.), which may refer to John Ramsey serving his country at Subic Bay Training Center in the Philippines where he was stationed as a new pilot. Without question the killer portrays John as having military connections—present and maybe past.

In summary the deeper message here is that someone resents the United States and, more subtly, the military and men in general (who are usually equated with the military). This is along the same lines as the slam "bussiness." Indirectly the killer is very subtly saying, "I don't respect men—businessmen or soldiers."

We can see why Patsy Ramsey might have resented men. If we stay with the idea of "country" as masculine and read the sentence as she wrote it, including the slip-up, the phrase becomes "but not the country (male) the 'bussiness' (female) serves." In a word, Patsy is telling us that as a woman she's tired of serving John, the man. What wife of a CEO hasn't felt that at times, particularly a trophy wife? (When we discuss the central part of the note, we will discover that Patsy had a stronger reason to resent serving John Ramsey.)

There is yet another way of looking at the same idea. If you ignore the slip-up "bussiness," the killer is saying that she respects John Ramsey's smaller interests (his business) but not his larger interests—his patriotism, his passion. She wants to keep him small, to put him down.

You can also look at "country" from another important perspective: Country hints at a feminine identity, as does the idea of serving. The Statue of Liberty—perhaps as much a symbol of America as the flag—is both feminine and representative of the Land of Liberty, of the Mother Country, even of Mother Earth. Patsy Ramsey may be saying that she also has very mixed feelings about women as well, that in the back of her mind lurks deep-seated resentment toward certain women, toward the fact *she* is a woman, toward serving womanhood.

One last way of reading "country" along feminine lines is that Patsy could also be saying that she resents the way John Ramsey serves her (his business served the country). Not only does Patsy serve John, but there may have been many moments in their marriage where he has served her, where she was in control. (Patsy possesses John and his money.) And there has been one major area where Patsy controlled John that she would have later deeply regretted. On a deep level, this could cause her to also see him as also weak and "feminine," which would also explain why she feminized his beloved "bussiness."

These probable meanings of this sentence may at first glance seem excessive and unrelated. In fact the opposite is the case. This wide variety of meanings shows the vast capability of the mind to give different slants on the same issue. Patsy Ramsey has many reasons to see men as lording power over women and vice versa. She has many reasons to resent men and to resent being a woman. And both Patsy and John have their own reasons for coming up with the sham of hating a country and those who serve it—they both hate being controlled—having to serve—and, indeed, they were in bondage.

Also we can see hints of how the cover-up might have begun with John suggesting to Patsy, "Write the note to me and leave you out of it." Trying to take her out of the limelight, however, he puts her in it. Even though John Ramsey may have made a few suggestions, it's still Patsy Ramsey's note even as she weaves John's ideas into her continued train of thought about putting men down—particularly underscored by her two key slip-ups in this part of the letter: "*don't* respect your *bussiness.*"

The Ramseys could have concocted another key part of the cover-up, the terrorist scenario, because of John's two military connections and because the very idea of a major foreign enemy that had terrorized United States forces was directly linked to JonBenét's death. Patsy's broken artist's brush used to make the garrote had "Korea" stamped on the handle. Korea itself symbolizes the divided Ramseys: a good pro-U.S. side and a destructive, controlling anti-U.S. side. Surely they both would have seen that word, and it would have struck a powerful chord in them as the killer tightened the garrote around JonBenét's little neck. *In a subtle way by introducing "foreign* (faction)*," Patsy links the ransom note to the crime scene something she will do again.*

"At this time we have your daughter in our posession [sic]."
We're only into the first four sentences of the note, but we begin to see even more clearly a powerful motive operating deep within the killer. She has been threatened by something concerning her femininity and what it represents to her, and this threat involved JonBenét.

"*At* this time we have your daughter in *our* posession." The two italicized words stand out because of their illegibility. For some reason the killer had a hard time writing "at" and the letters run together—as though the killer is saying that something is wrong with "at this time." It is as if "at this time" doesn't exist—which, in fact, was the case. JonBenét was already dead, and the killer didn't actually "have" her because she was gone.

The word "our" is poorly written and extremely small, particularly in comparison to "your" three words earlier. Minimizing and obscuring the word "our" may be the killer's way of saying, "I'm having a real hard time just saying that 'I' had something to do with this murder. I can talk about 'you' all day long, but not about 'me' or 'our.' " Patsy also may have minimized "our" to confess that it was really her fault—not "ours"—that JonBenét was dead.

"Posession"—A Third Major Slip-up

Even more striking is the choice of the word "posession." And it is *no accident the killer misspelled this word because it is one of the words in the note that tells the whole story in a nutshell.*

First of all it is a picture of a little girl who was trapped, a little girl who was someone else's *possession.* We will come to see just how much JonBenét was Patsy's possession. And we will see that John Ramsey said the same thing about JonBenét being a possession, an object, in a letter he wrote.

Judith Phillips, a family friend and photographer, recalls a comment Patsy Ramsey's mother, Nedra Paugh, once made. When Phillips asked Nedra what would happen if some day JonBenét decided she didn't want to do any more pageants, Nedra replied, "We (Patsy and her mother) say, 'You will do it.' "

Patsy's mother was speaking for Patsy and JonBenét as though they were both possessions and not people.

Is it possible that Patsy Ramsey has felt like someone's possession for a long time? Was she an abused child? Is this why she misspelled the word in the note, showing her contempt about being someone's possession too much of the time?

Nedra also reportedly said to others many times that JonBenét was her Miss America. Once again, JonBenét was *hers.* (But we can be sure she had said the same thing to Patsy as Patsy strove to be Miss America and fulfill *her mother's* dreams.)

The killer may be trying to deny that she is anyone's possession. This helps explain why she has such animosity, disguised as it is, toward John Ramsey—because, at times, she feels like his possession, his trophy wife. We begin to understand how much Patsy dislikes being in a serving role as she continues to hammer away at the idea. Along the same lines, she could have turned the tables on John and changed his "business" into her "bussiness" in order to possess him just like she feels possessed.

Most likely the killer misspelled the word "**pose**ssion" for several reasons. She could be drawing our attention to the fact that the whole note was a pose. Later we see Patsy Ramsey use the word "pose" in another key story, and, ultimately, we will see how it is one word that sums up who the Ramseys are right now—masters of the pose. If we can see through their pretense, we find deceit and terror—and two people who have been on the run a long time.

There is one last reason Patsy and John are holding a pose. *Posse*ssion implies **"posse"** and Patsy Ramsey knew that a posse was after her, something she would just as soon forget.

Last, it is ***interesting that in the two words the killer misspells, she adds an "s" in "bussiness" and leaves one out in "posession."*** This matches Patsy's style of trying to add something like a "bustle" to make up for a deficiency. Trying to overcome her inadequacy with an excessive show of power. That is the bottom line of this murder, revealed in two simple errors. The central part of the ransom note will take us to the heart of her deficiency. And once again there is a very subtle hint that it has to do with her femininity as an "s" is the closest letter to the hourglass shape of a woman.

In summary, three slip-ups—"don't respect," "bussiness," and "posession"—begin to tell a remarkable story. The fact that they occur so close together in the note tells us how strongly they are linked to each other. In addition, the fact that one of the slips "don't" (respect) was blacked out reveals that this was a chaotic moment for Patsy Ramsey—that she had great difficulty expressing her anger, and when she did she immediately attempted to cover it up.

IN THE GREETING AND THE FIRST TWO SENTENCES OF THE RANSOM NOTE, THE KILLER REVEALS:

• she needs order and neatness.

• she has an exceptionally controlling nature.

• a part of her that she doesn't understand caused her to kill JonBenét.

• she does not respect John Ramsey and his business.

• she feels left out in comparison to his success and resents being his possession

• she uses sexuality to gain power.

• she resents men and certain women.

• she resents John when he serves her as it makes him weak and "feminine."

• something she deeply fears is entrapping her.

Chapter Three
Money, Attaché, and Delivery

*"She is safe and **un harmed** and if you want her to see
1997, you must follow our instructions to the letter."*

O nce again two words stand out, and they tell us something has
happened to JonBenét. "Safe" is hard to make out with the "a"
obscured as though the killer is telling us she's lying. "Un
harmed" has a clear space between "un" and "harmed" as though they
are two different words and not connected. In other words, JonBenét
really was harmed.

The killer continues the sham, threatening the parents with the idea
that *JonBenét will not see the future—1997*—unless they follow instructions precisely.

But since the entire note is a ploy, the message is really about the
killer herself. The killer is saying that JonBenét's death (since it has
already occurred) had to do with the killer's being uncertain about the
future, with the killer feeling that she had to walk a tightrope and perform perfectly or she wouldn't live. For the first time, Patsy more
overtly begins to reveal the motive for the murder. *(The deeper mind
also communicates by linkages, saying, "Pay attention, these ideas of
death, uncertainty about the future, and having to be perfect are connected
and they reveal the motive.")*

Murderers virtually always inflict on the victim a trauma that has
wounded and still deeply wounds them. They re-create their terror in
the victim. When someone reenacts the past, either on someone else or
themselves, psychiatrists call it "repetition-compulsion."

Here, at the end of the very first paragraph in the note, Patsy conveys the desperate message "Be perfect or someone dies." We can
either read these words as simply a ploy—or as a confession: Patsy
feels this pressure herself.

A CLUE FROM THE KILLER: LISTEN TO THE DEEPER INTELLIGENCE

"... you must follow our instructions to the letter." Look at this sentence as a whole and read it in light of the fact that the killer has a deeper
intelligence that, without her knowledge, is speaking. Read it as if this part of
Patsy's mind is saying, "Listen for my hidden instructions in the letter—clues
that I have given—if you want to see the truth about what really happened to
JonBenét, if you want her to speak from the grave."

(Our deeper mind always has a clear awareness of its own

existence. Often at crucial moments in therapy when a patient's deeper mind solves a dilemma or gives clear guidance, the patient will talk about specialized radar, phenomenal computers, learning foreign languages, and the like. We will see the murderer do the same thing by referring to electronic equipment with special sensory devices. Deep down, Patsy knows that a part of her mind is telling the truth.)

The reference to paying incredibly close attention—"to the letter"—is a striking image. This is one of two sentences that, taken as a whole, seem undisguised when we give them a second look. This is also the only time the word "letter" is used. Again, anytime a word containing a clear reference to a message, to a reason, or to learning appears, it is a clue to "listen particularly closely"—it is a *message marker*.

This kind of clue is used six places in the ransom note, and each time we find vital information. In this particular sentence, we find two message markers *("instructions" and "letter")* that contain the ideas of both learning and message— this is a particularly important sentence.

This sentence reveals that the killer knows that there are "hidden instructions" in the note, instructions that give her away. In the back of her mind, Patsy knows that if the ransom note is examined closely for clues, she will be revealed. *(Later Patsy tells us how to catch her.)*

MONEY AND PRESSURE

"You will withdraw $118,000.00 from your account. $100,000 will be in $100 bills and the remaining $18,000 in $20 bills."

Once again the tone of voice is very precise and controlling. The killer is trying to inflict this suffocating rigidity and control on someone else (exemplified in using a decimal and two zeroes). *On the heels of the two message markers in the previous sentence, we would expect the killer to give some tremendously important information here—and she does.* For the first time Patsy boldly reveals some personal information: $118,000 was precisely the amount of John's bonus. John may have made the suggestion to give this number since he probably would be much more familiar with the exact amount of his bonus, but Patsy, for her own reasons, probably liked—and used—his suggestion.

Here Patsy really took a chance. She reveals that she knows a great deal about John Ramsey and also reveals another personal motive. Ostensibly the killer is a terrorist, angry with a wealthy John Ramsey and his capitalist country. She knows what his bonus was and, in effect, doesn't want him to have it.

Patsy is also suggesting that she was deeply divided about John Ramsey and his money. Patsy unconsciously reveals a personal matter—she herself doesn't really want John Ramsey to have his bonus. He has something she wants—power, since money means power.

The idea of someone withdrawing money from an account is a clear reference to losing something valuable. An account is connected to a bank, and the bank and the account are symbols of Patsy having lost her power. It would have been much simpler to say, "Get $118,000 by tomorrow morning at 10 o'clock." But the killer elaborates on a loss, a painful withdrawal from a place where valuables were kept—she is telling us about a tremendous blow to her identity. The loss is a big one but also a bit by bit loss—withdraw a $100,00 in hundreds, and $18,000 in twenties. You can picture someone slowly eating away at a bank account, removing one bill after another.

The killer gives a comparison here with money: The larger amount ($100,000) is to be in larger bills, and the smaller amount ($18,000)—the remaining amount—is to be in smaller bills. The killer is conveying a comparison, a larger amount has larger bills and the "leftovers" are smaller bills. It is not a stretch to identify John Ramsey with money and Patsy Ramsey with leftovers, the "remaining amount" or "remains." These words reveal that Patsy was deeply troubled by a severely damaged identity and saw herself as "remains." She saw herself as small bills in comparison to John's big bills—and she deeply resented it.

All of these ideas go to the heart of the JonBenét murder case, including the personal reference to John Ramsey. They tell us that Patsy was also out to destroy John because of a deep-seated deficiency in herself.

DAMAGED FEMININE IDENTITY: A DOWNHILL SLIDE

"Make sure that you bring an adequate size attaché to the bank. When you get home you will put the money in a brown paper bag."

Still more control—do this, do that. "Make sure"—"bring an adequate size"—"you will put." The money is going into an attaché, and it is coming out of the bank. Then it is going into a bag.

A bank account, a bank, an attaché, and a bag—all containers. In a sense they're all feminine symbols similar to a woman's PURSE, and they all symbolize the ultimate feminine container, the uterus (as well as the vagina). A woman's uterus is her NEST within, and a bank is where we keep our nest egg. All of these traditional symbols are mixed with orders and control.

Women instinctively tend to be gatherers—even while playing little girls gather their things together while little boys often build things only to scatter them far and wide. Likewise, mothers must learn early on to be emotional containers for their children's powerful emotions. A container or a gatherer is such an accurate picture of a woman in so many different ways. Think of bank accounts, banks, attaches, or paper bags as containers, as ways of gathering different items. Remember particularly the word "gather" as linked with feminine identity because we will see the killer use it later at a crucial point in another letter.

"Attaché"? Certainly this is a sophisticated killer who is not thinking briefcase, but attaché. Attaché is also an upper-class word. At the same time, Patsy reveals concern: The attaché might not be big enough. The killer is really concerned that her femininity or her familiar substitutes for it—such as money—might not be adequate to get the job done.

And just for good measure, the killer tells us one more time about her female-identity woes in another striking image: a *brown paper bag*. Deep down, Patsy sees herself as a plain brown paper bag. She's gone from a hefty bank account, to a valuable bank, to an attaché (although an inadequate one, too small for the job), to a plain brown paper bag. It's one steady downhill ride. Earlier Patsy had called herself leftovers (smaller bills), she will repeat this idea when she refers to "remains," and later to a stray dog, another degrading feminine image of a woman "who is a dog."

CHANGE

Just so we don't miss the message, the killer says to change the money from an attaché to a brown paper bag. She is subtly stressing the idea of *change* to reflect the change in identity that she has undergone. She has talked of other changes—of 1996 becoming 1997, of someone losing value (losing money), of changing a large bank account into small bills, and of changing a small amount into even smaller bills. The repeated reference to things being changed (into smaller things) conveys that Patsy was struggling with a major *belittling* change in her life prior to the crime.

Just the first few sentences of the ransom note reveals a great deal about the killer. At least one of the multiple killers—the writer of the note—is a woman who is threatened to her core about her femininity. She is very divided about John Ramsey, knows him personally, and uses control in proportion to her vulnerability.

SUCCESS AND DANGER: WHAT GOES UP MUST COME DOWN

There is another self-revealing message in this part of the note: Patsy links vulnerability to her husband's economic success. We speculated earlier that money is a powerful subject for the killer, and here we see just how powerful.

Having extraordinary success—particularly economic success—puts incredible emotional pressure on individuals, however pleasant their lifestyle seems on the surface. The greater the success, the greater the fear because, deep down, a universal Murphy's Law of success whispers, "If you have great success, somewhere shortly down the road lies an equivalent amount of pain." As Shakespeare put it, "Uneasy lies the head that wears the crown." Becoming very wealthy is, in many ways, like getting crowned.

In the ransom note, the killer specifically draws our attention to John Ramsey's economic success that year. In the Ramsey family 1996 Christmas letter, Patsy told everyone that her husband's company, Access Graphics, had just gone over the $1 billion mark. In other words, both Patsy and John had attained incredible financial success in the year preceding JonBenét's murder (and in 1995 John was Boulder Entrepreneur of the Year), and Murphy's Law—alive and well in the back of their minds—would naturally be telling them that they would pay dearly for it.

Time and again I've seen people get a promotion or come into money and suddenly become obsessed in disguised ways with the fear of dying or of some trauma occurring. As much as Patsy (and John) loved their newfound wealth, as much as she wanted to brag about it in her Christmas letter, deep down it was a death-related experience in their minds. Both Patsy and John were naturally wondering why so many bad things had happened to them lately, and both would have naturally come to the conclusion—in the back of their minds—that success was to blame.

Unconsciously a second reason Patsy chose such an odd number ($118,000) for the ransom was to convey the "odd"—unusual— pressure of success. A $118,000 bonus symbolizes significant wealth. The Ramsey's *personal success* was driving them crazy—thus the very *personal* reference to money.

How Patsy Copes: Money Is Power

Consider, in this light, another observation by Judith Phillips, who took hundreds of photographs of JonBenét, Patsy, and the Ramsey family—including Patsy's mother, Nedra. According to Phillips, after Patsy and her mother had bought a terribly expensive antique rocking chair for JonBenét's bedroom, Nedra said, "As long as John Ramsey keeps making the money, we don't care. We love to spend John Ramsey's money."

We love to spend John Ramsey's money. Nedra again speaking for Patsy—and spending Patsy's husband's money. Patsy was hers and so was Patsy's husband and his money. It's clear that, just like the killer who wrote the note, Patsy and her mother didn't respect John's money. This is evidence that Patsy had, for a long time, experienced mixed feelings about John and had a tendency to degrade him by seeing him as just a *possession.*

John himself had frequently commented about how quickly Patsy could go through his money. Not only was this her way of showing her power and disrespecting her husband, it was also her way of bailing out of the success space by diminishing her own bank account.

At stressful times such as this, marriages have great difficulty. When a couple experiences success as a dangerous trap, the spouses tend to move away from one another. Apparently the Ramsey's marriage was strained to some degree. There is evidence that John had a prolonged affair the year after Patsy was diagnosed with ovarian cancer, and that gave Patsy a reason to really doubt herself, down to the most basic way she coped—by showy femininity. It was also natural at a time like this for Patsy to turn to another form of power—money. I venture to guess that Patsy Ramsey became more extravagant than ever before in 1995 and 1996.

ATTACHÉ AND JONBENÉT

The ransom note reveals another striking, even eerie, revelation from the killer's deeper mind. Look at "attaché" again. That word stands alone as the only word in the entire note with an accent. It has caught the attention of many examiners who have commented on it as the mark of an educated killer trying to disguise his or her identity.

Some people question whether the killer really wrote an accent in the word. It appears that the accent is really just the tail end of the letter (a "y") in the sentence above it—which may well be the case. *But the way Patsy wrote it, the word effectively has an accent—it's too coincidental to be otherwise.* The killer wants and at the same time doesn't want to put an accent in the word. Only someone very familiar with such an accent would want to cover it up and yet unconsciously want to leave it in. Patsy is confessing both the crime and the cover-up.

Look closer. *The accent is over the seventh letter of the word attaché. JonBenét had a trademark accent in her name—over the seventh letter.* The killer is telling us that she is someone who is used to writing a word with an accent on the seventh letter. A mother who had committed such a crime would want to cover it up—but her deeper mind wouldn't let her.

Just so we wouldn't miss the connection, the killer writes "make sure ... adequate size attaché" to bring to mind by contrast the idea of a small attaché, a small container like a small little girl. And then the attaché (with the money in it) is to be swapped for little JonBenét directly, making the JonBenét/attaché connection undeniable.

Not one time in the entire note does the killer use JonBenét's name—which suggests that it was simply too painful to write her name. An indirect reference was the only way JonBenét's mother could write her name: She alluded to her by calling her a small attaché and put an accent over the seventh letter so we couldn't miss it. If you're *not convinced so far, say "attaché" out loud and see how perfectly it rhymes with* JonBenét.

There are two other subtle hints that Patsy Ramsey wrote this note. The word "daughter," specifically "your daughter," is used six times, by far more than any other word in the ransom note. Using the phrase repeatedly is Patsy's way of confessing to us that this was her daughter—another way of saying JonBenét's name without saying it. The obsession with "daughter" also reflects Patsy's ongoing preoccupation with femininity.

The killer, in a poor attempt to disguise her handwriting, writes her "t"s like reverse "j"s that have an upswing umbrella appearance at the bottom (similar to Patsy's handwriting at times). Since "j" is the only letter with such a characteristic, the "t"s remind the reader of a "j" that reminds the reader of JonBenét. Far and away "t" stands out more than any other single letter in the note. By choosing such a disguise, Patsy reveals that she is obsessed with JonBenét and what she has done to her. She continually reminds us by drawing our attention to the first letter in JonBenét's name.

Attaché also suggests attachment, and there is no question that Patsy Ramsey was quite attached to JonBenét. Perhaps John thought up the idea of an attaché, and Patsy just used his idea, but this would only tell us how attached John was to JonBenét as well. Sadly, too much of the time both parents only saw JonBenét as a little possession, like an attaché.

The killer hints that—for a very long time—she often saw herself the same way. This is Patsy's second reference to size in two sentences—first small bills and now a small attaché. Size or comparison plays a big role in Patsy's life and explains the two defining aspects of her identity—being a Miss America candidate and the desire to be the mother of a Miss America, which are all about constantly comparing herself, constantly measuring herself against other women.

The final clue the killer reveals in choosing the word "attaché" is that an attaché is also a staff member of someone in the diplomatic service. The word conjures up the image of someone privy to secret information, of couriers carrying leather attaches containing secret information attached—chained—to their wrists. Once again not only a picture of little JonBenét, her will controlled for the moment by being chained to Patsy Ramsey (and John)—but also a striking picture of JonBenét on the last night of her life, her small dead body all tied up. How appropriate that she leaves the world this way, so consistent with how her parents, often unknowingly, tied her up during her brief life.

Attaché also depicts the entire ransom note—papers filled with secret messages. The word "attaché" demonstrates to us how Patsy's deeper mind first looked at JonBenét and then looked at the note and chose one word to vividly portray what it saw in both.

DELIVERY

"I will call you between 8 and 10 am tomorrow to instruct you on ***delivery***. *The* ***delivery*** *will be exhausting so I advise you to be rested. If we monitor you getting the money early, we might call you early to arrange an earlier* ***delivery*** *of the money and hence. a earlier (****delivery****—crossed out) pick up of your daughter (spelled* ***daug hter****)."*

Quickly glancing at these three sentences (which the killer tried to turn into four), one word leaps off the pages—*delivery*. Delivery is used *four* times, so close together that Patsy is clearly preoccupied with it—so preoccupied, in fact, that she has to say it again in a slip of the pen.

If there's one word that symbolizes the essence of femininity, it's delivery. It's the peak of a woman's life. It's the one thing that only a woman can do—deliver a child. But there are definite limitations—windows of time—that determine when a woman can deliver a child. Every woman has a ticking biological clock, an end to her fertility.

A very common emotional stress for many woman is when they "hit the wall," reach the end of their potential for motherhood. And the killer is obviously obsessed with the idea of delivery. Patsy Ramsey had just lost her cancerous ovaries and uterus after surgery and radiation—suffering both symbolic (aging) and literal blows to her femininity.

"I will call you between 8 and 10 a.m. tomorrow to instruct you on delivery." The very first time the word "delivery" is used, it's within a very narrow time range—the killer's way of saying that the idea foremost in her mind about her delivery, her femininity, is that there is a window of time to it. Even the phrase "I will call you" implies someone who is passively waiting for a life-and-death event to happen, at the mercy of someone—or something—else: Time. Note this is also the first time Patsy uses the word "I" seemingly wanting to emphasize that this issue particularly applies to her.

Look at what comes next: "The delivery will be exhausting." The killer has just told us how exhausted she is trying to deal with her declining femininity. Patsy is trying to deliver herself from the terrible, psyche-shattering burden that has consumed her. Brick upon brick, painful idea upon painful idea, we are moving toward one consistent picture, one big house of ideas built upon one fear.

"... so I advise you to be rested." A killer telling a victim to get rest seems absurd, which means that the idea of "rest" had a personal meaning for the killer. In the ransom note, Patsy was pretending to put the parent through an exhausting process—which has proved to be the case in reality. Patsy has put the authorities and herself (and John) through an exhausting process. Here we see that, deep down, Patsy recognized that this bizarre "delivery" of JonBenét she was undertaking, this special way she was dealing with the horrible blows to her core identity as a woman, was going to be exhausting. She knew the investigation would come, and she knew there would be a huge price

tag in the end. Also, Patsy wrote the note when she was exhausted. By using "I," Patsy seems to be saying that being rested has a particularly important meaning to her.

Maybe Patsy's tired state contributed to her bad judgment about writing the ransom note. Doesn't it all seem so preposterous that on Christmas night, a group of terrorists, who leave no evidence of entry, kidnap a wealthy businessman's daughter, and hold out for a ransom—precisely that of his bonus—for some reason caring more about making a point than about making money? In the end they change their minds and kill JonBenét—but decide to leave the ransom note anyway, a note they practiced writing. The whole idea of such a ransom note was a sham, reflecting not only neophyte killers but also desperate ones who couldn't come up with a better idea. The ransom ploy is a hidden confession in its own right.

THE HIDDEN CONFESSION IN THE RANSOM NOTE FURTHER REVEALS:

- the "kidnapper" has already killed JonBenét.

- Patsy inflicted her own deep emotional wounds on JonBenét.

- Patsy left hidden instructions to police: how to catch her.

- Patsy is a damaged woman.

- Patsy is obsessed with the sudden loss of her feminine identity.

- Patsy left a major clue: attaché rhymes with JonBenét.

Chapter Four
The Killer Slips Up

*"If we monitor you getting the money **early**, we might call
you **early** to arrange an **earlier** delivery of the money and
hence. a **earlier** ['delivery' crossed out] pick-up of your
daug hter [sic]."*

T his simple sentence contains major slip-ups by the killer—the
slip-ups that everyone has been hoping for. The slip-ups are far
beyond that of John Ramsey accidentally providing the police
with a practice ransom note (if indeed that's what occurred).

The slips of the pen reveal the killer's deeper perceptions: Patsy's
own shock that she's now a murderer, what set her off, her brush with
insanity, her unique emotional pain, her unexpected need for a cover-
up, having a partner in crime, her guilt, once more her severely damaged feminine identity, and yet another confession. Amazingly, most of
the slip-ups come in rapid-fire succession, and the entire note is one big
slip-up.

THE CONSUMMATE KEY WORD: "EARLY" WHICH MEANS UNEXPECTED

The words "early" and "earlier" appear *three* times in the first half
of the sentence, followed by an *accidental period* before a *fourth* reference to *early*. Since JonBenét is already dead when the killer wrote
these words, they reveal a deeper meaning: Patsy is extremely preoccupied with "early" events, "unexpected" events. First, money is unexpectedly obtained from a bank by John Ramsey and unexpectedly delivered to "the kidnapper" with eventually the unexpected delivery or pick
up of JonBenét. Since the last "delivery" is so unmistakably connected
to JonBenét's body, Patsy is revealing that "earlier delivery" means
"unexpected death".

Patsy also reveals that the unexpected death of her child came
about as the result of another unexpected happening ("getting the
money"). By repeating "early" again and again, Patsy shows just how
shocked she is—her murderous impulses caught her completely off
guard.

TWO PEOPLE INVOLVED

Coincidentally this is the first time in the paragraph that the killer
uses the word "we," and she uses it twice in succession. *We* monitor you

getting the money early and *we* might call to arrange an earlier delivery.

Patsy again reveals that more than one person is involved in the plan. In the first part of the note she says, "*I* will call you" or "*I* advise you," *but at this crucial point when the subject of an unexpected event and the delivery of JonBenét are introduced, she uses "we."* Later in the note Patsy makes a slip-up that further implicates John Ramsey in the murder.

In some ways the idea of a catastrophic event occurring early and having to come up with money earlier than expected fits with the theory of Dr. Cyril Wecht, a famed coroner from Allegheny County, Pennsylvania. Wecht believes that JonBenét was accidentally killed in a perverted sex game that she had been forced to play repeatedly. This would suggest that John Ramsey had a cover-up plan of a contrived ransom note if anything ever went wrong. But by and large this story just doesn't fit with all of the evidence—and certainly not with the information revealed in Patsy's ransom note.

CLUES TO THE EVENTS OF THE LAST NIGHT OF JONBENÉT'S LIFE

The main ideas in this sentence, follow a clear sequence: *unexpected gratification (getting money), chaos, unexpected delivery (death) of JonBenét.* Breaking down the main ideas provides a clearer look into each idea.

CHAOS: THE ACCIDENTAL PERIOD AND THE CROSS-OUT

The first and most striking slip-up in the sentence—and one of the most prominent in the entire note—is a period after "hence." *A period that is so strikingly out of place, so far away from where it should be, that through a slip of the pen the killer is drawing us a picture, a literal show-and-tell of what happened that night: Patsy temporarily lost touch with reality.* Doesn't this bizarre accidental period, so far out of bounds, fit the equally bizarre story of a loving mother murdering her child?

Here Patsy reveals just how far over the edge she went by using the word "early" three times in rapid succession, which tells us how stunned she was, and by topping it off with *a completely out-of-place period*—all in the first half of the sentence. The second half of the sentence indicates that Patsy is even more overwhelmed—beginning with the accidental period, almost half of the slips in the entire note (four out of nine) are in this half sentence. Again, she is telling us to pay particularly close attention to the deeper meaning of this sentence.

The killer follows this with an even more convincing sign of chaos— *she conspicuously crosses out a word ("delivery"), the second word in the entire note that's crossed out (and by far the most glaring), and when she crosses it out she leaves a large black chaotic spot that distinctly stands out.* Combining this cross-out with the misplaced "psychotic period," we have the two most blatant slip-ups in the entire note back to back, indicating maximum chaos. This reveals the precise moment when the killer's mind is overwhelmed. Patsy is saying, **"This is where I lost it."**

These slip-ups not only reveal that Patsy Ramsey was beyond her mental limits during her attack on JonBenét, but also that she is now badly overwhelmed with guilt. These slip-ups are her way of confessing.

Thus we have two major indicators of chaos—two art-word forms (combining words or punctuation with "art"—other marks such as cross-outs or unique spacing—to convey a special message). Even when we get to the key story in the note (see Chapter 6) we will not see the killer as chaotic as she is here. Therefore, we must pay exceptionally close attention to this sentence. Here Patsy is defining the specifics of carrying out the ransom and arranging for the swap—she is getting to the heart of the matter. This is precisely when we would expect her to be overwhelmed and when we would expect her to tell why she erupted.

THE KEY SUBJECTS IN THE CHAOS

The sentence begins with the seemingly innocuous idea of John Ramsey being "monitored" getting the money out of the bank early. However there is a hidden message here about something powerful enough to drive Patsy Ramsey momentarily crazy. *The message suggests that prior to the murder Patsy unexpectedly came across her husband molesting* JonBenét—*taking her valuables from her, intruding into JonBenét's "bank." This follows our previous line of reasoning and stays with the same symbolic meanings: "Bank" is a woman, and the woman we're talking about is JonBenét.* Another meaning for "early" is "young"—JonBenét's valuables were removed before she was of age.

A second mention of money and *unexpected* gratification (earlier delivery of the money) connected to "delivery" suggests another interaction between a young woman and John Ramsey. A young woman has unexpectedly delivered her valuables to him. Was JonBenét delivering what Patsy felt she couldn't anymore, her appealing femininity? These are very subtle clues at this point in the sentence, but *when we look on the other side of the chaos—after the period and the cross-out—the clues are much stronger*—this was precisely what was going on that night.

John Ramsey has no prior history of sexually abusing children, and the police reportedly are leaning away from a sexual abuse scenario precisely because they don't see that pattern in his life, but people change—particularly in the face of powerful circumstances—and John was under inordinate stress prior to JonBenét's murder.

ANOTHER SLIP: JONBENÉT CHANGED INTO A "PICK-UP"

Another invaluable slip in the phrase *"pick-up* of your daughter," hints even more strongly that something sexual was going on between John and JonBenét (and Patsy). The killer has moved from being pre-occupied with "delivery" and "early" to "pick-up." She misspells "pick up," putting a hyphen between the two words instead of leaving them separate—Patsy wants to make it one word or one idea. Since "pick-up" is slang for sexual promiscuity, she is confessing that JonBenét is the one being "picked up" by John, something sexual was going on between them.

The sentence begins with two disguised references to sexual activity followed by two signs of severe chaos—signaling that the killer is overwhelmed—and another strong hint of sexual activity between father and daughter. The sequence itself, ending with such a strong sexual reference (pick-up), adds enormous credibility to seeing the first two references in the sentence—gratification is clearly linked to John Ramsey and JonBenét—as being sexual. Patsy's deeper mind seems to be saying, *"I'm going to provide you with the strongest possible sexual reference and link it specifically to John Ramsey and JonBenét so that you will see this whole sentence is about sex."*

This follows an extremely logical train of thought: Patsy unexpectedly comes across John molesting JonBenét, is temporarily disoriented, concludes that John is using and degrading JonBenét, and finally loses control. *Only something as emotionally powerful as sexual abuse could cause such profound and repeated slips.*

"Pick-up" also refers to Patsy and John's ongoing sexual exploitation of JonBenét through pageants. And it refers to a subtle sex game that was going on whereby Patsy helped create the seductive little JonBenét and pushed her toward her father in a sexual way. Here Patsy's actions speak louder than any words, as JonBenét was most certainly a little seductress.

Together Patsy and John Ramsey had changed JonBenét into a pick-up. Remember once again that it is JonBenét's mother writing this note and she loves her child enough to tell the world what she has done to her—how wrong she has been. No matter what the mother has done or what the child has done, a mother cannot stop loving her child, cannot stop being a mother.

Patsy Ramsey knows, deep down, how she has degraded herself and JonBenét in the past. By changing the word from "delivery" to "pick-up" Patsy is also revealing that she has become a "pick-up" in her own way. She is confessing that she has changed from a nurturing mother to the cheapest kind of woman imaginable, a woman who first encourages her daughter to behave like a prostitute and then murders her.

By writing "pick-up" Patsy Ramsey was referring not only to

symbolically prostituting JonBenét through the pageants but also to using JonBenét in a much more perverse way—something confirmed by the other slips in her note. The very next slip-up reveals just how powerful the emotions and chaos were that night.

"Pick-up" has one other crucial meaning. Patsy Ramsey's deeper mind *picks up* on reality in vastly superior ways to her conscious mind. "Pick-up" also subtly implies a message—the deeper message that Patsy Ramsey was picking up on.

THE RESULT OF THE DISCOVERY: "DAUG HTER"

Yet another slip-up packed into this invaluable sentence completes the story of the last night of JonBenét's life. The killer is strongly suggesting that witnessing the sexual abuse was a vicious wake-up call that resulted in JonBenét's death. Patsy says that the raw power of seeing JonBenét being used like a prostitute threw her over the edge and made her lose control.

She reveals this in several ways. First, immediately after the crucial word "pick-up" the word *"daughter" is written with such a gap in the middle that it looks like two words, "daug" and "hter."* The killer has literally torn the word apart.

If we compare this use of the word "daughter" to the numerous other times it's used in the note, it stands out more clearly. By doing this to the word "daughter" at this particular point in the note (when Patsy's talking about the perpetrator of the crime delivering the daughter), she's showing us again in an art-word form how JonBenét will be delivered: torn in two. She tells us again in no uncertain terms that JonBenét is already dead—and thus, that at the very moment it is being written, the ransom note is a ploy. Following the flow of ideas, the messages are unmistakable—the murder of JonBenét was directly related to JonBenét being treated like a pick-up, which created phenomenal chaos in the killer.

The *sheer brutality* that emerges in the next few sentences reveal a drastic change in the note and underscore the fact that this is where Patsy Ramsey lost control of her rage. We will try to understand why Patsy could direct her rage over her husband sexually abusing JonBenét at JonBenét and kill her.

"HENCE": PROSTITUTION AND DEATH (OF JONBENÉT)

"Hence," which occurs immediately before the "chaotic period," is a striking word on its own, meaning "therefore" or implying a *conclusion* based on what had gone before. First we must understand that the killer didn't want to see the conclusion, as the premature period tells us. She didn't want to see JonBenét's unexpected death—the period, the end of her life. Patsy didn't want to see JonBenét being turned into a little prostitute or see the chaos that erupted in herself.

"Hence" reveals that this sequence of *chaos, prostitution, and death* came about because John Ramsey got his money out of the bank early—JonBenét's bank. Once more, Patsy is revealing that John did something that unexpectedly set her off.

"Hence" is a verbal high-lighter used immediately prior to the chaos (the psychotic period and the darkened cross-out) to let us know that chaos was an inescapable result of what just happened—a natural result of John Ramsey's gratification. This is the third time in Patsy's ransom note that one of those crucial "message markers" appears, (after "*Listen carefully*" and "*instructions* to the *letter*"), indicating a key message follows.

"Hence" is not a particularly common word, and its use reflects someone with an education. Interestingly it is a word Patsy Ramsey later used in her 1997 Christmas message (see Chapter 19) recognizing the one year anniversary of JonBenét's death. In that letter, just like this one, "hence" points to a key sentence. In both the ransom note and the 1997 Christmas letter, "hence" is a subtle confession.

These are the only two places Patsy tells us, *"Here is the conclusion."* In the ransom note, she uses "hence" to say: Conclusion—the immediate trigger for her rage was catching John sexually abusing JonBenét. In her 1997 Christmas letter she will use "hence" to tell us: Conclusion—the main underlying motive for her rage (as we will see in Chapter 6). "Hence" in two key places signals the heart of the whole story.

SLIP: "DELIVERY" CROSSED OUT—MORE INVALUABLE MESSAGES

"... to arrange an earlier delivery of the money and hence, an earlier ['delivery' crossed out] pick-up." In a chaotic moment the killer writes the word "delivery" and then crosses it out, giving us another reason for her turmoil. This is a picture of Patsy on many different levels. She is eliminating "delivery" just as her feminine identity has been damaged—a picture of losing her ovaries. The assault she herself experienced on her core identity as a woman—when her "valuables" were taken—pushed her beyond the bounds of reality. It also helps explain why she might have directed her anger at JonBenét instead of at John.

The most chaotic moment in the note, the cross-out of "delivery," is also an art-word of the sudden murder of JonBenét by the killer—immediately following a completely unexpected event. The murder was unexpected, but so was the event that triggered it.

There is yet one other message hidden in the crossed-out "delivery." Following the red flag of the misplaced punctuation mark, the killer, after talking about Mr. Ramsey delivering the money, means to say (in what should be the second part of the sentence) that Mr. Ramsey can now "pick up" his daughter "early" but instead says "deliver" his daughter and then scratches out "deliver."

If we read it the way it was first written, Mr. Ramsey is delivering the money and then the daughter. *In other words, the one who delivers the money is the one who killed the child.* The one who appears to be being blackmailed is secretly the killer. This also hints that John Ramsey (since he was to deliver the money) was somehow involved in killing his own daughter.

Another specific reality of the situation might have forced Patsy to make the slip-up about delivering the child. There is good evidence that John had to "deliver" JonBenét to the basement in his arms where Patsy and John staged the murder.

A previous slip has additional messages. The markedly out-of-place "accidental" period tells us that the whole ransom note is phony because it occurs in the sentence that specifically defines the exchange of the ransom. The story really ends before it gets started. *The early punctuation mark secretly reveals that the literal story that comes after the accidental period—the alleged ransom—is false.*

There is indeed a striking hidden story that follows the slip of the pen. The misplaced period is a secret confession that Patsy and John were way out of bounds. By separating the two parts of the sentence, the definitive punctuation provides yet another picture of their split identity—and the finality of their separation from JonBenét.

FINE TUNING: MORE MEANING

"... we might call you early to arrange an earlier delivery of the money and hence. a earlier (delivery)/pick-up of your daughter." Between the two ideas of gratification (getting money) is the idea of "we might call you early to arrange" it. We can read this as Patsy Ramsey telling us that after discovering her husband's sexual gratification/abuse, she unexpectedly then had to communicate with him—call him—and this caused the situation to escalate.

But there may be an even more ominous meaning. Patsy may be trying to tell us that, deep down, she recognizes that *she* had a stake— if only indirectly—in this secret gratification *(sexual abuse).* Unconsciously she had helped arrange it. Patsy is suggesting that deep down she had known that some sort of explosion leading to JonBenét's death was going to take place, and that it still had consciously occurred unexpectedly—"earlier." Patsy also links the murder to two people here and brings in John more directly in very specific ways.

Had Patsy been secretly—unconsciously—monitoring what was going on between John and JonBenét, knowing that at some point things would reach a crisis and yet consciously still shocked when it came on "earlier" or unexpectedly? In the ransom note, "monitor you getting the money" strongly suggests Patsy not only closely observed sexual abuse the night of JonBenét's murder but unconsciously knew it was going on. *Studies reveal that family members are usually aware, deep down, of what's going on—which certainly fits with what we've learned recently about the ability of the deeper mind.* If John was sexually molesting JonBenét, Patsy knew about it deep down—and sanctioned it as the evidence clearly shows.

SUMMARY

The killer's train of thought in this crucial sentence is very revealing. **This is the single most important sentence in the ransom note for its sheer breadth.**

First, we have two thoughts of subtle sexual gratification involving John Ramsey (getting and delivering money early) connected to women in general and JonBenét specifically—gratifications that are closely monitored. This is followed by two major signs of chaos (an accidental period and a cross-out) immediately connected to a much more powerful sexual gratification—JonBenét becomes a "pick-up"—again clearly linking her with John Ramsey. Following these three thoughts of sexual gratification and chaos is the picture of a dead/broken JonBenét ("daug hter").

Patsy's train of thought was: sexual gratification (involving John and JonBenét), sexual gratification, chaos, more chaos, sexual gratification (again involving John and JonBenét), and the death of JonBenét.

In summary, the markedly out-of-place accidental period (preceded by a preoccupation with "early" and followed by three other slips, including the inappropriate spacing in "daughter") suggests a secret story: The ransom note is a phony. JonBenét is already dead, killed unexpectedly by the killer/mother (and by John, too) who temporarily went over the edge, becoming enraged when she unexpectedly discovered her husband sexually abusing JonBenét *(after they both had exploited her sexually)*. Now Patsy is deeply guilt-ridden and must confess.

TRIGGER MOTIVE, DEEPER MOTIVE

As we find level upon level of meaning in this marvelously condensed document known as "the ransom note," we must recognize that the killer has taken us to one of the central questions in the story—what exactly happened that night?—and has answered it blatantly by a repeated emphasis on an "early," or unexpected, death. The killer has also answered the question by suddenly crossing out a feminine symbol ("delivery") directly connected to JonBenét as well as suddenly putting in an "impulsive period" where one shouldn't have been.

The main message here is that the murder was impulsive and not planned. Something caused the killer to lose control. We must keep in mind, however, that we are only talking about the *immediate* trigger that set the killer off. *Still to come is the central story at the heart of the note which will tie everything together and reveal with extraordinary clarity the killer's main motive.*

IN ONE CRUCIAL SENTENCE IN THE RANSOM NOTE
CONTAINING FOUR SLIPS, THE KILLER REVEALS:

- a disguised train of thought: sexual gratification *(involving John and JonBenét)*, chaos, more chaos, more pronounced sexual gratification *(again involving John and JonBenét)*, the death of JonBenét—describes the specific events the night of JonBenét's murder.

- a preoccupation with the word "early" telling us several events happened unexpectedly: the sexual abuse of JonBenét, the killer's rage over discovering it, the murder of JonBenét.

- Patsy was temporarily insane emphasized by a totally out of place "psychotic" period and a huge cross-out.

- Patsy lost control when she caught John sexually molesting JonBenét emphasized by the slip "pick-up."

- Patsy deep down knew abuse had been going on.

- Patsy contributed to JonBenét's sexual abuse by pushing her toward John.

- a hidden confession through a slip, the cross-out "delivery," telling us the one who delivered the money also had the child.

- the crucial message marker "hence" which emphasizes this is the conclusion, the answer to"what happened that night."

Chapter Five
A Sudden Execution

"Any deviation of my instructions will result in the imme-diate execution of your daughter. You will also be denied her remains for proper burial."

"The two gentlemen watching over your daughter do (not— added as an afterthought) *particularly like you so I advise you not to provoke them."*

T he killer's tone clearly becomes far more ominous with these two powerful references to death—"immediate execution" and "her remains." The hidden meaning behind the killer's slip-up when she wrote "daug" "hter": JonBenét has just been suddenly executed and all that's left is her remains.

The killer has now gone into more detail. The killer's use of "early" in a previous sentence hinted at impulsiveness. In this sentence she explicitly highlights someone losing control and killing. Impulse control is totally gone. *Someone has deviated, causing the death of JonBenét, and that someone is John Ramsey (since that's who the killer is speaking to).* What the killer is really saying is that she was surprised, caught off guard—by John and JonBenét's failure to follow rigid instructions—and thus she unexpectedly killed JonBenét. The sequence of ideas hints at the sexual taboo—rigid instructions—being violated.

A few sentences later the killer writes that JonBenét would be *"beheaded"* if anyone speaks to the authorities. Beheaded fits sudden execution perfectly. The killer is revealing that a battle erupted over clear but rigid instructions not being followed and that she lost control and suddenly killed JonBenét—"beheaded" her by hitting her in the head with some object and then "beheaded" her again by strangulation. The autopsy confirmed that JonBenét was first knocked unconscious by a violent blow to the head and then she was asphyxiated.

THE BIGGER PICTURE: MORE OF THE KILLER'S PERSONALITY TRAITS

"Any deviation ... will result in the immediate execution... denied her remains for proper burial." These two sentences reveal again the killer's excessively *controlling nature* and her tremendous emphasis on perfection, on not making the slightest deviation. This is very consistent with the overall tone and particularly harkens back to "you must follow instructions to the letter" from the first paragraph of Patsy's ransom note.

"Immediate" also repeats the idea of a very tight time frame and hints at a biological clock—or even a life-or-death clock. The killer appears to be terrified of the slightest deviation from a particular norm and attaches the gravest of consequences to such an event: immediate execution.

"Execution" is commonly linked not only with helplessness and death but also with *guilt*—such as a sentence of capital punishment followed by execution. The killer is suggesting that the particular event that set Patsy Ramsey off was also an extremely guilt-laden one, further pointing toward a sexual event. "Slightest deviation" is yet another hint that the immediate trigger for the killer's rage reminded her of something she could not tolerate at all within herself. Patsy Ramsey was extremely uptight about sex. For her, sex was taboo.

The killer's harsh intolerant tone suggests that deep down she judged herself in the same way. Thus not only does the immediate trigger for the killer's rage point to a deep sense of guilt, but her underlying motive also had a lot to do with guilt. Prior to the crime the killer may have been living under a death sentence herself, a sentence to which she attached a great deal of guilt.

One more connection between "execution" and guilt is that in light of her having just murdered JonBenét, the killer has a new fear: She can be "executed" for her crime.

THE WRITER IS TALKING ABOUT HERSELF

JonBenét is already dead and the whole fictitious ransom note is a fascinating hidden description of the killer's psyche. **The more the killer writes, the more she reveals about herself**—and she eventually reveals the central story that ties everything together, the events leading up to the murder and the details of the murder itself.

"Immediate execution" is followed by "you will be denied her remains for proper burial." The word "remains" has a sense of mutilation, of leftovers, of something that's no longer intact. It's another hint that, deep inside, the killer is enormously concerned about her own body being damaged. "You will be denied" even the remains of a body suggests the killer is herself concerned about her own body being destroyed so badly that absolutely nothing is left. Something in the back of the killer's mind is eating at her—and she suspects it's her own body.

The abrupt shift into the primitive ideas of bodily harm following the suggestion of a sex-related trigger (see Chapter 4) point to sexual molestation as the primary motive. Discovering JonBenét being sexually molested would push many of Patsy Ramsey's psychological buttons, particularly the deep sense of inadequacy she felt as a woman.

A Woman's Touch: Proper People, Two Gentlemen

The connection between a severely damaged woman who is beheaded and "in remains" implies that the killer is a devalued woman. The feminine wording of the ransom note continues to reveal that the killer is a woman, a mother, JonBenét's mother, Patsy Ramsey.

The emphasis on "proper" (burial) gives the note a definite feminine cast. This is a familiar phrase, but in the context of the ransom note it reveals the killer's preoccupation with doing the "proper" thing, something a woman—especially a mother—would have on her mind. This once again points to a deep emotional split in the killer and suggests that she (and her husband) would present a strong outward show of being civilized and genteel.

Patsy and John liked to portray themselves to the world as the height of kindness and Christian character. So much so that Lou "The Fox" Smit, an ace investigator and former Colorado lawman who came out of retirement to consult with the local authorities on the JonBenét murder case, was initially fooled by the Ramseys' proper demeanor. Reportedly, after interviewing the Ramseys, Smit came to the conclusion that they were "good, honest Christians who were incapable of committing a murder of such ferocious brutality." Smit added, "They're the most unlikely people to have done this that I've ever seen." (He later changed his mind.)

John Douglas, famed ex-FBI profiler of mostly serial killers, was fooled just as badly as Smit. The Ramseys hired him allegedly to profile the killer. After spending four or five hours interviewing the Ramseys *together*, Douglas declared on *Dateline* NBC, "I just don't believe in my heart that he (John Ramsey) did this." He added that if the Ramseys were guilty, "they have to be the biggest liars in the world."

This shows just how charismatic and convincing the Ramseys are—and how cold-hearted. Wouldn't we expect Patsy and John Ramsey to be persuasive, given their backgrounds? In different ways they had both been "selling" themselves for years. Isn't this what beauty pageants are all about—mostly externals? Not really looking at the inner character, but mainly interested in the pose? The contestants are always smiling, always looking good, never admitting to any discomfort. The impulse is so ingrained in Patsy that she can continue this pose even after she has brutally murdered JonBenét.

"The two gentlemen watching over your daughter do (not—added as an afterthought) particularly like you so I advise you not to provoke them."

This is another confession that two people are watching over JonBenét, most likely *literally* observing her remains right in front of them as they contrive the ransom note. It's also a further confession that the "group" of people who took JonBenét's life are really a group of two. Once again Patsy cannot stop herself from telling the real story.

"Gentlemen" is a very refined term, a "proper" term, and almost certainly a word a lady would use. Identifying the killers as two "gentlemen" also reveals yet again Patsy Ramsey's secret desire to have "male-like" powers.

No one will really believe that gentlemen would commit such a crime, but once again the killer is confessing and telling us to look for the two (figurative) gentlemen behind this crime. Look for the cover-up, expect it, and be able to recognize it.

Expect the murderers to appear exceptionally genteel—as they certainly did on CNN right after JonBenét's murder as well as five months later, in May, when Patsy and John Ramsey made a joint television appearance as respectable grieving parents and the voice of reason, pleading for help in finding the killers. Once again though, while trying to conceal the truth, Patsy revealed it. As the cameras honed in on Patsy and John, Patsy suddenly holds up two fingers and reveals that there are two people involved in this killing. One who did it, and one the killer told—*how did Patsy know that?*

ANOTHER REVEALING SLIP: I LIKE YOU

The slip-up "do like you" instead of "do not like you" (referring to John Ramsey) reveals that something inside the killer caused her to admit that really she liked John Ramsey. Patsy committed the exact opposite slip in a previous sentence when she confessed that she really didn't respect John's "bussiness" (see Chapter Two).

Why does the killer make this positive shift toward John? Because now they're partners—in crime. As both stand looking at JonBenét's corpse, there's no other person for Patsy Ramsey to turn to in the entire world than John. And the same goes for him—and continues for both of them until this day, which helps explain their insistence on being interviewed together and their constant clinging to each other.

A second powerful reason for this slip can be understood if we eliminate one simple letter: "The two gentlemen watching over you(r) daughter do particularly like you." Imagine two parents standing over the dead body of their own daughter they have just killed. Surely they would want to say, *"But we loved you."*

Yet their actions said they didn't. "Do like you"/Do not like you" is another art-word form where Patsy Ramsey wants to show the loving side of herself and John, but as an afterthought admits they have a downside, too.

One last aspect of the slip again points toward Patsy Ramsey. When the killer inserted the left out word "not" in "do *not* like you," she used an inverted "v" instead of an upward pointing arrow to show the left out word "not" above the line. This use of an inverted "v" is indicative of someone with prior experience in editing and exactly the opposite of the way an average person would point out a left out word (with an upward pointing arrow). Patsy was a *magna cum laude* graduate in journalism from West Virginia University and would have often used the inverted "v" when she copy edited or proofread written material. Additionally, her handwriting overall is exceptionally clean, often printed, plainly spaced, extremely legible, and well punctuated with *proper* paragraphs, etc.—all marks of someone with a great deal of experience in writing and particularly editing. The neatness itself reveals the killer's personality.

"I advise you not to provoke them." For the first time in several sentences, the killer returns to using "I" and—on the heels of extensive references to JonBenét's dead and damaged body—she writes about someone being provoked. Has she returned to using the single person "I" to tell us specifically that she was the one who was provoked and who killed JonBenét?

This sentence is the first of several hostile warnings. But it's a *specific* warning, allegedly addressed to John Ramsey. Is Patsy Ramsey, on another level, warning John himself to watch out lest he provoke someone—namely her? Surely the warning is a reminder that someone (because of something connected to JonBenét's death) has leverage over another person. (Patsy will read the entire note to John Ramsey before leaving it, and she knows he is capable of hearing such a message on some level.)

SUDDEN EXECUTION: NO ROOM FOR ERROR

*"Speaking to anyone about your situation, such as Police, F.B.I., etc., will result in your daughter being **beheaded**. If we catch you talking to a stray dog, **she dies**. If you alert bank authorities, **she dies**. If the money is in any way marked or tampered with, **she dies**."*

First, the killer warns that there will be *zero* tolerance for talking with any law enforcement person. Then the killer becomes increasingly brutal: Speak to anyone, and JonBenét is beheaded. Talk to a stray dog and she dies. Alert bank authorities and she dies. Tamper with the money and she dies.

These threats reveal the killer's inordinate need to control, with someone's life hanging precariously in the balance if she is disobeyed. The killer continues to demonstrate her obsession with the slightest boundary being crossed. Four times the killer says "she dies" if the slightest false move is made.

We know JonBenét is already dead, so what is Patsy so concerned about? She gives us a clue in writing that a female body would be mutilated (beheaded) and a female would die. Once again this reveals the heart of the killer, who is obsessed with the idea of a woman dying. This is powerful evidence that a deeply threatened woman wrote this note—someone who was threatened as violently as the violent tone of the note. Patsy feels violent pressure in her life.

The three images connected to "she dies" all relate to Patsy. First, the repetitive idea of tremendous pressure not to deviate in the slightest is attached to a *stray* dog. Clinton Van Zandt, formerly head of the FBI Behavioral Sciences Unit, told *Newsweek* that this was related to some cliches from the movie *Dirty Harry*. Van Zandt described the killer as a novice who was trying to sound like a hardened criminal.

JonBenét's killer is sounding tough and possibly used some phrases from a movie. It is significant that she thought of them at this particular moment in time and either they came out of her mind or she gave approval to the idea from her husband. Whatever its origin, the idea of a stray dog is not coincidental. *Every word, every idea in the ransom note is important if we keep in mind that Patsy's deeper intelligence is guiding the communication.*

Likewise the idea of money being marked or tampered with is not coincidental. Read it as something very valuable being damaged or changed—and also set apart, marked. These two simple ideas of "tampered with" and "marked" also fit precisely with Patsy Ramsey's personal story.

"Alert bank authorities and she dies," is the third idea in a row connected to sudden death. Bank authorities link to someone who has authority over banks, someone who knows how to handle the valuable items associated with banks, someone who knows the code to get into the bank's secrets.

If we go back to the idea that "bank" in the ransom note refers to a woman, then we see how someone who knows how to handle women, in this case one woman in particular, can bring about the death of a woman. **Here Patsy Ramsey is talking about herself and what will bring about her downfall, her conviction: Someone who knows where her valuable secrets are, someone who is alert to her secret communications. Someone trained to decode her valuable messages.**

The word "alert" draws our attention to the mind, a subtle hint that the deeper mind is the key. Here Patsy Ramsey reveals her Achilles heel—her deep-seated fear of death that burdens her—and how vulnerable she is to confessing, if the authorities can only understand her fear. Her repeated idea of the slightest talk resulting in someone's sudden downfall reveals that she knows, when the right buttons are pushed, that it won't take much to bring her down.

She also reveals that speaking to the "Police" (whom she sees as quite powerful with a capital "P") or the F.B.I., etc. (note her characteristic precise punctuation again revealing how thorough and strong she sees the Bureau) will immediately result in a death, directly linking her vulnerability to being interviewed by the authorities—just as she linked her vulnerability to bank authorities.

The idea of someone speaking in the most innocuous way—to a stray dog—is simply another revelation of her secret vulnerability that she elaborates on in the phrase "catch you." She knows how vulnerable she is to being caught, which is why we have seen the Ramseys fight so strongly against being interviewed a second time. At first John insisted that Patsy not be interviewed because of her grief, and later, that she not be interviewed alone. *(Patsy is most vulnerable when she is alone with someone who understands her deepest motives. She would be most vulnerable at a grand jury hearing where she would be the least protected.)*

THE HIDDEN CONFESSION IN THE RANSOM NOTE REVEALS:

- further evidence that the murder was an unplanned rage killing.

- Patsy repeats that she is a frightened woman.

- Patsy admits to bashing in JonBenét's head.

- Patsy greatly fears death herself.

- Patsy used unique editing and precise punctuation to reflect her journalism background.

- Patsy made a unique slip-up to show the killers are secretly attached to JonBenét.

Chapter Six
The Key to the Killer's Identity

*"You will be **scanned** for electronic devices and if any are found, she dies. You can try to deceive us but be warned that we are familiar with Law enforcement countermeasures and tactics. You stand a 99% chance of killing your daughter if you try to out smart us. Follow our instructions and you stand a 100% chance of getting her back. You and your family are under constant scurtiny [sic] as well as the authorities."*

Here the killer reveals that it is impossible for John Ramsey to escape with the slightest deviation, impossible to get by with the smallest item hidden on his body—because of a scanner. When you think of a scanning device that would surround someone and detect the smallest abnormality connected to their body, what do you think of? If you're Patsy Ramsey you think of one thing—the scanner that picked up her advanced ovarian cancer, the scanner she repeatedly visits to determine if her cancer has returned.

"... if any are found she dies" is the language of a cancer patient. Did they find cancer? Will they find it in the future? "Find" is a very crucial word for cancer patients—it's the one word that says it all. The ransom note contains a plethora of cancer-related words, almost a complete lexicon.

The scanner is at the very heart of the treatment of advanced ovarian cancer. At the very beginning of treatment an ovarian cancer victim has a CT scan of the abdomen to determine how much the tumor has spread. The patient is repeatedly scanned to determine the effect of chemotherapy and the length of time it is to be used and then has repeat scans every three months for one to two years to make sure the cancer is still in remission. If the patient remains cancer-free after two years, she continues to be scanned twice yearly for two more years.

The scanner comes to symbolize the verdict for the cancer patient—pass or fail, live or die. Now we can see why this brief story about a scanner fits Patsy Ramsey hand in glove. Deep down she would see herself confined to a scanner for five years—if she lived that long. Like all cancer patients Patsy both loves and hates that scanner. The scanner would see into deep crevasses where no one else could—simultaneously a blessing and a curse—a literal picture of death.

This is what is driving Patsy (and John, in his own way) insane. This is what has haunted her. She is terrified, moment to moment, that she as a cancer victim—is going to die.

She claimed in an interview that God had "healed" her, but that was her conscious mind speaking. Deep down she's terrified that her cancer could come back at any time, and with good reason. She had a particularly malignant form of ovarian cancer and it had spread to her liver. She had very poor odds of surviving.

The very minute Patsy Ramsey incorporated the seemingly clever idea of a scanner into the phony ransom note, she exposed herself as the killer. The scanner that constantly reveals whether she lives or dies sums up the whole note and Patsy's predicament.

When all is said and done, the "scanner story," the story within the story, will bring Patsy Ramsey down. It also points to a larger "scanner," the search for justice that awaits her with a jury and jail.

Virtually every part of the note points toward the "scanner" and Patsy. At the beginning of the note she wrote about monitoring someone for an early event, which parallels the idea of early detection of cancer. How many times had Patsy been surrounded by monitors during her numerous hospitalizations at the National Cancer Institute in Bethesda, Maryland, where she went for experimental treatment for her invasive cancer? Always concerned if they were going to *pick up* any more cancer in her.

The ransom note continually refers to defective women and declining femininity. Patsy's cancer went right to the heart of her femininity, her ovaries. And to her uterus, her nest. With her cancer she lost her ability to *"deliver"* as a woman, lost the very essence of her identity—and suddenly not only had an empty nest, but no nest at all.

Patsy also lost her hair. For a woman who prided herself on her hair, who would wear elaborate wigs to make a grand show, losing her hair was *the equivalent of being beheaded*, as was the cancer itself.

Patsy's friend Judith Phillips took pictures of Patsy immediately after chemotherapy, just as her hair was starting to grow back. Patsy was nearly bald and had lost her famous beauty. Judith had to talk her into getting her picture made without her wig, as Patsy dearly loved her wigs and wore them, as some friends said, "like Dolly Parton."

Patsy groomed JonBenét, a little girl to look like a twenty- five-year-old model with big blond hair. In JonBenét's pictures her hair looked twenty years older than she did. And Patsy loved JonBenét's hair, so much so that she was willing to have it bleached—and then lie to Judith Phillips about having it bleached. As we will see, it wasn't a far step from admiring her daughter's hair to having it bleached, to lying about it, to envying it as much as she took pleasure from it. Now we can see even more clearly how Patsy used JonBenét to have the hair she had lost—and the life she thought she had lost.

CANCER: ALL THE ASSAULTS

Think of all the assaults on Patsy Ramsey's body: loss of her hair—everywhere (including the pubic hair that distinguished her as a fully developed woman). A catheter in her chest to receive her chemotherapy. Surgery twice, as she put it "from stem to stern," to remove her ovaries and uterus leaving behind vivid scars as a constant reminder. Her pale skin from the anemia, and the weight loss that left her a skeleton of her former self. All of this caused her to perceive herself deep down as a plain-brown-paper-bag sort of person, a *stray dog* who has already been abandoned and is about to die, someone who had been greatly tampered with and who was now a marked woman, a beheaded carcass, "remains" ready for burial—if she wasn't eaten up so completely by cancer that there was nothing left to bury.

Another friend of Patsy's, Pamela Griffin, confirmed the toll that Patsy's cancer had taken on her identity as a woman. Pamela told Geraldo that Patsy once said to her in the middle of her treatment, "How feminine do you feel when you have your head in the toilet, and the head that's in there is bald as an eagle."

Most of all Patsy's cancer left her terrified, a woman constantly on the edge of death, with uncertainty constantly eating at her in the back of her mind just as cancer itself. If the slightest flaw was found hidden anywhere in her, there was no hope. That is also what cancer does to the patient's psyche.

No wonder Patsy is preoccupied, in her own warped way, with "delivery"—obsessing both about her femininity and even more so about her hoped for delivery from cancer. But as she wrote in the ransom note, "the delivery will be exhausting." *As a chemotherapy patient, Patsy stayed exhausted physically.* She is still exhausted emotionally, constantly haunted by the nightmare that her cancer is coming back.

Her psyche ties all of this exhaustion, pressure, and fear to her *performance.* Patsy thinks that if she crossed the slightest line, she is doomed. In one part of her mind she is a perfectionist, thinking that she has to perform to stave off cancer—subconsciously thinking that the cancer had been caused in the first place by her own failures. This is how driven people think, particularly when they have cancer.

Patsy Ramsey frequently linked her children with death. She told the *Colorado Woman News* (now defunct), "I asked God, 'Why did you give me my two kids if I was going to die?'" Death also means a possible separation from her kids—God giving her something and then taking it away from her. Also, God giving her a life and then taking it away.

Could Patsy Ramsey, deep down, be angry with the same God she desperately clings to at moments? Right after Patsy's chemotherapy, Judith Phillips took a poignant picture of an almost bald Patsy wearing sunglasses and biting on a small metal cross. Does this not reflect anger at God—even if the pose was not Patsy's own idea originally?

And Patsy is angry at others too. She sees herself as a woman with a black mark on her, the same black mark she showed us in the note when she so blatantly scratched out the word "delivery" just like her ability to deliver had been destroyed. Somewhere in her mind she hates herself for being a woman. She would have been angry at JonBenét for also being a woman and simultaneously for getting to go on living. And Patsy was angry at her husband, who didn't have to suffer like women did.

THE BEAUTY QUEEN AND CANCER

For a woman like Patsy Ramsey to have her beloved body wracked with cancer was to attack her most vulnerable point, her beauty and her body—her beauty-queen identity. Now everything she had ever considered important was lost, including, she thought, her life. Patsy decided she was going to live *through* her children. As she said, **"They became my reason to live."** Now more than ever, driven like she had never been driven before, this meant living through JonBenét far more than through her son, Burke.

Many friends noticed how much more attention she paid to JonBenét. Of course she could more easily identify with a little girl, especially a little beauty queen. In addition her favoritism reflected her being threatened, particularly at the time, by males and her anger at them.

PATSY CONFIRMS THE NOTE IS HERS

At the heart of the ransom note is a woman terrified of cancer, as Patsy herself confirms. Patsy told the *Colorado Woman's News* in a 1994 cover story exactly what her cancer was like to her consciously. On the July 4th weekend of 1993, Patsy was a judge in the Miss West Virginia pageant. During that trip she discovered a mass in her abdomen and was evaluated the next day when she returned to Atlanta. She was immediately diagnosed with stage 4 ovarian carcinoma (the most advanced) and underwent a hysterectomy and began chemotherapy. From being a vibrant and still beautiful thirty-six year old woman, Patsy *"went through menopause in five days. It was a total and unequivocal nightmare."* A total and unequivocal nightmare—one that still hasn't gone away. Cancer caught her completely off guard at a young age.

There is a second part to the story of how cancer blind-sided Patsy Ramsey: Unconsciously she links cancer with her (and her husband's) extraordinary success—as a sort of punishment (see Chapter 3).

The day before she was diagnosed with cancer, Patsy had returned to her days of glory, now elevated to the status of a judge, still striking and beautiful—a mountaintop experience reminiscent of the biggest mountain she had ever personally climbed—and she had been struck down in the batting of an eye. Patsy's mind formed an unbreakable connection between the great success and major disaster. (Patsy's 1996 Christmas letter [see Chapter 15] reveals that this crucial and distorted idea still lives in her mind.)

THE MOVIE *RANSOM*—IDEA FOR THE NOTE?

Some authorities have suggested that the killer got the idea for the ransom note from the Mel Gibson movie *Ransom*. In the movie, after his child was kidnaped, Gibson's character was told in the *ransom* note to be prepared for a "rigorous" ordeal. The writer of the JonBenét note had the same idea but put it "the delivery will be exhausting," a phrase much closer to Patsy Ramsey's situation and much more consistent with her repetitive fixation on feminine symbols that have been devastated—reflecting a woman who has exhausted her resources. Once again, it really doesn't matter if Patsy borrowed some ideas from movies or another source because when and how she used them and shaped them would reflect her own unique thought processes.

The comparison to *Ransom* is so strikingly obvious that it strongly suggests a possible origin of Patsy and John Ramsey's cover-up, but a very juvenile origin not only in its paper-thin creativity—consistent with the rest of the cover-up—but in its outright stupidity. There are very few kidnappings these days simply because it is so hard to pull off. In 1995 the FBI recorded a minuscule number of kidnappings in comparison to 22,000 murders. This suggests that the killer's judgment was impaired by the popularity of the movie *Ransom*, which temporarily made kidnaping appear to be so feasible.

This Hollywoodization of the crime suggests that JonBenét's killer was prone to live in a fantasy world, someone who was quite familiar with the camera and the world of illusions it creates. This once again points toward Patsy as both the killer and the originator of the ransom note cover-up. The idea of kidnaping is also fairly real to wealthy businessmen who are more vulnerable to such threats and points to John as does the fact that the lead character in *Ransom* was a man..

Patsy and John Ramsey would be the type of people who, in a pinch, might be prone to concoct a kidnaping ransom story. The whole idea is one big confession.

Deep down JonBenét was Patsy and John's ransom. She paid a price for them that they couldn't pay. They both were in a terrible death trap from which they desperately needed to be freed—ransomed. The whole idea of a ransom note and the tone of this one particularly communicated "You are surrounded by impending death, and you're helpless."

While their idea of a ransom note may have been juvenile in ways, this ploy didn't occur by accident. Patsy and John Ramsey needed to be set free from a horrible trap.

THE KILLER KNOWS HER DEEPER INTELLIGENCE HAS CONFESSED

"You can try to deceive us but we are familiar with Law enforcement countermeasures and tactics." Anticipating the authorities' counter-measures and shrewd tactics, the killer's mind goes to the thought of the authorities as having electronic devices that can listen in on conversations or secretly follow someone and discover their strategy. Ostensibly the killer has a scanner that can outsmart the authorities, but deep down she knows different.

Once again the killer has used *two more message markers* in one sentence ("countermeasures" and "tactics") that have to do with reason, strategy, and communication. These message markers are particularly linked to Law enforcement which means that this is a very special message to them. *The killer is telling the police that if they will shape their strategy around the two major clues contained in the scanner story—revealing the central motive (which points to others) and how to detect it (utilizing the deeper intelligence)—they can outsmart the killer (or killers).* She knows that the reference to the scanner is a tip-off to her identity—it reveals that her cancer is behind the murder of JonBenét. And she knows that *someone with a different kind of scanner can detect this and overcome any means of deception, including her own.*

The killer is referring to the deeper intelligence, the force within us that constantly scans our environment, subliminally picking up on clues our conscious mind misses, secretly listening in on deceitful plans, and encoding special messages revealing the truth. Specifically the killer is referring to her own deeper intelligence, which is secretly observing her motives as she tries to write a deceptive ransom note.

Once more, the killer's deeper intelligence is secretly giving the authorities key tactics they can use to overcome her deception: scan the note properly—decode her messages. *Thus the "scanner story" takes on even more importance. It is not only a killer's confession but also an advisor's recommendation about how to catch her.*

The killer knows she will be caught. She shows this by capitalizing the authorities' identity—"Law enforcement"—just as she did with "Police." She knows that if the police pick up on how great her vulnerability is and where it is, she stands a 99% chance of being "killed"—being caught. She sees law enforcement as having incredible power.

This vulnerability leads the killer to try to compensate in a familiar way: by insisting upon how brilliant she is. Again and again the ransom note says "don't overlook me" or "don't undervalue my ability." Patsy knows she is going to match wits with the police, and on the surface, she thinks she can do it—but, deep down, she knows she can't.

MORE PREDICTIONS

We can predict what is coming next in the note: more pressure, more images of being under pressure, more efforts at deception that would backfire and shine the light on the killer even more clearly. *The very fact that this is such an unusually long note is a tip-off itself—the killer was under a lot of pressure before the murder because of some personal crisis* and she needs to talk to get rid of the pressure.

Extreme desperation drove both Patsy and John Ramsey to the point of killing their daughter and covering up the crime. Prior to JonBenét's death both parents felt wall-to-wall desperation, however quiet or hidden they kept it: the desperate child beauty contests with a very seductive child *(was it sexual abuse that gave her that seductive edge?)* and always, in all things, the desperate mask of perfection.

Patsy and John have continued their same desperate modus operandi as they proclaim their innocence in the murder of JonBenét. The criminal attorneys, the public relations campaign, the reward, the private detectives to muddy the waters, the battle of wills with the police, the extreme religiosity, the extreme pseudo-grief. Why can't John and Patsy take one simple lie-detector test? It's an opportunity that innocent people leap at, as did the Ramseys' own housekeeper, among others—it's something the F.B.I. uses to *eliminate* suspects.

POOR SURVIVAL RATES

Here, right next to the very heart of the note, to the biggest clue as to the identity (and motive) of the killer, is one of the most blatant parts of the confession: *"You stand a 99% chance of killing your daughter."* These words come straight out of the mind of the killer—it is another confession from Patsy Ramsey's deeper mind pointing to herself and John. In essence the killer is saying that John Ramsey has a 99% chance of being involved in the death of his daughter. It is a very unusual phrase to use. I cannot imagine a kidnapper telling any parent "you will kill your child"—maybe "you will be responsible for your child's death," but not "you will kill."

The whole sentence (including "if you try to outsmart us") reflects the killer's deeper recognition that one day she (and John) will be caught and will pay with their lives. She knows that she and her partner in crime cannot continue to outsmart the authorities nor can she outsmart her own deeper mind.

This idea of trying to outsmart someone and getting caught follows the idea that the police have a lot of tactics and weapons. The killer is consciously in denial of getting caught and is obviously trying to make "someone else" appear to be the one in danger of getting caught, but she knows that someone is going to get caught no matter how slick they are, even if they know the latest tactics.

"Follow our *instructions* and you stand a *100% chance* of getting her back." Stand back from the words themselves just a bit, and consider the underlying ideas: life or death, with the odds given in percentages. Who in our society most commonly talks like that? *Doctors and patients talking about survival rates.* Criminals, "real" criminals, don't discuss their crimes in such specific, clinical terms. They just say, "Try something smart and your daughter dies. Do what I tell you and she lives."

But somewhere in this criminal's mind is the idea of "99% chance of dying." In the killer's mind she was a walking dead person. That's why she radically (consciously) insisted, in public that she was completely healed. Patsy probably thought about survival rate a million times a day because her prognosis is so poor. She has been told her odds aren't good and that extreme measures such as experimental treatment were necessary. If there's one phrase that encapsulates Patsy's life it's a 99% *chance of dying.* Down deep that's how she sees her odds.

This sentence also contains a *message marker* ("instructions"), which means the killer is giving another major clue. Patsy is saying that if we break the secret code of the ransom note and understand the survival percentages as her motive, then the police can approach her with this strategy and confront her about how she killed her daughter. She is cluing us in that she can barely stand to consider the truth that "you, Patsy Ramsey, killed your own daughter." With this strategy, she will break—100% guaranteed as she tells us. It's the way to get JonBenét back—to have her speak from the grave. And strangely enough it will allow Patsy to get her back in her own way as well. She can then appropriately grieve the loss of her daughter instead of spending so much time utilizing the cover-up as a form of denial.

A Very Conditional Survival

Once more the killer ties survival with *performance.* "Follow our instructions" is the condition that survival depends upon, delivered in a very harsh tone. The killer reveals again that when she thinks about chances of living or dying, she thinks about performance. And not just any old performance, but a perfect one: Instructions must be followed to the letter. You must look so straight ahead that you can't even glance at a stray dog. Make the slightest slip, and the scanner finds it.

When being observed and judged combines with having to be perfect, disaster looms. The killer's choice of words shows us that she's combining these two ideas in her mind: Patsy Ramsey with cancer who thinks that any minute now the scanner is going to find a defect in her—the slightest defect—and then it's curtains. Isn't that what cancer victims and their families live with—the constant fear of the defect, however small, being found by the scanner?

Part of Patsy's mind thinks that somehow, magically, she can ward off this cancer by being perfect—the second she isn't perfect, she's a goner. *Perfect performance wards off danger.* In other words, the key to a perfect (cancer-free) body is being a perfect person—perfection to the letter. This is why she had to perform, to constantly "sing for her supper"—indeed, for her life.

The struggle for such perfection, the constant "posing" is not only futile, but also terribly exhausting for both the body and the emotions. Deep down the killer knows she can't keep it up—so she went ahead and "got it over with," erupting in a rage at JonBenét. Deep down she realizes she is on a suicide mission. But now she (and inevitably her husband) suddenly find themselves facing a very different type of game: If they can just lie convincingly enough and keep posing perfectly, they think they can get away with the killing. Same idea, different setting.

Both Patsy and John are very deeply divided individuals and completely awash in guilt even *before* JonBenét's death, no matter how many ways they tried to deny it. Many of their acquaintances would tell you how conscientious they are, but they are simultaneously evil, destructive, and terribly afraid. Their unhealthy selves co-exist with their healthy selves.

SAME SONG, FIFTIETH VERSE: CONSTANT SCRUTINY

"You and your family are under constant scrutiny (as well as the authorities)." We could have predicted this—*constant scrutiny.* You and your family. *A disease like cancer* indeed affects the whole family. Just another image of the killer's motive—that every moment of her life she feels under constant scrutiny of the most extreme kind.

JonBenét was also closely scrutinized—judged—either by Patsy or by John. Think of the multitude of reactions that must have gone through JonBenét's mind in her final moments (possibly reflected in her scream that a neighbor recently reported): helpless, totally controlled, condemned, betrayed, victimized, terrified, and hopeless. None of these reactions were new to John or Patsy—they were only passing them along. It certainly doesn't excuse what they did, but it does shed light on how they could end up this way.

By connecting the idea of constant scrutiny with the authorities, the killer is reminding them that they should study what being under "constant scrutiny" means to her. It also reflects the pressure she is constantly under because the authorities are scrutinizing her closely.

Patsy disliked the idea of scrutiny so much that she misspelled the word. She made the letters "r" and "u" run together—she made them indistinguishable except for the slightest hint that they have been reversed. First, Patsy clearly wants to obliterate the word because she doesn't want to be under scrutiny. The very idea overpowers her normally meticulous nature, so much so that she has *another brief chaotic moment.* Reading the slip like she apparently intended it before she was completely overwhelmed, scrutiny becomes "scurtiny"—Patsy wants to skirt the whole issue of judgment and guilt. Characteristically she also feminizes whatever threatens her and, as a former journalism major, demonstrates her skills as a word smith.

FROM BEGINNING TO END: A CANCER NOTE

More than a killer's confession, this ransom note is really from beginning to end "a cancer note." The very first sentence, "Listen carefully," refers to cancer being a wake-up call in Patsy's life. The introduction, "Mr. Ramsey," hints that Patsy isn't around and suggests that Mr. Ramsey might have to go it alone one day soon. The idea of terrorism reflects the secret terrorist in Patsy's life—cancer. The cancer in her body is a "small foreign faction," a foreign entity that was exceptionally small but wreaked great havoc and made her terribly uncertain of how much of 1997 she would see. The killer claims to possess the Ramseys' daughter, and cancer possesses Patsy. "If you want (her) to see 1997" reflects Patsy's continual uncertainty about living another year.

The references to remains (money or a body) and to sudden executions suggest bodily damage and loss of value—all unquestionably tied to cancer. Money being tampered with—something extremely valuable that has now been disfigured or changed in some sinister—way recalls how Patsy's cancer tampered with her body. Cancer set Patsy apart as a marked woman, and the doctors use cancer ˆ to follow her tumor, to see what they can pick up on. While her body might have looked good on the outside, inside cancer was hiding.

The killer makes repeated references to *"small"* in the note: a small foreign faction, small electronic devices, a small scanner, remains, small attaché, small bills, small or shorter time frames, slightest deviation, the shrinkage of an attaché to a paper bag, underestimations, and later small cells that grow (brain cells). Even a small—insignificant—stray dog. In the back of her mind, Patsy constantly saw the small but powerful force of cancer about to erupt inside her. Even her explosion at JonBenét was a picture, in its own way, of cancer. This also helps us see why she thinks of large bonuses and later "fat cats" as a way of coping with her smallness, her perceived deterioration. And short time spans, being monitored, under constant scrutiny, survival percentages, exhausting delivery along with repeated references to dying all point loud and clear to cancer.

The end of the note contains hidden references to the body and to cancer. Even the very ending of the note points toward two ideas related to cancer: helplessness, the outcome of an event being up to someone else ("It's up to you, John")—and the idea of "Victory." Wherever you turn in the ransom note, whatever the superficial cover-up idea may be, you will find cancer hidden behind Patsy's words and between the lines.

A PORTRAIT OF HER CANCER

Patsy Ramsey the artist (her hobbies include painting) also provides a vivid portrait of her cancer in the ransom note. The black mark she used to cross out "delivery" *(cancer destroyed her fertility)* stands out just like a black spot stands out on an X-ray. If we want to get creative, we can interpret the small black spot over the only other crossed-out word at the top of the first page has spread and become a larger black spot on the second page. Cancer that spreads is the kind that scares a cancer victim the most, as Patsy is telling us when we see her black spot getting bigger in this art-word portrait of herself.

Looking at Patsy's self-portrait from a different angle, the largest black mark covers "delivery"— the self-portrait of a woman who has been destroyed. The smaller black mark on the first page, where she covers over the word "don't" in *"don't respect your bussiness,"* portrays Patsy's hidden anger at her husband.

THE HIDDEN CONFESSION IN THE RANSOM

NOTE REVEALS:

- the key to the note: The story of the scanner shows the killer is a cancer victim.

- entire note points to cancer: scanners, monitors, survival percentages, etc.

- fear of cancer returning drove Patsy Ramsey mad.

- Patsy knows the police have clues to catch her.

- Patsy tells us to look for clues in the note.

Chapter Seven
Patsy Blackmails John

"Don't try to grow a brain John. You are not the only fat cat around so don't think that killing will be difficult. Don't underestimate us John. Use that good southern common sense of yours. It is up to you now John!

Victory!
S.B.T.C."

T he last sentences of the ransom note reveal more clues about how the killer sees John Ramsey and some hints about John's role in the tragedy. "Don't try to grow a brain John," is the first time the killer uses John's first name or speaks to him so intimately. The killer previously showed that she has some significant personal knowledge about John Ramsey (his bonus), but this is the most overtly personal moment in the note so far.

Yet this intimate connection comes in the form of a controlling put-down—and one that contains a warning. The killer talks about John Ramsey being under constant scrutiny and now continues to warn him that he cannot outsmart her or "them." This subtle message suggests that Patsy has knowledge that she can use against him.

This same tone continues for three sentences: "Don't try and grow a brain," "You are not the only fat cat," and "Don't underestimate us." By speaking in a very personal way to John at the end of the letter the killer reveals that something powerful is going on between them.

Ostensibly the killer is telling John Ramsey, "Do this to save your daughter." But read another way the message is "Do this to save the life of a woman, namely Patsy." If ever anyone's neck was on the line and needed saving it was Patsy Ramsey's.

So why is Patsy telling John not to think, not to do anything out of the ordinary, not to get creative? Either John was up to something or she feared he would be. Patsy knows how crafty and ruthless John could be in a pinch—and how he loved a good battle. She obviously fears that John will try to think his way out of this situation and perhaps place all the blame on her.

The killer (Patsy) had just bashed in the head of JonBenét (her own child) and while someone had to strangle the unconscious JonBenét as a cover-up, Patsy knew full well that John could blame that on her even if he did it. Since Patsy was the one who had lost control and made the major assault, John could choose to blame her for the whole thing, it would be credible. She knows how cool John can appear under fire, and it would be his word against the word of an obviously half-deranged mother.

She also knows that John loves murder mysteries and that he can very easily—as he is prone to do—come up with a new plan on his own without consulting her. Patsy wanted no surprises. They had come up with a story, and she would insist that they stick with it. The hostile threat, "Don't try and grow a brain," again implies she had distinct leverage with him.

BEHEADING JOHN

John Ramsey's brain led to his successful business. Of all his attributes, John Ramsey's mind, his smarts, would be most responsible for his success and in a real way be the most outstanding thing about him. Notice that the killer uses the idea of a "growing" brain, an expanding brain, a head that grows.

Seen in the context of all the earlier sexual symbols, the brain here is a phallic symbol certain to evoke resentment in a damaged female when she has been unable to bolster her own identity in her usual competitive ways. This harkens back to the killer's feminizing John's "bussiness" and not liking him (see Chapter 2). Now the killer more blatantly puts John down and at the same time reminds him that she has power over him.

Taken more literally, the killer's sexual imagery (growing a brain) could be hinting that it was not just John's brain that she held over him but also his genitalia. The killer reveals that she knew he was sexually abusing JonBenét. JonBenét's body showed evidence of sexual abuse—not just vaginal irritation—chronic inflammation—but damage to the hymen and vaginal wall. In medical findings these two different types of evidence suggest more than coincidence, especially erosion of the vaginal wall strongly suggests penetration. Dr. Wecht, the experienced Pennsylvania coroner, told the local newspaper *Daily Camera* that indeed this was evidence of sexual abuse. Dr. Robert Kirschner, a child-abuse forensic pathology expert, told *Vanity Fair* that "the genital injuries indicate penetration, but probably not by a penis, and are evidence of molestation that night as well as previous molestation."

The killer is telling John Ramsey not to think, just act. The real message here may be "Just continue the charade." Maybe Patsy's reminding John that he has a lot to lose if he starts to think—i.e., to think independently. This suggests that Patsy and John have worked out a plan, and she is strongly recommending that he not rock the boat. Apparently she's secure enough in the hold she has over him to subtly put him down while warning him. However much Patsy's trying to disguise her identity as a terrorist, the use of the name has a wifely quality about it. Ironically the first put-down is detoxified somewhat because it uses his first name.

ANOTHER LINK TO CANCER

The idea of someone growing a brain can be seen in another revealing light. Brains don't really grow, certainly not in adults—and if they do, you're in trouble because there's cancer growing. The very last thing a cancer patient wants is any growth to take place in the brain (or elsewhere). "No signs of any growths are the magic words" for cancer survivors. Ovarian cancer patients are particularly concerned about cancer spreading to the brain because it is often the first sign of recurrence. Stage 4 ovarian cancer patients like Patsy Ramsey, whose cancer has already spread in the abdomen, are even more concerned.

Thus Patsy would have had an incredibly strong wish not to grow a brain. The unusual phrase draws our attention once again to the human body, the killer's way of telling us that the assault on JonBenét's body is directly related to the assault on Patsy's own body. The killer's preoccupation with "brain," added to the previous "beheaded," is another confession—it points to JonBenét's damaged brain.

Embedded in this idea of growing a brain is one more picture linking it to JonBenét and to Patsy: JonBenét's hair that Patsy had groomed and bleached, the hair that symbolized the secret (Patsy's lie about coloring it) and not-so-secret sexual exploitation of JonBenét, Patsy hating to lose her own hair during her chemotherapy, and how badly she wanted it to grow back.

On a deeper level, it was no accident that Patsy struck JonBenét in the head. *The blow to the head is another signature of the killer* and another reason to think it came first—something Patsy is trying to tell us by repeatedly focusing our attention on the head. (This preoccupation indicates that the ransom note was written by one person.)

Also, Patsy and John would have discussed JonBenét's brain the night Patsy struck her in the head—whether or not her brain injury was fatal and what it meant. One of them could have reminded the other that brains never grow back or that damaged brains swell—grow—and that's why people die from head injuries. It would be natural under those conditions for Patsy to wish that JonBenét's brain wouldn't grow.

Most subtle of all is one last message—about *success*. Not using your brain, and not thinking, normally leads to failure in life. Patsy later reveals that she would have wished away John's success.

ANOTHER CUT: FAT CAT

The killer continues the note's hostile theme but in a much darker tone: "You are not the only fat cat around so don't think that killing will be difficult." The basic message is "Don't think you are above me, I can strike at what's nearest and dearest to you in a heartbeat." This put-down—which repeats the previous warning ("don't grow a brain") but so much harsher—indicates just how threatened Patsy felt. She is terrified that John will turn her in.

She is sending John a special message that if he tries to think his way out of this and leaves her holding the bag, he had better think again. She's reminding him that she won't break and that she will take him with her. In "don't think killing will be difficult" Patsy is informing John just how vicious she can be. Along with "beheaded" and "she dies," it's the most overtly hostile thing the killer writes.

These words imply that Patsy is unquestionably guilty, that John is intimately involved in the cover-up, and that she has enough on him to destroy him—and won't hesitate to do it. The stronger the threats, the greater the killer's vulnerability—the more she has to hide. And the greater her rage. The killer makes it more and more apparent that John too has something terrible to hide.

ANOTHER MOTIVE—ENVY

"Don't think you are the only fat cat" reeks of envy and points to another important issue between John and Patsy. The former beauty queen has turned fat and forty. Forty, in our culture, is a kind of death symbol in itself—the final loss of youth. Patsy is not the same woman as in her glory years, certainly an even harsher blow for a beauty queen—particularly one as desperately competitive as Patsy—than it would be for the average woman. She's literally telling us that one of the things that's eating at her is getting fat, her metabolism changing as most women's do at forty, particularly those who have had ovarian cancer and are thrown into premature menopause.

"Fat cats" is also a put-down of her husband, which fits perfectly with the fact of her declining beauty. The two ideas go together and shed further light on Patsy's motives for killing JonBenét. What is a fat cat? A "big shot," a wealthy or successful person whose prominence has gone to their head.

Patsy Ramsey is again telling us that she was enormously threatened by her husband's power and wealth—Mr. Fat Cat himself—at a time when she was most vulnerable. The competitive spirit could not be louder or clearer: "You, John Ramsey, are not the only fat cat around." You're not the only one with power.

The killer part of Patsy Ramsey is revealing another one of her central motives—envy—and linking it to ruthless, cold-blooded murder. She tells how easy it was on one level to carry out her hostile act and warns John that the cold-blooded part of her could easily kill him too.

Pictures of Patsy Ramsey's mother, Nedra Paugh, reveal where Patsy got at least part of her ruthlessness and raw aggression. Both

Nedra and Patsy at moments have the same chilling look. Patsy's friend, photographer Judith Phillips, saw that ruthlessness and heard it the day Nedra omnipotently informed Judith that if it came down to it JonBenét would have no choice as to whether or not she entered the pageants— she *would* do it.

Patsy had shown ruthlessness early on when she continually communicated to many of her high-school classmates (in Parkersburg, West Virginia) how superior she was. Groomed to be a beauty queen, smart, good grades, part of a championship debate team, and a cheerleader to boot—Patsy Paugh was certain she was above the crowd. She was obsessed, too, with becoming successful and rich. Unconsciously she practiced for the beauty contests by walking down the halls of her high school with her nose in the air, and she demonstrated more than her share of gall and viciousness. For a long time Patsy Ramsey has known she was a fat cat who had a comeuppance awaiting her—one that deep down she thought she deserved.

In the ransom note the killer (Patsy) warns John that, "When I think of losing my power, and being unable to repair my defective self, that's when I get cold. That's when I get brutal. Don't ever forget how brutal I can be."

FAT CAT JONBENÉT

When the killer wrote "fat cats," she was also referring to how she saw JonBenét becoming a fat cat—becoming the important one, the one who got all the attention, the one who had all the glamor. On one level Patsy "merged" with JonBenét—but on another, Patsy retained her ruthlessness and desperation. The "fat cat" side of Patsy wasn't about to let JonBenét think she was the only "fat cat" around.

"Fat cats" can be young cats who fatten up and fill out. "Fat cats" can also be pregnant cats. And Patsy Ramsey saw all those cats in JonBenét—a young beauty who was becoming a fat cat before her time and who one day could be a fat cat who had children. And in those terms, Patsy would never be a fat cat again—a bitter pill for someone who thought her very life depended upon her being a fat cat. On a deep level JonBenét greatly threatened Patsy.

"Fat cats" and ruthlessness suggest one other image Patsy had of herself deep down. Cats are extraordinarily quick when attacking and tend to pounce on their victims. Is it totally coincidence that Patsy Ramsey has thought up the idea of a fat cat, someone who pushes their weight around, and connected it to herself at this moment in time? Is she finding yet another condensed way to tell us exactly what happened that night? That in the blink of an eye she pounced on little JonBenét, fueled by envy and rage as well as other terrors? *Don't we usually think of cats as feminine and describe a fight between women as a cat fight?*

All along law enforcement authorities reportedly have felt that Patsy was the weak link, but here she tells us, that at the time she wrote the note, deep down she thinks that she is tougher and, by implication, John is the one most likely to break.

The killer has seemingly revealed two contradictory things: She is telling us just how tough she can be and is prepared to fight until the bitter end, but if the right buttons are pushed she will fold. John Douglas, the former FBI profiler, has noted that every killer has a weakness—Patsy Ramsey has revealed hers.

SUCCESS ENVY

The killer underscores another key motive by linking "fat cats" to "killing"—she links successful people—"fat cats"—with being destroyed. This reveals that Patsy saw her cancer as payback for being so successful. *"Don't think killing will be difficult" is also exactly what she saw her cold-blooded cancer saying to her.* Since Patsy viewed success as causing suffering, success was responsible for making her a cancer victim and as much as she craved success, she also saw it as incredibly dangerous.

Patsy Ramsey, the beauty queen, knew something about the envy and competitiveness of others toward "fat cats." Both Patsy and John Ramsey, each in their own way, have seen the dog-eat-dog world coming after them because they were fat cats. Instead of facing their pain and helplessness, both of them inflicted it on little JonBenét.

There is one more obvious meaning to the killer's threat "Don't think killing will be difficult." Patsy realized better than anyone how quickly and easily her aggression had gotten out of control—the slightest provocation had enraged her so much that she suddenly, unexpectedly, brutally murdered JonBenét. Patsy is saying, "I didn't mean to do it."

FROM FAT CATS TO A STRAY DOG

"Don't underestimate us John" provides another revealing look at the killer's deep feelings of being underappreciated. It's another stray dog image: damaged, unimportant, unappreciated, overlooked, fighting to be recognized. *Being underestimated—deemed insignificant—is also another reference to cancer and what it did to her.* Once again Patsy ties her pain to John—his success and prominence made her feel by comparison inconsequential.

This is what drove Patsy to seek beauty-queen prizes: her deep feeling of insignificance that cancer (and her husband's success) magnified exponentially and that she would try to surmount with increasing desperation. She was so desperate that she would paint her living room five times in one week just to find the perfect color. Desperate to the point that she would control her daughter's life without giving it a second thought—as apparently her mother did hers.

That may have prompted Patsy to create a stray dog image of herself deep inside, an image of a person who wasn't really important except to the degree they could be controlled and meet someone's else's needs for power. Did this set Patsy up to explode at her most vulnerable moment years later and to inflict the same worthless stray dog mentality on JonBenét?

Impulses like these, magnified by a terror such as cancer, can turn an "ordinary" person into a full-fledged monster. The potential was there all along. Nedra—and apparently Patsy—treated John with the same ruthlessness at times. As we saw when Judith Phillips commented on the expensive bedroom chest Patsy bought for JonBenét, and Nedra responded, "As long as John Ramsey keeps making the money, we don't care. We love to spend John Ramsey's money." Nedra said, "We," speaking once more for her daughter as if Patsy had no voice of her own and degrading John at the same time.

Did Patsy learn from her mother how to treat a man? Did she have a deep hostility toward men (because secretly she felt that they underestimated her)—and did her primary feminine role model, her mother, share the same mentality? The killer reveals that hostility in the previous sentence, "killing (JonBenét) will not be that difficult." In human development, tendencies for bad or good can be nourished in either direction, and combined with life's stresses they can produce a monster or a saint.

Patsy Ramsey's deep feelings of being underestimated led to her passion for JonBenét's beauty contests and the ever-present posing. It's the same passion that caused her to go to the Miss America pageant a year before she was in it *to take notes*. Was the sense of loss over not winning "it all"—Miss America—still driving Patsy all those years later? Did she want it so badly that in desperation she groomed her daughter to fulfill her Miss America dreams?

ONE LAST REMINDER: "JOHN"

There is another possibility to "Don't underestimate us John." A "john" is a man who uses a prostitute and the killer may be speaking for both herself and JonBenét, reminding John that he has treated both of them as prostitutes. First, he used Patsy as a trophy wife, and more recently he used JonBenét sexually. In "John," we find another subtle hint of abuse.

Patsy may also be revealing exactly what she holds over John's head. *By repeating John three times in rapid-fire succession, she may be drawing attention to the fact that "John is a 'john.'"*

Going one step deeper, Patsy uses the words "don't" and "John" *three* times at the end of the note. She could be alluding not only to the *threesome* she and John had created that led to the predicament they were in, but also hinting at something she had wanted to say then and now, "Don't John." Don't in the sense of not doing what John did with JonBenét and also "don't think about confessing."

All this sexuality follows immediately after "don't think that killing will be difficult." Patsy is subtly but powerfully linking sex with violence—one more way of hinting that the two are intricately related in this crime.

A DIFFERENT KIND OF PERSUASION: CHARM PATSY STYLE

The killer appears to be enormously driven by the time she wrote the last part of the ransom note. She repeatedly reminds John in one way or another to be careful.

"Use that good southern common sense of yours" sounds like it came from someone who knew John intimately, who recognized his common sense—calling it good and southern in an admiring, almost seductive, way. Although the killer is still cautioning John, the approach is drastically different from the decidedly hostile tone of the preceding two sentences. Was this how Patsy related to John—alternating between a subtle hostility and charm, all the while attempting to control him?

Certainly the killer was not southern—southerners rarely describe each other as "southern." It would be logical, particularly with John's quiet demeanor, for Patsy to think of him as southern, in contrast to herself, because he was in Atlanta when she moved there and met him. And wouldn't she particularly have recognized his common sense? Successful in business, not outgoing at all, his common sense—his business acumen—was his greatest asset.

Patsy was not altogether lacking in common sense, but she was the one who spent his money foolishly. She was the one who continuously repainted the same room and indulged in expensive furniture. In moments of stress her common sense was in scarce supply.

Also, "southern common sense" is an unusual phrase. Although southerners have common sense, they aren't particularly known for their common sense—but rather for their charm, good manners, accent, etc.

The killer seems fixated on getting across a message, about thinking things through. First,"don't think too much, don't try and grow a brain—think it through, but in the end, don't think." Now "think about it again—this time use your common sense." Patsy clearly wants John to think about something *particular.* Doesn't this sound like Patsy felt the day would come, and soon, that John would think about doing something that

Patsy didn't want him to do—such as confess and blame her?

LAST SENTENCE: POINTING TO THE MOTIVES

"It's up to you now John!" more strongly puts the entire burden on John. As in "From now on, once the authorities come in and the note is found, it's all up to you." This implies that John now has something to hold over Patsy's head. The literal message in the note is a warning, allegedly from the killer to John: If you do something foolish and get caught, somebody will die. But the real message is from Patsy herself to John and is addressed exactly as a wife would if he does anything foolish (like confess) she (and now he) will die.

The killer ended this sentence with an exclamation point, which is significant. The ransom note contains *three* exclamation points: The first is at the end of the first sentence ("Listen carefully!"), and the second and third ones come at the very end—after the last sentence, and after the one-word closing. Thus from beginning to end the entire note is surrounded by exclamation points like prominent displays at the entrance and exit of grand theaters or stadiums—dramatic, attention-getting symbols. The number "three" provides another clue—there is a threesome.

The exclamation point is the most expressive, and most phallic, of punctuation marks. It fits perfectly with "it's up to you now John." By placing the exclamation point right next to John's name, Patsy is saying, "I'm going to give you one last picture of the real story by placing a striking phallic symbol right next to his name to remind you that 'yes, he was a john.'" In addition, by choosing such a grand ending on the heels of such desperate warnings, the exclamation point represents the "phallic" power Patsy now holds over John. She is reminding him that she holds his sexual behavior over him.

The killer's deeper mind has communicated indirectly that sex is indeed the issue in four ways—a punctuation mark, two expressions ("a john" and "it's up"), and a linkage to John Ramsey. At one of the most crucial places in the note—the every end—where the killer has one last chance to tell us what this murder was really about, Patsy leaves no doubt in our mind that it had to do with sex. She ends with three sexual symbols in a row to make it plain that sex was behind her explosion.

The message is highlighted by a verbal message marker, *"good sense right before it."* "Good sense" is contrasted with "evil sexuality," and Patsy is appealing to John to *keep up the pose of a "Good John"* or she will expose him, bring him down, castrate him. It's another way of telling him, "I can kill you in a minute. I know your 'Achilles of all Achilles.'"

The killer is also saying that she has John right where she wants him. Patsy has turned the tables on "evil men" her mother taught her about—men who want only one thing from women. *(Later we will see how this fits with the idea that a shadow side of Patsy actually wanted John to be involved with JonBenét. It then gave her a perverse power over both of them—just when she needed a power boost the most.)*

With the exclamation points, the killer also tells us something about herself. She begins the ransom note with a dramatic phallic symbol and ends her note in the same way—as if to say, from beginning to end this is about a perceived deficiency in herself that she is trying to overcome with bold strokes, bold moves, moves designed to give one the sense of power, to bolster her vulnerable, failing self-image—just as she did with the flamboyant accent in JonBenét's name. *(In other letters, we will see what a characteristic trademark of Patsy Ramsey's an exclamation point is.)*

And it worked—temporarily. But Patsy always needs another fix. The nation's attention is focused on her and she can keep the game going, being suspected but not caught she can keep some support coming. What better cover than doing good, going to church, and appearing to be deeply spiritual?

It is no accident that in the next to last sentence, for the only time in the ransom note, the killer uses the word "good." As she gets ready to sign off, wanting to be "good" is on her mind. Eventually it will be this very battle in her soul between the "bad Patsy" and what's left of the "good Patsy" that will determine how much longer she "can keep it—the charade—up." Patsy comes from a family of competitors *extraordinaire*—they could pose for hours.

THE HIDDEN CONFESSION IN THE RANSOM NOTE REVEALS:

- Patsy was secretly blackmailing John Ramsey.

- Patsy ends the letter with three sexual symbols confirming that John Ramsey was sexually abusing JonBenét.

- Patsy Ramsey saw JonBenét. as a rival—and the last night a catfight broke out between them.

- Patsy was uncomfortable with success.

- Patsy specifically feared her cancer could spread to her brain and quickly kill her.

- Patsy continually links the murder to a conflict in a threesome involving herself, JonBenét., and John.

Chapter Eight
What is The Killer's Victory?

(...It is up to you now John!)
Victory!
S.B.T.C.

The note is signed "Victory!" What is the killer telling us? Certainly it's the language of competition, even of war, and Patsy is a ruthless competitor to the end. By getting away with this, she has experienced a distorted victory—over JonBenét, over millions of people she has fooled, over death, over judgment, over boundaries, over cancer. Boundaries are the last thing people who are terrified of death want because boundaries connote death. Death is the ultimate boundary.

Patsy Ramsey wants to burst out of all boundaries, to rise above them, to be the winner. She ends the ransom note with a flurry of capital letters (the first letter of the last two words and "S.B.T.C.") and striking punctuation marks. Even the neatly punctuated ending with the four capitalized initials repeatedly says, "I want to stand out, notice me." It's exactly what Patsy did with JonBenét's name by using two capital letters, the prominent accent mark, and the French pronunciation.

More than anything else Patsy needs a victory over cancer, over what she feels was a certain death sentence. This is the first and most obvious personal meaning of "victory" for her, but the word has other meanings. For spiritual comfort Patsy watches the television program *Victory.* And her favorite Psalm (118) implies victory and deliverance from enemies (cancer) and death. Some translations use the word victory, "Hark, glad songs of victory in the tents of the righteous: The right hand of the Lord does valiantly ... I shall not die, but I shall live" (Ps 118: 15-17, RSV). "He is my strength and song in the heat of battle, and now he has given me the victory" (Ps 118: 14, Living Bible). The ending of the ransom note has Patsy Ramsey's signature all over it.

OEDIPUS: THE RAMSEY TRIANGLE

Other psychological victories also come into play in JonBenét's murder, including the oedipus complex. Years ago Freud hypothesized that there is a competition in families across gender lines with the males in the family competing for the females, and the females competing for the males. This was true for sons competing with their father for the mother, and daughters competing with their mother for the fathers. It's a taboo subject we feel uncomfortable talking about, but if we observe families closely we see it in many disguised (and not-so-disguised) ways.

Patsy grew up as the oldest of three highly competitive sisters. Only four sets of sisters have competed in the Miss America pageant. Patsy and her younger sister, Pamela, are one of those four. Patsy's mother, Nedra, likewise is exceptionally competitive. Combine her mother's strong competitive spirit with the possibility of sexual abuse and other probable traumas in Patsy's life, and Patsy would have gotten the message loud and clear that it wasn't safe to compete for men. Yet compete she would—and she showed fierce determination to win pageants.

Patsy also showed her competitive spirit in her attraction to a significantly older (by thirteen years) John Ramsey who was thirty-three, divorced, and the father of three children—just as her own father was. John embodied significant elements for her to be a father figure, and he also provided the satisfaction of being able to win and keep a man another woman couldn't—even their names were similar. John's first wife was Cindy Pasch, and Patsy's maiden name was Paugh.

The essence of the oedipus complex is that to compete with your same-sex parent for your other parent is taboo and punishment supposedly awaits the competitor. If by some chance an "oedipal victory" occurs, where in fact or fantasy (including symbolically) the competitive child displaces their parent, danger ultimately awaits them and revenge invariably will be the payoff.

Winning such a competition (even symbolically) puts incredible pressure on a child because any minute could be payback time. Since we tend to react the same way in similar situations, an oedipal victory can predispose someone to be very uncomfortable with victories in general—although they don't realize it consciously.

The Ramseys had the making of a potboiler of an oedipal battle— with all kinds of problems and anxieties surrounding "victories." Seductive little JonBenét, most assuredly put up to the task by her mother, perhaps wins too much of her father's attention. On the one hand this was exactly what part of Patsy might have had in mind—she could easily have enacted her own secret oedipal wishes through JonBenét, she could have enacted her own sexuality that she was uncomfortable with deep down. On the other hand Patsy despised the little seductress she had created because JonBenét was an insult to her fading beauty and severely damaged feminine identity. Under such tumultuous circumstances Patsy would act out both sides of the oedipal conflict.

Most likely Patsy was already looking over her shoulder and thinking that any minute could be payback time because of her many victories over other women who in some way symbolized her mother.

She would have seen her devastating cancer as a payback for her triumphs. Remember, she first became aware of her cancer when she was judging the 1993 Miss West Virginia contest. And she would have continued to wait for the other shoe to drop, as she clearly reveals in the ransom note.

By killing JonBenét, Patsy could have been killing the guilty child-adolescent competitor in her—a powerful hidden motivation behind her rage, a payback victory. And if Patsy had been sexually abused (see Chapter 10), she would have had an even greater reason to condemn herself over her sexuality, thinking it was somehow her "fault," as kids invariably do. Patsy desperately needed a victory over death, and her beloved child who was simultaneously her rival provided a perfect outlet for her typical way of coping: competition and winning. Of course Patsy wouldn't have known all this consciously—which makes it all the more dreadful because without her being aware of what was happening, the tension was building daily as she watched the young and beautiful JonBenét flourish.

If indeed JonBenét was involved with her father sexually, Patsy would have been stirred up more, even if she tacitly encouraged the sexual relationship. The most logical scenario is of the oedipus complex played out large: The young beautiful daughter seduces her father (while her ill mother is on the sidelines), and in a moment of rage, the mother one day takes the daughter's life. In the end the mother is victorious—thus another plausible meaning of "Victory!" in the ransom note. Oedipus doesn't get any plainer than that.

JonBenét's Hero: Daddy

We are all familiar with little boys who are going to "marry Mommy" when they grow up and little girls who are going to "marry Daddy." JonBenét showed the same disguised wishes shortly before her death in a dream that she revealed to her friend, Ariana, the daughter of Linda Hoffman (the Ramsey's housekeeper). JonBenét dreamed that she had a baby and lived with her mother in a castle that was surrounded by a high wall; her father did not live in the castle.

Some commentators focused on John Ramsey being left out of JonBenét's dream, but they missed the point. He was very much in the dream, but in a disguised fashion—which is typical of such dreams (the wish and the disguise). The castle with the wall around it, followed by the specific mention that her father wasn't there, indicates JonBenét's strong need to put up a barrier between herself and her father. First, she wants to hide her threatening fantasy (because of mother) that her father is the father of her baby, and secondly, she may want to further distance herself from him because of his sexual abuse, which could be stimulating her "natural" wishes to marry Daddy. She resolves this dilemma through compromise. She still has her baby, but she and her mother rule the kingdom away from all men. This also suggests that she indeed sees herself as a little princess.

Children are incredibly sensitive, and JonBenét appears to have already incorporated her mother's style of dealing with men: Use them to get your babies and then dominate without them. She also reflects Patsy's inordinate preoccupation at this time with having babies.

Overall this dream suggests another powerful variation on the oedipal conflict. JonBenét was strongly preoccupied with having babies and, thus, indirectly with sex.

Add to the information revealed in JonBenét's dream several other known facts: JonBenét was extremely attached to her father, describing him as her hero on one beauty pageant application. He was reportedly very gentle with his children. On top of it all her mother had a grave illness and she wanted to cling to her father even more—which would only intensify JonBenét's longings to replace Mommy with Daddy.

JonBenét was very seductive, which may be how she won a victory over all the tumultuous forces in the Ramsey family that she would undoubtedly have sensed. Kids always know what's happening—deep down there are no family secrets.

Lastly, to consider all possibilities, it is very likely that JonBenét felt guilt-ridden herself about competing this way with her mother, particularly since her mother had recently been ill. Children commonly feel hidden guilt about their wishes, and it's possible that this guilt could have caused JonBenét to provoke her mother in order to be punished, the punishment being death.

There was also at least one other third party—besides JonBenét—in Patsy and John's marriage, a sign that Patsy's cancer significantly affected her marriage. Although never greatly affectionate, a good friend observed them becoming more distant physically. John may have had an extramarital affair during Patsy's illness—Kim Ballard, a woman from Phoenix, initially came forward and reported having an affair with him, although later she refused to talk further to the media. It would not be the first time John was unfaithful in marriage. If there was another "third party," Patsy had a greater than ever need to win a victory over a rival—and her fear and rage would have intensified.

At least three powerful forces would have exerted recently great pressure on Patsy and John to dissolve their marriage or subtly withdraw from each other: the deaths of John's loved ones, cancer, and major business success. Any one of these three major stresses alone could have created a significant distrust of intimacy and commitment.

As separation-sensitive as Patsy was at that time, she also could have been her own worst enemy, pulling away from any sexual intimacy and pushing a seductive JonBenét toward John—undermining the very marriage she desperately wanted.

Patsy's final act of rage could have been a test to put John in a double bind so that he would stick around, and in a way she would have him all to herself. If he turned her in, he would have been shamed both from the notoriety and from the exposure of his secrets. And if he didn't, she would have him all to herself: a partner in crime.

S.B.T.C. AND JOHN RAMSEY

Right below "Victory!" the killer signs off S.B.T.C. The ransom note writer attempts to cast the killer as a member of a radical foreign anti-U.S. terrorist group. S.B.T.C. could refer to John Ramsey's military experience at Subic Bay Training Center—but it's doubtful. Even so, the direct reference to foreigners and indirect reference to the military is enough to make a clear link with John's military experience in a foreign country.

While stationed in the Philippines, John had a powerful emotional experience that he most likely discounted, as pilots are prone to do. He was far away from home, "entrapped" in a foreign country where terrorists could strike, a new pilot, on his own for the first time—all what we call death or separation experiences. As he was just making his way into the adult world, in particular as a pilot, he would have been reminded of his struggles with his father who was a decorated World War II pilot. A young child thrills to hear about his father's dangerous exploits in a great war while feeling very uncomfortable on another level. It is a vivid reminder of the father's vulnerability and the possibility he could die.

John strongly identified with his father as evidenced by his becoming a pilot. But there would have been the usual father-son competition that typically gets buried and creates hidden guilt because of the strength of the competitive drive. Thus John's Subic Bay experience would have triggered painful memories in the back of his mind of his father's mortality and of his competitiveness with this man he idolized. John would have been looking over his shoulder expecting something to go wrong.

The fact that John thought of this experience thirty years later when he was trapped, facing his daughter's death and helping his wife—the killer—contrive a cover-up, reveals how he really saw Subic Bay deep down. John thought back to all his death experiences in the Philippines—and he still needed a victory over death. Like Patsy, John would have easily resonated with the idea of terrorism since each of them had been through the terror of death in their own way. Also like Patsy, John could shout "Victory." But their victory over death on December 25, 1996, the night Patsy killed JonBenét, was a false one.

There is another possible reason John closely identified with his father. After John's mother died, his father very quickly married Irene

Pasch, John's former mother-in-law who was then a widow. That meant that if John had stayed married to Lucy Pasch, his father would also be his father-in-law. Unusual to say the least, and a hint that John's father had a subtle tendency toward impulsiveness and triangulation (involving himself as a third party in a familiar one-to-one).

The thirteen-year age difference between John and Patsy also suggests a subtle father-daughter attraction from John's side, a tendency that manifested itself more prominently later in John's relationship with JonBenét.

Whether JonBenét's murder happened suddenly in a fit of rage or whether it was a sex game that got out of control is, for the moment, beside the point. Given a multitude of possibilities, both Patsy and John collaborated on a "ransom note" cover-up. Which reveals a great deal about what was in their minds at the time of JonBenét's murder. Both of them felt imprisoned by enormous, engulfing fear, and both desperately needed a victory, some "ransom" to release them from the captivity of their pain.

S.B.T.C. AND PATSY RAMSEY

Other clues in the ransom note link "S.B.T.C." with Patsy Ramsey. "Victory!" with its exclamation point and the six capital letters, including S.B.T.C., at the very end of the note reflect Patsy's flamboyant mind. Thus while there is the extremely remote possibility that John Ramsey may have had his reasons for suggesting the closing words, Patsy had final veto power so the words are hers as well. *Most likely "S.B.T.C." originated exclusively from the mind of Patsy Ramsey as several possible meanings connect uniquely to her and to "Victory!"*

The crime scene itself suggests an immediate meaning for "S.B.T.C." along spiritual lines with an important twist. In the center of John Ramsey's desk in the Ramseys' large bedroom the police found his King James Bible opened to Psalm 118. A source reveals that the Bible had been in the same place for days—open to the same page. The observer had the distinct impression that John never used his desk.

It is well known that the 118th Psalm was Patsy's favorite and she had claimed several verses in it as hers in her battle against cancer including, "I shall not die, but live, and declare the works of the Lord." (v 17). *Healed of Cancer*, a book by Dodie Osteen, which repeatedly emphasizes the 118th Psalm, greatly ministered to Patsy during her cancer treatments. Eventually Patsy was consciously convinced that God had healed her of cancer. Fundamental to the healing was the requirement that Patsy had enough faith and continued to have enough faith to trust that God had healed her—God didn't reward doubters.

The Bible open to the 118th Psalm on John's desk was at the very least a constant reminder to Patsy to keep trusting God for—claiming—

her healing. As busy as she stays, Patsy probably has little time for reading. Keeping the Bible in one place, John's desk, would enable Patsy to easily sit down and read her favorite Psalm to boost her faith— which almost certainly she does from time to time. Patsy knows Psalm 118 like the back of her hand.

Having known all along that the 118th Psalm was Patsy's favorite, many following JonBenét's murder have been drawn to one verse: "God is the Lord, who has shown us the light; *bind the sacrifice with cords, even unto the horns of the altar.*" (v 27) Does the verse in any way relate to JonBenét's murder?

The evidence definitely suggests a Patsy Ramsey rage-killing and not a planned sadistic murder. But it is indeed eerie how the bound body not of JonBenét resonates with that particular scripture verse.

Deep down Patsy was aware that the escalating tension in the Ramsey home was heading toward an explosion (see Chapters 15 and 16), and she would probably be looking at her favorite Psalm in a deeper way. The entire 118th Psalm might have suggested subconsciously to Patsy how she could escape the troubles that were weighing on her. The way Patsy reacted to stress both before and after the murder—particularly how she brought God into the equation—strongly hints at how the 118th Psalm fits into JonBenét's murder.

Patsy ran to God when she was diagnosed with cancer, openly ran to God the minute John brought JonBenét's body up from the basement (see Chapter 17), and also impulsively ran to God before a 1997 national television appearance (see Chapter 10) when she discussed JonBenét's death. *After impulsively killing JonBenét, the first place Patsy would run, upon halfway coming to her senses, would be to God. And she would handle her failures before God just as she did all her other failures—whitewash as much of it as possible and make lemonade out of lemons. Without missing a beat, Patsy would continue to think that she was the anointed one—albeit one who had temporarily dropped the ball although for good reason in her mind—enabling her to shift the blame.*

She would be telling herself that "God knows it was an accident," and she would recall the 118th Psalm through the same distorted lens: "His mercy endureth for ever." (vv 1, 3, 29) "The Lord hath chastened me sore, but he hath not given me over unto death." (v 18) (Patsy probably picked up her Bible for comfort that very night and read Psalm 118.)

Having quickly bypassed the hurdle of her tremendous guilt in typical Patsy Ramsey manic fashion, she would embrace the idea that God was in charge and he would handle this crisis. "The right hand of the Lord is exalted; the right hand of the Lord doeth valiantly." (v 16) In her mind Patsy would immediately be one with God again and His plans. "Open to me the gates of righteousness; I will go into them, and I will praise the Lord. (v 19) She would have again drawn on her past attachment to these comforting words, "I shall not die, but live, and declare the works of the Lord." (v 27)

Now back in God's good graces and willing to follow his plan, it would be only a short step for Patsy to see through her flawless beauty-queen eyes "His plans" especially laid out *for her* in this very Psalm. Now Patsy could see plainly—God knew this was going to happen on Christmas Day: "This is the Lord's doing; it is marvellous in our eyes. *This is the day which the Lord hath made*; we will rejoice and be glad in it." (v 23-23)

Possibly, maybe even probably, Patsy wondered if God had allowed all of this to happen because he was going to raise JonBenét from the dead, which makes verse 27 even clearer: "God hath shewed us light; bind the sacrifice with cords."

Patsy would know that the familiar 118th Psalm referred to two other special children and two other resurrections. In the Old Testament story, Abraham bound his special son Isaac to sacrifice him on an altar according to God's instructions (identical to verse 27). At the last minute God intervened and stopped the sacrifice—"resurrected him." Many Christians have long considered Isaac to be a picture of Christ who would be bound on a cross/altar and resurrected after His death. The 118th Psalm (one of twelve special Messianic Psalms that many feel prophesy the life of Christ) uniquely points to the resurrection of Christ as the Apostle Peter makes plain in his New Testament letter (I Pet 2:8). Peter refers back to Christ in Psalm 118 as the overlooked cornerstone of the church, "the stone which the builders refused [rejected and crucified] is become the head stone of the corner." (v 22)

In her desperate distorted self-centered thinking, Patsy easily could have uttered these words as she stood over JonBenét's body, "This is God's will. He is going to do something good. He will deliver us—'God hath shown us the light.' *He is going to resurrect JonBenét, the special child accidentally slain on Christmas day, like he did his special sons Isaac and Jesus. 'This is the day that THE LORD hath made.'"*

Patsy brought up this very idea the second John laid JonBenét's body on the living room floor (see Chapter 17). Patsy Ramsey was certain that God was going to raise little JonBenét from the dead, just like she was certain He had healed her from cancer, and she claimed her victory. **Name it and claim it—everything depended on that. And so very possibly she did exactly that with S.B.T.C.—Sacrifice Bound (with) The Cords.** Just as he did with Isaac, just as he did with Jesus, He would raise JonBenét from the grave. God was going to use JonBenét to point to Christ's great sacrifice.

After Patsy bashed in JonBenét's head (see Chapter 16), and perhaps thinking that she was already as good as dead since she was severely brain damaged, Patsy encouraged John "in obedience to God" to go ahead and finish her off—bind her with the cord around her neck—as a sacrifice, so that God could raise her whole from the dead. Just like Jesus healed people and made them whole.

Patsy Ramsey can dream big, and never in her life did she need so big a dream as she did the night of JonBenét's murder. She would know that if her dream was to come true, it was now up to her. And so she secretly named it and claimed it for the world to see in S.B.T.C. and in asking for a ransom of $118,000. *The 118th Psalm was all about sacrifices—ransoms—and how fitting that JonBenét the sacrifice should wear the same number that Christ the sacrifice (and Isaac the sacrifice) wore—118.*

Knowing Patsy Ramsey, she would also think of how she too had been a sacrifice bound with the cords of cancer—and saved. Given her inability to accept her flaws and her capacity for grandiosity, Patsy could easily have put this kind of spin on the entire matter.

Later Patsy could rationalize that if God was not going to raise JonBenét from the dead, then he would use the tragedy to give her the chance to testify to his Grace—which she did in her 1997 Christmas letter.

On a deeper level, it is very possible that Patsy Ramsey unconsciously "plotted" all along to use JonBenét as a sacrifice. As more evidence unfolds, it will be quite clear that she was looking for a sacrifice (see Chapters 10,15, and 17).

MORE POSSIBILITIES

In light of the brilliant capabilities of the deeper mind, there are other possible meanings to these puzzling four initials at the end of the ransom note.

"S.B." is common slang for "s.o.b." which has several meanings itself. People use this expression when they're in a jam. Used as a degrading term it literally means son of a bad woman or not quite so literally, the child of a bad woman. "S.o.b." also expresses hostility. All of these possibilities fit Patsy Ramsey. In a condensed way, as she signs off the ransom note, she could be telling us that she recognizes that she's in a huge jam. She is a bad mother who has just expressed tremendous hostility toward her child and has degraded her child, that she herself feels degraded by those who raised her, and that she has just expressed a hostile and masculine part of herself.

Patsy could even be revealing that, just as her exhibitionism revealed, she had turned JonBenét into a masculine sort of person for the purposes of gaining power—she had symbolically turned her daughter into a son. This fits with the showy finish of the ransom note.

"T.C." could refer to "T.L.C." *(tender loving care)*, almost the exact opposite of "S.B." Here Patsy could be revealing her other side, the good mother. The S.B./T.C. split could represent Patsy's bad mother/good mother split, with Patsy's evil part coming first.

"T.C." is not far from "T.S." *("tough s—")*, an incredibly common expression that suggests Patsy is confessing that life was cruel to JonBenét (and to her as well). Maybe that's how Patsy viewed her cancer—"T.S." and she inflicted that same bad break on JonBenét.

In addition to these unconscious meanings that can be attributed to S.B.T.C., Patsy had conscious reasons for choosing to sign off with these letters. "S.B.T.C." is directly connected to "Victory!" and may share the same hidden meaning. For Patsy "Victory" meant her religious faith and remission of her cancer. As she writes the closing lines of the ransom note, she would naturally be wondering if there was anything she wanted to add, especially considering the horror of her deed. On a deep level she wants to salvage some semblance of self-respect as she "talks to the whole world—and to God." Whatever Patsy may have said to God about her cancer, she never quit talking to him.

She wants to put as positive a spin on JonBenét's murder as she can. As she thinks of her utter terror about what's she's done, she instantaneously thinks back to a not so long ago time of terror seared into her mind when she was diagnosed with cancer. Patsy had a victory over cancer—victory was inseparable in her mind from cancer and from God who had delivered her from cancer. Being who she was, Patsy Ramsey would have thought about God looking down at what she had done, and just as Patsy later put her "good mother's" touch on her deed at the crime scene, she would have been desperately searching to find some way God could put his "good mother's" touch on her. There was no question in Patsy Ramsey's mind that she was still living only because of God, and she still wanted to go on living.

Various Christian endeavors use "T.C." to mean "through Christ" or "Through the Cross." A capitalized "T" even looks like a Roman cross (on which Jesus was crucified). **"S.B.T.C." may also mean "saved by the cross."** Another possibility is "salvation belongs to Christ"—Patsy Ramsey was certainly looking for salvation. This fits in even a deeper, almost certainly unconscious way with the idea that Patsy's "S.B." side is taken care of through forgiveness. Also, Patsy Ramsey always tried to put an absolutely perfect spin on things, and Christ represents perfection in the face of her imperfection. She has just failed horribly at something she took a lot of pride in—her mothering ability. After JonBenét's funeral Patsy told someone that her daughter is better off in heaven. Deep down Patsy knew what she was doing to JonBenét and that in many ways she had destroyed her long before the last night of her life. In short, Patsy wants to turn JonBenét over to the perfect mother—in heaven. But at the poignant moment of separation as Patsy ends the ransom note, she comes face to face with her deed.

To see JonBenét again, Patsy is claiming S.B.T.C. (Saved By The Cross) for herself as well. S.B.T.C. may be one of the most important parts of the ransom note because Patsy Ramsey is acutely sensitive to separations, and S.B.T.C., the only way she will be reunited with her daughter, is of utmost practicality to Patsy Ramsey. Her spiritual faith may well be the only thing that will make her tell the truth.

ANOTHER POSSIBILITY

Patsy or John Ramsey may simply have come up with the initials "S.B.T.C." on a whim, as a random choice. Perhaps they adapted the initials from something like "TCBY" yogurt. One thing is certain, S.B.T.C. came out of their deeper minds which strongly points to yet another possible explanation.

From beginning to end the ransom note hints at cancer, and it's only fitting that the ransom note end with a capital "C" since cancer is known as "the big C." "T.C." could easily represent "the cancer" to Patsy (and John). "Slain by the cancer" explains the crime in a nutshell. "S.B." and "T.C." could also represent "Son of a B_____" "The Cancer." "Saved because of the cancer" is another possibility as, in the beginning, the cancer did open Patsy's eyes to the next world and more important matters, although she later lost her spiritual vision.

Surely the initials have some significance to Patsy Ramsey. Being the artist that she is, Patsy likes to put a special hidden message into her communications, particularly at the end of an event because she is acutely sensitive to separations.

THE ENDING OF THE RANSOM NOTE REVEALS:

- Victory and S.B.T.C. point to Patsy's cancer in two ways: God delivered her and remission.

- S.B.T.C. also hints Patsy used JonBenét as a bizarre sacrifice.

- Patsy's characteristic trademark punctuation: Exclamation points.

- key message in very last letter: "the Big C."

- Her spiritual convictions may be the only reason she would ever confess.

Chapter Nine
The Killer Guides the Police

We have witnessed the striking ability of Patsy's deeper mind to observe her own deeper motives, communicate about John's contribution, and secretly talk to the police—all at the same time and all while she's consciously attempting a cover-up. Patsy's need to confess undergirds all these messages.

Had the police known about the deeper mind's ability and integrity—and how it responds so quickly to the immediate situation—they would have asked themselves at the crime scene: "Is the killer trying to tell us where the child or the body is?"

We can now ask the same question, *"Was Patsy trying to tell the police the body was in the house?"* Patsy's ransom note gave the police clues as to what happened and how to break her during an interrogation, but were there messages in the note specifically for the police the day they searched the Ramsey house?

Yes—the killer's deeper mind did give the police specific clues in the note they read on December 26, 1996. Patsy knew the police would immediately read the ransom note, particularly since the note says the killer will call them. Patsy's opening, "Listen carefully!" speaks volumes. Her third sentence refers to people serving their country, but this is not far from the police who serve the community.

Her disguised **"police marker"**—means that she *is unquestionably talking to the police* and she wants them to pay attention to what comes next in her note. "At this time we have your daughter in our possession" were as true as any words in the letter. The killers had JonBenét in their possession the very moment the police read those words. The police could have picked up on the immediate nature of the statement and immediately begun trying to read between the lines—looking past the superficial messages. Right away they should have been leery of Patsy and John Ramsey.

Specifically looking for messages to them, the police would have looked past "She is safe and unharmed" because obviously the child had at the very least been harmed emotionally by the "kidnaping." "You must follow our instructions to the letter" would have gotten their attention too—the killer or kidnapper was instructing them to pay attention to the details, another variant of "Listen carefully."

CLUES FROM THE KILLER: LOOK IN THE BASEMENT

Next Patsy's ransom note makes several references to money and containers: a bank, an attaché, and a brown paper bag. These can be read: *Go where the money is, look for something hidden in a container, in a vault.* Right away the police would have followed up on their earlier instincts to search the house and thought about *what part of a house is like a vault.* Attics, basements, or tool sheds come to mind. Patsy gave these vivid images directly after "follow instructions carefully" to point the police toward where to find the body in the Ramsey house.

"Brown paper bag" was Patsy's warning to the police to not overlook the valuable body or child hidden in a plain part of the Ramsey house. Since it was obvious by now that the killer was asking for money in exchange for JonBenét, the police could have substituted "child" or "body" for the word "money." Patsy was saying that the money (the valuable)—JonBenét—was contained in a plain place—the basement. A more thorough search of the basement would have led to the discovery of JonBenét's body.

Patsy's deeper mind continued to send the police one clue after another in the note. "I will call you between 8 and 10 a.m. to instruct you on the delivery (of the child)" was a striking message since Patsy knew the police would be in her home at that time, if they hadn't already discovered the body on their first search. If they had known on December 26, 1996, how powerfully the mind of the killer or kidnapper wanted to help them, the police could have said to themselves, *"The kidnapper is telling us that this very morning we can find clues about where the child is,"* and they would have looked for the hidden message in the note. Also when the killer didn't call, the police's suspicions of the Ramseys would have been heightened.

An "exhausting delivery" and "I advise you to be rested" call to mind an image of a tired JonBenét who is lying down somewhere. Patsy was telling the police to, "Look in the basement and see if she's lying down somewhere."

JonBenét Is Dead, Look for Her Body

Next the killer shifts to the possibility of an "earlier delivery." If the police had realized that Patsy's deeper mind was sending them hidden messages, they would have realized that *the killer was telling them how to find JonBenét earlier than they might otherwise.* Patsy repeats herself as she talks about "a earlier pick-up of your daughter." The police routinely *pick up* criminals or suspects, a clue that could have doubly gotten their attention.

"Any deviations of my instructions will result in the immediate execution of your daughter" was Patsy's way of telling the police that JonBenét was already dead. Recognizing the very real probability that a deviant person had already suddenly executed JonBenét, investigators on the scene would have known to look for her body.

Now the police could have shifted into overdrive. Experience would have told them that most times when people are home and a child is murdered, a family member did it. This should have been the reddest of flags, particularly since the killer specifically addressed the message to them. "Any deviations" would have been easily translated into "contacting law enforcement." "You will be denied her remains for proper burial" moves more toward the idea of a corpse and once again calls to mind the idea that the body is hidden, buried somewhere—nearby.

"A corpse is hidden away" was Patsy's secret instruction to the police to immediately look closely for a body "buried" on the premises. Then JonBenét could have a "proper burial."

"Two gentlemen watching over your daughter" has the ring of immediacy, and it accurately describes exactly what was going on at the moment. Patsy and John Ramsey were posing as gentlemen, but they were really two criminals watching over their daughter's dead body— literally standing one floor over it in the kitchen. The police could have heard the message, *"the body is right in front of you if you will look—and so are the killers: 'two gentlemen.'"*

TO THE POLICE: THESE MESSAGES ARE FOR YOU

The killer's slip-up in the same sentence, "the two gentlemen ... do [not] particularly like you," could easily have been read as a part of the killer that is secretly on the side of the police—likes them deep down— and wants to help them since the police are indirectly mentioned in the same sentence (the warning not to call them). By continuing the warning against "speaking to ... Police (capitalized), F.B.I." so vehemently, with repeated references to them *("police markers" back to back)*, Patsy was alerting them that she is particularly talking to them and "... result in your daughter being beheaded" and "catch you talking to a stray dog and she dies" that follow, then become crucial messages to them. By now they could have been almost positive that JonBenét was dead from a head injury and realized that her body was off by itself somewhere in the house where a stray dog might stay. *By following Patsy's clues the police would have looked even harder in the basement* since they missed the body the first time.

"... alert bank authorities, she dies" is yet another reminder that the deceased child is in a vault to which the police themselves have the key if they use it. *Appreciating that Patsy was talking to them in code was the key to the vault where JonBenét's body was hidden.*

One last threat "if the money is ... tampered with, she dies" was just another reminder that JonBenét's valuable body had been tampered with and she was indeed dead. Patsy is shouting at the police, *"Can't you see what I have done? I have killed my daughter—hurry up and find me out."* Patsy repeated the word "daughter" to get the attention of the police.

Perfect Chance to Catch the Killer: Look at the Family

A warning against scanning for electronic devices—an abrupt shift in ideas on Patsy's part—and connecting these devices to "law enforcement countermeasures and tactics" contained a hidden, valuable clue especially for the police (because the killer is talking specifically to them). By utilizing their right brain and "reading" for symbolic language—*knowing how the mind works*—*the authorities could read "scanner" and "electronic devices" along with "countermeasures" as an instruction to look for something hidden.* Linking a scanner with an X-ray says: Look for the body in a small hidden dark place. The police would have been convinced the body was hidden nearby, and the killer's "instructions to the letter" could have compelled them to keep searching the house until they found JonBenét's body.

"You stand a 99% chance of killing your daughter" tells the police that "there's a 99% chance the parents did it." This would have reminded them of what they already knew: The percentages are great that most of the time when a child is killed with family members home, the family members are involved.

"Follow our instructions and you stand a 100% chance of getting her back" was an enormous encouragement from Patsy's deeper mind. This would have alerted the police that a crucial tip from the best possible informer was coming up. *Unequivocally Patsy was telling the police that they could discover where the body was* if they decoded the hidden message her deeper mind had written "between the lines" of the ransom note.

"You and your family are under constant scrutiny as well as the authorities." Once again Patsy was talking to the police and had repeated herself, telling them to scrutinize the family closely because that's where they will find the killer—100% guaranteed.

The Killer's Final Advice: Use Your Common Sense

Patsy gives the police one last piece of advice: "Don't try and grow a brain" and "use that good common ... sense" *was wise counsel not to get fancy but to just think about the most logical explanation for the crime.* Boulder (Colorado), a murder rate of one, Christmas night, parents home, no phone call from the "kidnapper" between 8 and 10, bizarre motive, etc. The police could read "don't think killing will be difficult" and "don't underestimate us" as *another striking instruction: Don't be misled by appearances, don't underestimate the Ramseys, don't think it wouldn't have been easy for them to have done it.* And "you are not the only fat cat around" tells the police one of the motives: The Ramseys were two fat cats who thought they could behave any way they wanted to. They had gotten too big for their britches.

The repeated messages not to overlook the family were all linked specifically to John Ramsey. The final refrain "It's up to you John" surely told the police that everything around the heart of this crime centered on him—where the killer puts him in the ransom note.

Given that, the police could have really put John under the microscope that day and made him think, made him talk. Likewise they could have interrogated Patsy about John's relationship with JonBenét. On that day the Ramseys were still alienated from one another and investigators could have quickly picked up on the issues if they had separated the two of them. After telling the police where to find the body, the killer was then giving the police the second part of the plan to catch the killer—focus on John.

Reading Patsy's ransom note letter and looking for hidden messages to the police has revealed that the deeper mind of a killer can help the police investigate a crime. *There is no question that Patsy was speaking directly to the police in her magnificent contrived ransom note and trying to help them find JonBenét's body.*

SUMMARY

We have read the ransom note from a slightly different angle to see if in a criminal investigation the mind of the killer can be an asset to the police. Based on our understanding of the deeper mind, we would expect that to be the case. This is exactly what we have found. There is no question that on another level of the extraordinary ransom note the killer was speaking directly to the police and trying to help them find the body.

THE RANSOM NOTE REVEALS:

- Patsy's deeper mind was constantly guiding police.

- Patsy told the police that JonBenét was already dead.

- Patsy told the police how to find the body the first day of the investigation.

- Patsy told the police to look for the body hidden in the basement.

- Patsy warned the police not to overlook her and John as suspects.

- Patsy reminded the police to use their common sense.

- Patsy revealed one motive to the murder: she and John had become fat cats (and above the law).

- Patsy told the police to focus on an incident between John and JonBenét to solve the crime.

Chapter Ten
Patsy Ramsey's Other Side

One of the fundamental questions in the JonBenét murder case is the motive. Patsy continually portrays herself as a grieving, caring mother who under no circumstances could ever harm her child. Admittedly the case can be made that Patsy didn't demonstrate a pattern of overt hostility or of losing control emotionally—something her attorneys will make the foundation of her defense should the case ever go to trial.

On the surface Patsy is the epitome of graciousness, and at first glance we cannot find a hint of anger or contentiousness anywhere. Which simply means that if we are really going to understand Patsy, we have to look deeper. We have to read between the lines, look behind her appearances—and when we do, a different Patsy Ramsey emerges, a Patsy Ramsey she herself would never recognize or acknowledge.

We must first understand that Patsy was her mother's child, Nedra Paugh's *first* child. Besides her nurturing traits, Nedra has variously been described by those who know her as aggressive, domineering, outspoken, coarse, and tacky. In a *National Enquirer* interview, she came off as vindictive and mean-spirited—blatantly accusing Patsy's former housekeeper, Linda Hoffman, of the murder and proclaiming that she'd never liked Linda. One person who knew Nedra observed the same inappropriate outspokenness, recalling how Nedra would impulsively tell a stranger she barely knew, "You'd better watch what you eat. You'll lose your figure, and you know that's the only thing men are interested in."

Patsy would have heard her mother make comments like these over and over, and she would have reached certain conclusions about the world around her based on her mother's comments. Mother didn't think much of men, who only used women as sex objects. Mother didn't think much of women either since she saw them as vulnerable to being dependent on men and then abandoned by them. Mother was obsessed by women's physical appearances, which were their only defense and security. How do we know this? From Nedra's comments and particularly her obsession—beauty pageants.

Nedra was more than determined that one of her three daughters would be Miss America—and when they failed she next turned the fire that burned inside her on her granddaughter, JonBenét. Nedra coped with vulnerability by shining *through her children* for all men to see, strutting her stuff—but only on a look—don't touch—basis. Nedra didn't desire for her daughters to establish real relationships with men but instead wanted them to become a man's ultimate fantasy. She encouraged her daughters and granddaughter to become objects,

Barbie dolls, not persons. They were to appear sexual at moments, but only to appear that way—they were never to *really* give a man what he wanted because maybe, just maybe, he ought to be paid back for the power he has over women.

This gives an inkling why, years later, despite all her beauty-pageant trophies, Patsy Ramsey complained to her housekeeper that she didn't like sex. Deep down Patsy believed—as her mother taught her—that men were not to be trusted. Patsy Ramsey's mother forced her identity upon her, stealing Patsy's life from her just as she later stole JonBenét's. Nedra bore and bred Patsy to be a beauty queen.

BEAUTY-QUEEN PERSONALITIES

Recently a perceptive young lady in her thirties told me about her experiences with beauty queens who were obsessed with the world of pageants, some of whom were her good friends and could laugh at themselves on occasion.

My friend said that *above all, these women are vain and always on stage. They are more interested in appearances than anything else.* For example, they would learn a foreign language to impress someone, not for personal satisfaction and enjoyment. They go to great efforts to *appear* casual and carefree, but they are incredibly competitive, particularly with other women. One former beauty expressed the idea that as much as she wanted a daughter, "God must have been looking out for her" and gave her only sons because she would have been too competitive with a girl.

Beauty queens handle pressure well, and they are perfectionists to the extreme. Their inability to tolerate criticism and own up to faults is so all-powerful that they construct a fantasy to handle the imperfection—the greater their failure, the more elaborate their fantasy.

They have a particularly hard time handling aging. From my vantage point as a psychiatrist, I would add that beauty queens are frightened of true intimacy since so many of them have been deeply wounded emotionally.

Let's see how Patsy Ramsey matches up with these generalizations.

PATSY RAMSEY, BEAUTY QUEEN

Patsy Ramsey makes a striking first impression. Almost everyone who comes in contact with her is initially charmed. She is engaging, and first impressions of Patsy Ramsey are universally positive.

Patsy's energy and charisma cover a multitude of sins—cover them so completely that it takes a while to see them. A few friends gradually began to see beneath Patsy's polished facade. Her friend, photographer Judith Phillips, eventually saw Patsy's dark side, but she continued to be her friend for some time. Judith told another friend about the time she and her former husband, Robert, traveled with Patsy and John along the West Coast in the wine country. During the trip she realized that Patsy was not only well-organized but also controlling. Patsy had personally laid out the whole itinerary without any discussion with John, Judith, or her husband.

Judith also came to see Patsy's self-absorbed, manipulative, quietly domineering side. Patsy was a master at getting others to go along with her plans. JonBenét could not stand up to such power, and though the party line (according to Patsy) may have been that JonBenét wanted to compete in pageants, it's likely that Patsy secretly chose for her.

Patsy appears to be an open book. Warm and friendly, she seems never to meet a stranger. Part of her charm is giving the appearance of telling all. Indeed, Patsy Ramsey cannot keep a secret well.

Patsy was always busy, compulsively busy, in relatively laid-back Boulder, Colorado. Busy doing charity work, church work, social engagements, parties, PTA, all the while being a Supermom carting her kids here and there—as well as having been extensively involved with JonBenét's pageants, including photo shoots, costumes, and travel.

This degree of compulsiveness invariably covers significant emotional pain. Patsy's busyness may be her way of running from something painful. By constructing her own busy world, Patsy could maintain control.

Patsy's confident nature shows up in her religious faith. She wasn't trusting God to heal her—God already had healed her. In ways, she was past faith into certainty, into her own reality, her own fantasy world.

Patsy can also be touchingly generous at times. Two days before JonBenét's murder, on December 23, 1996, Patsy and John threw a spectacular party for more than forty friends at their house. Patsy had gotten personal gifts for each of the guests and added a special poem or message to each gift. She even arranged for a Santa Claus (just one of the people the Ramseys would later accuse of murder) to deliver the gifts. *But this generosity also enabled her to remain on stage—at her own home, with her lavish gifts and eight big Christmas trees strategically placed throughout the house.*

In 1994 the Ramsey home was on the Boulder Parade of Homes. Most homeowners on the tour left their home the day of the event, but not Patsy. She stayed to shine for all the guests, making sure her Miss West Virginia dress was on display in one room. Patsy never misses an opportunity to be on stage.

COMPETITIVE

Behind her warmth and gregariousness Patsy is extremely needy, which fuels her competitive spirit. She once spotted a big diamond on another woman's hand and immediately went out and bought a bigger one and wore it proudly (very much like her mother who once overtly compared her own diamond ring to Jane Stobie's smaller one). Underneath Patsy Ramsey the loving, doting mother lurks Patsy Ramsey competitor extraordinaire—even with JonBenét, particularly with JonBenét. Patsy and Nedra once went on a photo shoot with JonBenét dressed in her now familiar cowgirl outfit. Not to be outdone, Patsy—who had had her own hair done—brought along several dresses, with matching glamorous jewelry for each, and had a photo shoot of her own—a testimony to the vivid fantasy world she constantly tries to create.

But Patsy's excessive need to construct a fantasy world can lead at times to poor judgment that demonstrates her manipulative nature. After the murder, Boulder mayor Leslie Durgin attempted to reassure the city's residents with a public comment that there was "no killer on the loose." Patsy, the beauty queen, can't tolerate even a hint of possible criticism, and she immediately pressured a friend to call the mayor and ask her, "Why aren't you supporting the Ramseys?" The mayor replied, "I support the police, and you [the Ramseys] are protected like any other citizen."

COLDHEARTED PERFECTIONIST

Everywhere we look, we see Patsy Ramsey's perfectionism: The perfect parties, perfect gifts with the perfect notes, perfect home, perfect children, perfect mother with perfect glamor, including the perfect ring.

But with that perfectionism comes *an extreme intolerance of imperfection.* Judith Phillips described what happened when her former husband, Robert (who was in business with John Ramsey), pointed out to Patsy an error she made in a brochure she had written, a skill Patsy particularly prided herself on, having specialized in communications. Patsy never got openly angry or in any immediate way expressed any major displeasure—she simply didn't speak to Robert anymore. She also stopped inviting Robert and Judith to do things with them until, after a year, she seemed to get over it.

Patsy demonstrated the same coldness toward Judith after JonBenét's murder by completely cutting off contact with her. This was long before Judith released any photos of JonBenét and Patsy to the public. Judith once told a friend that Patsy could cut somebody off at the drop of a hat—when Patsy was done with somebody, she was done with them.

The Ramseys' best friend in their neighborhood, Joe Barnhill (who continues to believe in their innocence), was particularly struck by Patsy never once contacting him after the murder. A former housekeeper, who loved Patsy greatly, also felt that Patsy's response to her after the murder was extremely cold. The fact that the Ramseys included both of these close associates on their suspect list and, moreover, had them submitted to lie detector tests also indicates Patsy's coldness.

Friends from Patsy's past, all the way back to high school and even earlier, describe the coldness that could come over Patsy without warning—coldness you could scarcely believe coming from someone as outgoing and embracing as Patsy appeared most of the time. Yet no one describes Patsy as getting overtly angry. People who contain their anger so tightly frequently do so because they fear the violence they will unleash if they lose control. She could be incredibly harsh, but she always hid her coldhearted actions behind a mask of respectability. This points even more to someone who spoke brutally through actions the night of JonBenét was killed.

Patsy almost always expresses her anger through actions. External outbursts were extremely uncharacteristic, but she had two spats with JonBenét not long before the murder. Not only did she have two spats, but the two happened in one day, which suggests the tension was really building inside Patsy. Patsy just couldn't contain herself anymore.

SEXUALLY ALOOF

Patsy did the same thing with her sexual impulses that she did with her anger—she hid them. She hid them so deeply in the back of her mind that she never felt them. As she told Linda Hoffman, her housekeeper, she hated sex. Patsy's friends noticed how she would never flirt in any way, and didn't show any real interest in sexual matters.

But Patsy got on stage, often in revealing outfits, to show off her body, to attract the attention of (mostly) men in such a striking way that she would be declared the woman above all women. Patsy used her sex appeal well enough that it got her pretty much where she wanted to go. But since she wasn't really in touch with her sexuality, she really couldn't enjoy it.

WAS PATSY HERSELF ABUSED?

The idea of having to be perfect to ward off catastrophe would have been in Patsy Ramsey's mind long before she murdered JonBenét. Where did this obsession with perfection originate?

Her mother is an incredibly controlling and domineering woman who clearly abused her daughter emotionally. As acquaintances observed, she is the consummate stage mother. Patsy herself is a fiercely competitive individual, the oldest of three daughters in a driven family and probably feels deep guilt over her natural competitiveness with the other three women in the household. Surely this situation makes her guilt-ridden and perfectionistic about the normal kinds of failures we all experience.

Patsy's perfectionistic needs are so extreme that they *seem to point to some specific traumatic event years ago—an event so terrible that she developed the idea in her mind that it was her fault, that it wouldn't have happened if she had been a better child.* Out of this event could have come her lifelong drive for perfection—to be so perfect that nothing bad would ever happen to her again—typified by her need to be Miss America, to prove to the world she was indeed perfect. As I've seen countless times in my patients, such extreme rigidity is typical of traumatized youngsters.

From the harsh voice demanding perfection in her ransom note, and considering how forcefully she sexualized little JonBenét, it's likely that Patsy is trying to tell us (and even herself), "Look at what happened to me when I was a child some powerful adult used me as a sexual object, abused me sexually, and tried to cover it up." (Patsy's frigidity with her husband is another suggestion that she was sexually abused.) In the process of destroying JonBenét, Patsy was also destroying the guilty child-self within her, the child who—in her mind—had "caused" the early trauma by the shortcoming of not being perfect. When cancer came upon Patsy at such a vulnerable moment in her life—not to mention all the other defeats that naturally come with aging—she simply couldn't deal with it.

WORLD OF HER OWN

Patsy Ramsey has *a unique ability to enter a world of her own whenever she desires.* Patsy can quickly bury any uncomfortable emotion such as guilt without even recognizing it. This is not uncommon for women who have been abused as they frequently deal with their abuse by going somewhere else in their mind while it is occurring.

After the murder, we get a vivid glimpse—on nationwide television—of how Patsy thinks. One evening while watching *Larry King Live* with her mother, Nedra, she suddenly felt compelled to call him when the topic of paparazzi and the tabloid press came up in conjunction with Princess Diana's death.

As she's dialing, her mother asks her what she intends to say. Patsy confidently replies, "God will give me the words." God will give me the words.

Here's Patsy Ramsey, a guilty murderer running free, having broken one of God's most basic laws, having the gall to speak on God's behalf and say that He will speak through her. *She has equated her thoughts with God's thoughts, which essentially means she's equated herself with*

God. One thing's for sure: Though Patsy may believe it's God who's speaking, we know beyond a doubt that the choice of words is coming from her own mind.

Predictably Patsy railed against the guilty tabloids and the evil paparazzi who contributed to Princess Diana's tragic death. And she added, "I would ask in the memory of my daughter, JonBenét, America's people's princess—and the beautiful people's princess of Great Britain—to ask everyone worldwide to boycott [the tabloids]."

The immediate connection between Patsy and the subject on television is transparent: *Someone is to blame for the death of a beautiful, glamourous young person.* Patsy is so thoroughly guilt ridden that she must externalize that burden of guilt onto someone outside herself— the paparazzi were to blame. But try as she might to shift into a world of her own when faced with guilt, Patsy Ramsey can't quite pull it off.

Patsy also externalized her fear onto Princess Diana. In the back of her mind Patsy is riding around in a "car" that is about to crash—in a body that is about to crash with cancer and is now about to crash with an arrest.

How Patsy Copes with Fear: The Stage

Even in this brief outburst on national television, we see how Patsy copes with her extreme fear of death. She equates JonBenét with Princess Diana and then self-proclaims her lost daughter "America's Princess." Wasn't that one of Patsy Ramsey's deepest longings—to be America's princess, Miss America?

Doesn't it make sense for her to try to resurrect that sterling way of coping in her hour of deepest need? Is it any wonder that after she got ovarian cancer Patsy Ramsey chose to start entering JonBenét in beauty pageants? This is all she really wants to see about herself, and all she really wants us to see—the former beauty-queen mother reflected in the beauty-queen daughter. Why look at pain and deterioration of your body when you can look at beauty—a beauty so close to you it substitutes for your own?

Consciously this is what Patsy Ramsey wanted us to see—beautiful, now famous JonBenét. But deep down she is confessing and telling us really how much terror she lives with daily. *Her impulsive appearance on Larry King Live matched perfectly her secretly terror filled ransom note and her impulsive murder of JonBenét.*

Patsy indeed made little JonBenét into America's little princess and a martyred one at that, something our society lores. Perhaps Patsy is justifying it all in her fantasyland mind, telling herself that it was a small price for JonBenét to pay to become a celebrity for the century. Deep down Patsy herself felt like a martyr, unfairly suffering at the hands of cancer. And now JonBenét, a martyr for all the world to see, is secretly

Patsy the martyr—living through her daughter, both in life and in death.

With this brief look into Patsy's mind after the murder, we see how she keeps going, keeps coping—by the delusion that God is pleased with her, that she is so special that she can do anything she wants. Let others worry about consequences—Patsy is above it all.

We see the same patterns of coping and the same distorted thinking over and over again. When a couple's car broke down in front of Patsy's vacation home in Charlevoix, Michigan, Patsy asked them in and immediately shifted the conversation to JonBenét, inviting them to see her room. The same thing happened to artist Kathleen Keane who was painting near the same vacation home and upon meeting patsy Ramsey was quickly invited to see JonBenét's room. In a strange way Patsy Ramsey seems to be enjoying the attention and seeking it out—just as she did on Larry King's show. But this is not surprising since being center stage has kept Patsy's mind off her real pain for a very long time.

Whether in pain from guilt, shame or fear, Patsy splits it off and takes flight into an upbeat unconquerable mind set: Her guilt becomes her self-righteous protests, her terror of death become her worldwide stage (America's princess), her shame become notoriety and oneness with God. Patsy Ramsey flies into the face of pain in as bold a fashion as possible—a classic manic way of coping.

ANGER: ANOTHER BLOCKED-OFF EMOTION

Pain can cause people literally to lose their minds. And Patsy Ramsey lost hers the night of December 25, 1996, however briefly. The pressures on her had pushed her beyond all normal boundaries: of motherly love, of kindness, of self-respect, of human decency. And deep down her guilt is on her mind—as in "everybody in the world should boycott ..."

That extreme judgment gives us a clue to the extreme nature of Patsy Ramsey. When she focused that same judgment on another person, it would indeed be extreme. And this is precisely what happened that night. All the rage that had built up in Patsy Ramsey—rage reflecting a mountain of fear—came pouring out of her. Fear that she would die, fear that her beauty was fading, fear that she would be abandoned for someone else again. Gnawing, deep down gut-wrenching fear, fear so strong that she had to try and deny it with everything that was in her.

Patsy had so much leftover anger: anger at God for letting her get cancer, anger at her mother for controlling her, anger very possibly at someone who sexually abused her, anger at her husband for betraying her, anger over Christmas reminding her of losses, anger at JonBenét for replacing her—and for just being alive.

PATSY'S NEED FOR RELIEF

Just as Patsy didn't recognize her terror, her sexuality, her guilt, and her anger—she didn't recognize her need to be freed from these burdens. We can see her crying out for relief in her actions that terrible night and when she signed off at the end of her ransom note with one triumphant word: "Victory!"

Maybe it's no coincidence that the "victory" came on Christmas Day—the special day when the special child was born. For Christians, Christmas points toward victory in two ways—first, God joined his people as one of them, in human form, to deliver them from the curse of death. Secondly, he delivered them through a blood atonement, symbolized in Easter.

For Christians, Christmas and Easter are the two most meaningful days of the year. Patsy (and John to an extent) present a definite public face about being Christians. How sincere they are in their faith is another question altogether, but their faith is important to them.

JonBenét Ramsey—the special child who was now the very reason for her mother to go on living, the special child whose young beauty had sparkled in a hundred contests and a thousand photographs—was killed on Christ's day. Did Patsy by some twisted logic think the sacrifice of such an idealized child could make up for her own failures and deficiencies and that by destroying her rival of sorts she could restore, at least temporarily, her own power as the pageant beauty?

Did Patsy also somehow have the distorted sense that she herself was special because she was temporarily spared by cancer and was thus the anointed one—leading her to think that she could do what she wanted with JonBenét, just as her own mother had done with her? Was this idea of special privilege a way of rationalizing that she would not have to confess and pay for her crime as ordinary people do? Or in the back of her mind did she think that she had already paid for her crime with her cancer?

Since we must read between the lines to see Patsy's fear, guilt, and much of her anger, we must do the same thing to see her distorted cry for redemption. Her distorted anger—fueled by abject terror—was a cry for help.

Her anger festered deep down all those years, and in one instant Patsy directed it all at little JonBenét—the anger wasn't by any means all intended for JonBenét, but she was the only available target at the moment. JonBenét was in the wrong place at the wrong time. **Maybe the gold identification bracelet on her right wrist with the inscription "JonBenét" on one side and "12/25/96" on the other—and the small gold cross found around her neck—speak volumes about her being a sacrifice for Patsy's (and John's) shadow side.**

THE GREAT DIVIDE

Patsy has a *huge split in her personality*, about as total a split as we could imagine in someone who maintains such a positive public image. Powerful motives operate in Patsy Ramsey, and her psyche functions by powerfully splitting off unacceptable perceptions of herself and her predicament. For Patsy it's out of sight, out of mind.

If you can't admit you're afraid and have no room in your makeup for anger or imperfection of any kind, that anger hides *somewhere* deep inside. The cover-up can only play out so long, and the longer it does the more intense the anger until the day it comes out in the only form that's left if you don't own it and talk about it—actions. That's what Patsy Ramsey's anger did on December 25, 1996.

Behind Patsy's charm, warmth, generosity, and openness, hides another person who is self-serving to the extreme: domineering, over-whelmingly competitive, and most of all ruthlessly cold-blooded. As one person from Boulder said, **"Whatever Patsy Ramsey did, it was bigger than all Texas,"** *and when Patsy's shadow side finally came out, it did so in the same way.*

Patsy's children reflect the personality split that Patsy (and John) demonstrated. To the world, Burke and, particularly, JonBenét showed a pleasant, submissive, appealing face. But behind closed doors they revealed their split personalities (as we will see in Chapter 16). Like father, like son; like mother, like daughter.

A PERSONALITY PROFILE OF PATSY REVEALS:

- **Patsy has a dark shadow side to her personality.**

- **Patsy is highly competitive.**

- **Patsy can be cold and ruthless.**

- **Patsy uses sex for power.**

- **Patsy is uncomfortable with anger and expresses it through her actions.**

- **Patsy behaves like a sexual abuse victim.**

- **Patsy has zero tolerance for imperfections.**

- **Patsy covers up her flaws in flamboyant fashion.**

- **Patsy retreats to a vivid fantasy mode in the face of stress.**

Chapter Eleven
Who Is John Ramsey?

"Some say he's quiet—others doubt it."
John Ramsey
Okemos (Michigan) High School Annual, 1962

To comprehend John Ramsey's involvement in the murder of his young daughter, JonBenét, we must look specifically at who he was in December 1996 based on the events in his life during the preceding several years.

In 1991 John Ramsey moved from Atlanta to Boulder, assumed the presidency of Access Graphics, and the company's sales took off. He purchased a $500,000 home in an exclusive Boulder neighborhood and spent more than $700,000 remodeling it.

In 1992 Elizabeth, his oldest daughter from his first marriage, was killed in an automobile accident just months before her wedding. A few months later John's father died—one of the most significant events in a man's life and particularly when, as in John's case, the father is domineering. John had lost his mother to cancer several years before, and immediately following the catastrophic losses of his father and his daughter in 1992, his beauty-queen wife is diagnosed with advanced ovarian cancer in 1993. With a very guarded prognosis, Patsy began commuting between Boulder and the National Institute of Health in Bethesda, Maryland—the only place she can obtain megadoses of chemotherapy. Thus in the span of less than two years, John Ramsey is surrounded by death—engulfed by it.

All the while John's company, Access Graphics, is prospering beyond his dreams and in 1996, goes over $1 billion in sales. If ever a man would be inclined to link success with catastrophe in the back of his mind and be prone to developing a "success phobia"—a hidden wish to partially retreat from success—it would be John Ramsey in 1996. Despite the common link between success and punishment, *rarely do we see someone experience so much death at any one time, and far more rarely do we see the same person simultaneously experience such overwhelming success.*

As former Atlanta neighbor Joe Saportas put it, "He's had a lot of good fortune in the financial sense, but I wouldn't trade anything for all of that, given what he's been through."

Success issues are often linked with family competition. John obviously identified strongly with his very successful father, James Ramsey, who was a decorated World War II pilot and later became director of the

Michigan Aeronautics Commission—a job he carried out in such a controlling fashion that he was called "Czar Ramsey." James ran his home in the same military-like way, and John grew up quiet and intimidated by his father.

Every son competes with his father and wants to surpass (and supplant) him as much as he loves him. When a father dies the son literally surpasses him by going on living.

Enormous economic success occurring simultaneously with his father's death gave the potential to produce a tremendous amount of *hidden* guilt in John. With his dictatorial demeanor James Ramsey would have provoked far more than the usual underlying resentment and competition in a son—and far more guilt when the son surpassed the father. The additional suffering of a daughter's death, a wife's life-threatening illness increased John's tendency to see these traumas as pay backs for his success. The fact that John rose to the top of Access Graphics by defeating two rivals, one of whom was a father figure, added to his deep-seated guilt and his belief deep down that indeed punishment follows success.

The human mind tends to link events in a cause-and-effect way, and the enormity of both the traumas and the successes in John's life from 1992 through 1996 made him very vulnerable and guilt-ridden—although he would not have consciously realized it.

AN ENGINEER AND PILOT PERSONALITY

John's modus operandi is to damn the torpedoes and keep going, blocking out traumas and distractions. He is an engineer by background, and engineers tend to be people who don't deal very well with emotional issues. They are quite good at burying things and carrying on. They are high achievers but also very structured—which serves to keep their minds focused on issues they *can* control and away from painful emotional issues they *can't* control.

John is also a pilot, and pilots, like engineers, need structure and control. Pilots, however, are exceptionally good at blocking out fear—they treat it in a "counter phobic" way. In other words, they jump right into fearful situations as a way of convincing themselves they aren't fearful. Pilots are particularly good at denying or covering up death or trauma fears, good at hiding their vulnerability—thus the ice water-in-their veins reputation. Unfortunately this can lead to undesirable and self-sabotaging behaviors including substance abuse or "acting out" in other ways.

Pilots and engineers are *predisposed to speaking through their actions.* John demonstrated this tendency immediately after Patsy was diagnosed with cancer. His friends noticed that he became emotionally aloof, and reportedly he began having an affair. With an affair, he would have been expressing his hostility and fear by punishing his wife and seeing another woman just when his wife needed his fidelity most. In the back of John's mind loomed the terrifying idea that if he got close to anyone (i.e. have emotional success), a loss would occur immediately.

Therapists aim at freeing their patients from the fear caused by the unconscious link between trauma and success, but it is a very painful idea to uncover. Naturally we fight pain, and John was into control, big time. In the end John's fears controlled *him*.

EXTREME IDEALIZATION, EXTREME COVER-UP

John had been into denial for a long time before JonBenét's death. No one likes to show their more socially unacceptable sides, especially not John (or Patsy) Ramsey. The fact that they are both so over-the-top in their cover-up of JonBenét's murder means that they have a good bit to hide.

When talking about John, an old friend, Jim Marino, said, "I never saw him get mad. I never heard him cuss. I never saw him raise a hand to anybody." Even John's ex-wife, Cindy, went out of her way to tell everyone how gentle he was with his children.

But what about John's alleged affair—doesn't it reflect significant anger and destructiveness? It shows that John is a *hyper-controlled* individual who is very uncomfortable with his anger and has a problem expressing it directly. He must have a lot of anger bottled up—he must have been very tightly wound after suffering so many traumas. This makes him very vulnerable to acting out his anger in unhealthy ways. His extramarital affair was not so much about sex as about anger—and fear. Bonding with the wrong person is simply a matter of fear.

Some friends describe John as modest and taciturn, a person who stays in the background while his expressive, charismatic wife holds center stage. John's brother Jeff has noted, "He's not boastful." But John is described as inordinately ambitious by people who knew him in high school—John was a guy who knew exactly where he was going—exactly the way Patsy's high school friends describe her.

You don't accomplish what John has without an iron will and an unyielding determination. Jeff may describe his brother as "not boastful," but John was not shy about letting his actions speak through his lifestyle: a million-dollar-plus house, lavish parties, and his glamorous trophy wife.

A neighbor in Boulder noted that the Ramseys' house and its furnishings went way beyond the norm, even for the very affluent, and that a visitor couldn't help getting the impression they wanted to show off their wealth. John obviously chose to marry someone who was quite expressive: Someone who could do his talking for him, as Patsy did by bragging in her 1996 family Christmas letter about the financial success of Access Graphics. Contrast Patsy's public persona with the quiet, retiring John who presumably likes to go off by himself in his 34-foot sailboat named *Miss America* (secretly he wanted to be noticed). John tended to speak through Patsy, but deep down he was very much like her. He also spoke a great deal through JonBenét.

SEEING PAST THE MASK

The description of John Ramsey in his high-school yearbook is, "Some say he's quiet—*others doubt it.*" Some of his classmates describe a split in John Ramsey, who was an honor student and played in the band, but who also partied with the wild crowd. Many years ago, in a high school in Okemos, Michigan, people were already asking the question, "Who is John Ramsey, *really?*" And they answered themselves by suggesting that he's hiding a lot behind his surface "quiet." Very often, the deeper intelligence speaks remarkably clearly in the spontaneous jottings we find in high-school yearbooks. It's true in John Ramsey's case who was a master at hiding his true inner self (just like Patsy).

It is quite plain, in retrospect, that John Ramsey badly wants to be idealized—again remarkably like Patsy. Their "oppositeness" is like flip sides of the same coin. Their personalities fit together hand in glove.

It was John's ambition that got him where he wanted to go. But once he got there, he discovered that wealth offers any number of disguises. Once he had enough money, he could hide behind his beautiful house, his beautiful wife and children, his lavish parties, and his magnificent lifestyle.

As CEO and business magnate he was constantly surrounded by people who idealized him. But nobody really knows him—including himself. As one neighbor put it, in trying to reconcile the whirling pace of their lives with their external persona of relaxed, gracious hosts: "I always assumed the other neighbors must have known the Ramseys better than we did. But since all this [with JonBenét] has happened, I've talked to many who say they didn't know them, either."

John Ramsey knows how to hide, how to seize control, how to compete, how to stay focused on a task—but it comes at the expense of his heart and soul. And none of us, however privileged, can hide forever. When crunch time came his mask came off, but even *he* didn't know who he really was. John and Patsy's stresses unmasked the absolute worst in them both in 1996.

THE SHADOW SIDE LURKS

When people are as gifted as the Ramseys in keeping up a false front, it becomes easy to lose their true selves in all the image building. It began with the "ransom note" and continues now with attorneys, public relations gurus, and selected media appearances. But the eye of truth eventually prevails: particularly when it's their own "eye," the truth from their own deeper intelligence.

In twenty-five years as a psychiatrist, I have watched my patients' deeper intelligence tell me who they really are while on the surface they present a completely different picture. It's their own words—their own ideas and actions—that best show me the vast difference between their surfaces and their inner selves. In essence, the "other 90%" of them is alive and well and real—also vastly imperfect and coping with a great deal of fear and guilt.

Everyone has a shadow side, and as nice as John and Patsy Ramsey appear (and indeed there is a very nice part of them) they can, through a culmination of circumstances, also display a chilling degree of destructiveness. Such gracious fronts can fool experienced investigators including Lou Smit, the ace Colorado detective who came out of retirement to assist on the case, and the FBI's former top profiler of murderers, John Douglas. Eleven months after the murder, on the Geraldo Rivera show, investigator (and lawyer) Jennifer Kay, who had interviewed Patsy Ramsey privately, told how impressed she was with Patsy's charm and that Patsy was incapable of murder. Utilizing only her conscious mind and listening only to Patsy's conscious mind, Jennifer leaned toward believing her.

The bottom line is that people can greatly fool us. Listening to the hidden part of the mind—by far the largest part, the "other 90%"—convinces you of this, and experts in profiling killers warn us not to fall for a person's conscious persuasiveness or charm, no matter how convincing. Many have been duped by the Ramseys, including many of their neighbors and friends. All these folks are only too willing to buy into the fine, upstanding Christian image the Ramseys are so good at portraying—something that has enabled them to reach great heights. Wouldn't we expect such people to continue to use their main gifts and present the same strong front they've always done so capably? The more charming they have been, the more we would expect them to fool us if all we see is their surface mind and charm.

But we need only pick up the Bible, which the Ramseys claim to believe, to see abundant references to the shadow side of man. The Old Testament prophet Jeremiah, among others, stands side by side with Freud and the whole depth psychology movement telling us, in effect, "Look again. There's another side to us all—a shadow side." We must give up our naivete if we're to see the truth of who John and Patsy Ramsey really are.

We must also appreciate the clues the Ramseys themselves gave us about how skillful they are at covering up. Patsy Ramsey, in the ransom/confession note, has already clued us in on how genteel they can appear.

But like Patsy, John couldn't always hide his other side. People who knew him in the business world saw him as incredibly vicious at moments. In the late 1980's consolidation was the byword in John's particular niche industry (value-added resellers) in the computer field. Basically it was a "middleman" business. In 1988 John merged his company (Advanced Products Group) with two other companies to form Access Graphics. One company was run by an older man and the other by a younger one. Of the three companies, John brought the fewest clients to the merger and was originally named vice president of sales. Shortly into the venture, John and the other "junior" person in a two-on-one power play moved the older man aside. Then in a follow-up maneuver, equally as slick, John arranged for his contemporary to be scapegoated as the ruthless one for moving the "old bull" out of the way—while John gained support from the rest of the company's power structure. John Ramsey was named company president in 1991.

Prior to that, in the fall of 1990, *a few months after JonBenét was born*, the most crucial development in the history of Access Graphics occurred—Sun Microsystems (the workstation giant) named Access the principal distributor for 200 other value-added resellers, a "super middleman," to the other middlemen. In the back of his mind John Ramsey would have linked JonBenét with both phenomenal success and guilt. The birth of a child symbolizes a real success, and John had plenty of reasons to feel guilty about his business successes. Deep down JonBenét would come to symbolize the guilty competitor in him.

One employee of Access Graphics describes John Ramsey as a ruthless and vindictive person—known for getting even. Other people see this same coldness in John's relationships with his children. Several people have said that the kids' grandfather, Don Paugh, showed much more affection with Burke and JonBenét than John did.

JOHN AND JONBENÉT

Both John and Patsy spoke loud and clear through their youngest child, JonBenét. Even before Christmas night 1996, JonBenét reveals their shadow sides.

To clearly see John and Patsy's shadow sides, we have to dispense with a few myths. The first is that child beauty pageants are harmless, wholesome activities. More than one director of such pageants has said they are "more about what's *inside* the young girls than outside; we're interested in character." "Inside" rather than "outside"? "Interested in character?"

Then why on earth does their ritual insist on changing little girls into little women, aborting twenty years of social and emotional development? Why the swept-back, moused, bleached blond hair, the elaborately made up faces with lush eyelashes and exquisitely decorated eyes—combined with a knowing, come-on look? Why the seductive wardrobes—in JonBenét's case, an off-the-shoulder, black-and-white dress with matching black stockings, flashy dangling earrings, and a commanding black, white, and shocking-pink, feathered headdress? Or a low-cut short black dress with the thick fabric shaped to give a hint of a bust, complete with matching hat and heels? Or a tight *Las Vegas showgirl* outfit with sequins, plumes, and floor-length feather boas streaming from behind, once more with a hint of padding at the bust, exactly the amount they could "tastefully" get away with. And a body suit with a see-through wrap-around skirt that she peeled off like a professional showgirl/stripper.

Above all, that look—that *knowing* look. JonBenét had worked exceptionally hard on her pose, and some adult or adults had worked equally hard on it with her.

JonBenét's face stares at us from the covers of national magazines: her long beautiful blond hair flowing down on her shoulders, her half-smile accented by vivid red lipstick, the best makeup money can buy. She's a junior Farrah Fawcett without the junior. Deep down, *we know it just doesn't fit.* Look at a natural photograph of JonBenét from her daily life—if you can find one that wasn't scripted—and see if that little girl looks anything like the one on the magazine covers.

Pageant Abuse

Organizers of the larger statewide pageants routinely make $100,000 or more per contest. One annual Florida pageant, Sunburst U.S.A. International, regularly gives *$1 million* in prizes. Include all the custom-designed clothes for the important contests, and you have an industry in itself—tremendous economic motivation for all types of adults to enable these children, aside from the emotional gratification.

People magazine saw a "flirtatious, even provocative" JonBenét in her videos. The article quoted a Denver deputy sheriff who said, "It's impossible to look at these photos and not see a terribly exploited little girl." Many of these photographs and many of these pageants unavoidably amount to the sexual exploitation of children.

It's natural for kids to want to grow up too fast before they have time to build appropriate *internal* controls. A main rule of thumb for parents is that if you *in the least suspect* you're encouraging an undesirable trait or behavior in a child, you play it safe: You simply *don't do it.* The child-pageant industry should set off lots of warning bells in a parent's mind in that regard. In our sexually oriented culture, every parent has their hands full in helping kids stay within appropriate bounds, and the last thing you want to do is give a premature push to your kids' sexuality.

But that's exactly what John and Patsy Ramsey did. Don't think that

Patsy Ramsey (The Globe)

JonBenét, America's Royal Miss Pageant, 1996 (Zuma)

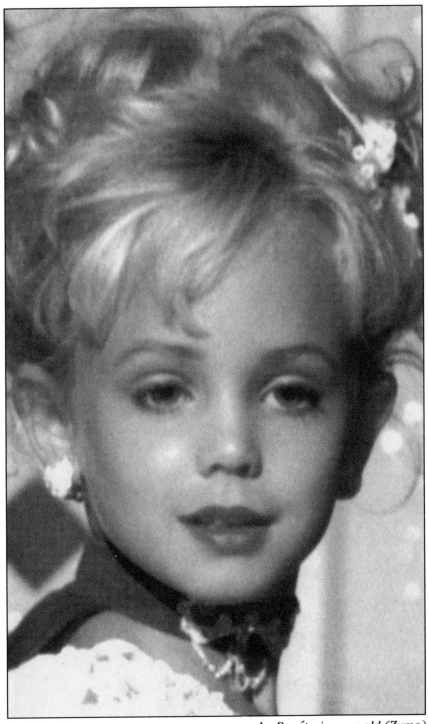

JonBenét, six-years-old (Zuma)

JonBenét, beauty pageant, 1996 (Zuma)

John didn't have a stake in these beauty pageants—he enabled Patsy to push JonBenét every step of the way. Through their actions John and Patsy told JonBenét: Because of our own needs, we want you to grow up much faster than you should. We want you to learn how to dress seductively, how to smile seductively, how to walk and move seductively. We will help you learn what turns people on, what they respond to, and how to play to their basest desires. Our need for this stimulation is greater than your need to progress slowly.

They used JonBenét and in the process abused her emotionally, but they taught her to think that it was good for her. They told her that being prematurely sexual is good and she should enjoy it. Smile, they told her, we know you'll like it. See? Just keep smiling. Keep giving the people what they want. Remember, you're just an object. You're just a performer—like both of us are.

JONBENÉT AND SEX

Patsy and John may have had many reasons to sanction JonBenét's premature sexuality. Patsy may have been reenacting a childhood trauma and the ensuing coping skills she herself used—appearing counter-phobic about sexuality. She may have been teaching JonBenét the same lesson she had been taught—to be an object.

Which of John's needs did JonBenét meet? Perhaps John used JonBenét to meet the sexual need Patsy had satisfied before her cancer. Or perhaps he used JonBenét to fulfill his secret need to stand out sexually. Perhaps JonBenét covered up an extreme inadequacy he had—appearing alive and dominant instead of weak and vulnerable. Was JonBenét fulfilling John's childhood fantasy of being a dominant sexual person? Was John so threatened by his traumas from adult relationships that he was all too willing to enable his daughter's sexuality? Was he in ways substituting an involvement with JonBenét for a relationship with Patsy (particularly in light of Patsy's frigidity)? Did it fulfill some sexual fantasy he had about JonBenét? Count on it: JonBenét's precocious sexuality fulfilled some perverted need or needs in John Ramsey.

JOHN'S HISTORY: ACTING OUT MOTIVATED BY FEAR

John is prone to act out his emotions instead of processing them—and to act out sexually, as his previous affair (affairs?) in his first marriage and possible affairs with other women in his second marriage reveal. *Why* would these latest supposed extramarital liaisons occur right after Patsy was diagnosed with what appeared to be terminal cancer?

It's understandable but all too simple to think that John simply would have turned elsewhere to gratify his sexual needs when Patsy was ill and unavailable. This may be true to a point, but John Ramsey's sexual acting out goes much deeper than this.

When intimacy becomes connected in our minds with pain, such as the pain of losing someone we love, it creates a powerful "intimacy phobia." It's at just such times of crisis that exactly this type of acting out—such as with a third party—becomes extremely common. By doing so John Ramsey would be experiencing temporary comfort and bonding while avoiding intimacy—which now, *in his mind, would be linked with death.* (The recent losses of his oldest daughter and his father reinforced the idea that closeness means pain.) In short, John's sexual behavior was motivated by fear in two ways—he would undo a sense of loss by being with someone besides his wife, and he would avoid the pain of loss by never really being truly close to this sex partner. By becoming involved with another woman, John would also express his anger at Patsy for threatening him so.

John is prone not only to act out sexually but *aggressively* which shows us his basic tendencies: back off from intimacy and act out sexually with third parties, particularly under stress. And John does it in a characteristic "good woman/forbidden woman" fashion (what psychiatrists call the Madonna/prostitute syndrome). In high school John was involved with a popular cheerleader for more than two years while seeing on the side at least initially, a wild party girl during his senior year, when high schoolers typically deal with separation issues.

While married to his first wife, the mother of his first three children, and stressed by marital problems, John had an affair with a young "forbidden" woman who worked for him. (Usually when someone gets caught in an affair, it is not the first.) John's acting out again extra-maritally with another, younger third party, when he is stressed by Patsy's illness, fits the same picture. John tends to "triangulate" when he's under stress.

At the time of JonBenét's death there were signs that his marriage was in trouble. There were strong hints of an affair. Additionally, Patsy was mentioning her sexual problem to her house keeper and openly wondering what to do about it—an indication she was worried about her marriage. And it would only have been a year or so since she had resumed sexual activity with John after her cancer surgery and chemotherapy.

If he was ever going to sexually abuse JonBenét, it would be at a time in his life where he was once again afraid of true intimacy and afraid of loss. This fear would have been greatly magnified by his tremendous success that he would automatically link with loss. *In the back of his mind he would be thinking about 1992 and 1993 all over again when his father died and his wife got cancer—right after he became the company president. Now he would have to wonder what was going to happen after Access Graphics had reached a billion dollars in sales.* Under these conditions, JonBenét could have served as a third party in the marriage and, just like John Ramsey's previous extramarital liaisons, simultaneously served to undo a sense of separation.

In December 1996 John Ramsey felt a lot of stress—and he tended to deviate under stress. It's not illogical to think that, under the right pressure, one type of sexual deviation could have lead to another—particularly since he had already sanctioned JonBenét's prematurely blossoming sexuality.

One more incident subtly indicates that John (and Patsy) would stretch conventional sexual boundaries. One month before the murder and before Patsy's fortieth birthday on December 29th, John threw an early surprise birthday party at a lavish Denver hotel, The Brown Palace. The striking event of the evening was the appearance of a male transvestite in drag who parodied Patsy. While John didn't select the transvestite—Patsy's friends did—he certainly sanctioned it (as Patsy did later) and prior to the party had told Priscilla White, "The sky's the limit."

That speaks volumes: A disguised attack on Patsy, hinting that her sexual identity was in many ways more masculine than feminine (an amazingly accurate perception) and that her sexuality was more about shock and power. On the surface Patsy took the joke in good spirits.

But don't miss the other messages. The transvestite could also have been a picture of how John saw himself—weak and ineffective, and running from his masculinity. Behind the avant-garde humor and the sex, transvestism is secretly about fear and hostility and pushing against boundaries. It's sexuality used to hide aggression and deceit, somewhat like the name of the popular Boulder band that played at the party, "The Four Necators." Most importantly, it draws our attention to the sexual abuse of JonBenét—both the ongoing sexual activities and the specific events the night of the murder—and how it was mostly about more than just sex.

ALL IN THE FAMILY: SEX SECRETS

Maybe John's sexual behavior reflected what was going on in the family as a whole. Three of the four members were using sex as a way of violating commitments and boundaries. All of them would have had natural urges to do so in light of the extreme stress the family was under—they were all living under a potential death sentence.

Patsy Ramsey had her own sexual secrets, as Jane Stobie, a former employee of John's company in Atlanta, revealed. Patsy's mother, Nedra Paugh, and sister Paulette Davis worked for Jane. Another employee told Jane that Nedra and Paulette were bragging to other employees about the size of Burke's penis, which suggests that in Patsy's family men were viewed as sexual objects to be used, reflecting a need for power. Jane herself heard Paulette Davis make inappropriate comments to a male employee about oral sex. While this may appear sexual, it was more a wish to flout the boundaries and shock than truly being sexual—which is consistent with Patsy's view of sexuality. What Paulette Davis did was also sexual abuse—a woman abusing a man, which reflected the way Patsy would have been taught to view men.

It is not hard to imagine Patsy, in some half-naive way, bragging to her mother and sister about the size of her young son's genitalia, behavior that is consistent with someone who is frigid while outwardly appearing very sexual. Throughout her life Patsy used sex much more as a powerful weapon rather than for true sexual enjoyment—and it seems that she learned it from her mother, her primary role model for sexuality and everything else.

A snapshot from Patsy's high-school days in a drama group captures a subtle glimpse into her sexuality. The picture shows five couples around a hot Chevy, portraying a fifties rock and roll *Grease*-like scene. The other four couples are in affectionate poses. Patsy Ramsey and her partner, the farthest apart of any couple, were not even touching each other. Patsy is sprawled on the top of the car in one of the most dominant places, smiling but subtly distant—eerily foreshadowing the future.

Since Patsy enabled JonBenét's seductiveness, she would have pushed JonBenét toward John. Why? The same reason John did—to avoid intimacy but to bond. It also fulfilled Patsy's power needs—she was the mother who had "created" this powerfully seductive young woman.

Dr. Julianne Densen-Gerber, who reviewed all the videotapes of JonBenét's routines, found a shocking performance JonBenét gave for a senior citizens group. Dressed as an elf, JonBenét put a saxophone between her legs and moved very suggestively—evidencing her instructions on how to be highly sexual. But JonBenét's sexuality, like Patsy's, was more about power than sex.

JonBenét's own power needs made the Ramsey family life a powerful firebomb of emotions that could go off at any time. Having such a sexually seductive child around such emotionally vulnerable adults could only end in trouble.

DOES JOHN RAMSEY FIT THE PROFILE OF A SEXUAL ABUSER?

One of the central issues the police and investigative reporters have pursued is the question of John Ramsey's potential for child abuse. Thus far no one has uncovered any prior history of sexual abuse. Reportedly the police have talked to authorities on sexual abuse and have been told that John Ramsey doesn't fit the pattern of a pedophile. John's daughter, Melinda, has insisted that her father never abused her and couldn't possibly have abused JonBenét. John's ex-wife, Cindy, implied the same thing as she described him as exceptionally gentle with his children, never disciplining them in any physical way.

Case closed? Hardly. In my own practice I have seen several instances of first-time child abusers (and often family members) being in their forties or fifties. Dr. Mark McKee, a child psychologist and former program director of a nationally recognized center for sex offenders in Chicago (CAUSES[2]) has seen hundreds of cases of sexually abused children. As he said, "A lot of sexual abusers are highly successful, fine upstanding citizens who control themselves extremely well except for one period of time (with one person). It's like they have this psychotic pocket in their personality." Or perhaps it's like a "foreign faction" living inside them. Richard LaBrie, Executive Director of CAUSES added, "Many times the profile of a sexual abuser is no profile. People want easy answers when there's not one." In other words, John Ramsey could fit the profile or non-profile of sexual abusers.

There is also the hint in John Ramsey of someone who is too passive, reluctant to discipline his own children, and commonly child abusers are passive. It suggests someone who is uncertain and not entirely comfortable with his masculinity, someone who deep down feels more comfortable with children. Combine this with a very seductive young JonBenét who Patsy would have unquestionably pushed toward her father, and we have a powerful force working on John.

Two of the ingredients in sexual molestation within families are often familiarity and unfamiliarity. A familiarity involving natural togetherness and physical contact that gets out of hand—sometimes due to unfamiliarity of another type. Typically the guilty father has not been exposed to a maturing adolescent female before, and it excites him. While John had two daughters from his first marriage, we can be certain

[2]Child Abuse Unit for Studies, Education, and Services

his first wife didn't encourage the seductiveness in them that Patsy Ramsey encouraged in JonBenét. And John was divorced and out of the home when his oldest two daughters were in adolescence. Thus a seductive JonBenét would have been a new experience for him.

Add to this the possibility that John had made a special effort earlier to comfort his little daughter when Patsy was sick, and we can see how both John and JonBenét might have clung a little tighter at such a time. Many family pictures show JonBenét standing particularly close to her father, often touching him in affectionate ways, far more than anyone else.

The bottom line is that John Ramsey does fit a definite profile of certain sexual abusers.

SEX DISGUISES ANGER AND PAIN

Keep in mind that John and Patsy's stresses (and thus their vulnerabilities) were major and ongoing: the uncertainty of Patsy's health, John's heightened sensitivity to loss caused by the recent deaths of his oldest daughter and his father, and his growing fear of punishment caused by his growing wealth and success.

At times John is an incredibly poor communicator. One friend has noted that Patsy is very outgoing but John could remain silent interminably if you didn't keep the conversation going. John's inability to express his feelings through words makes him especially vulnerable to "talking through actions."

Under such circumstances, it's more than conceivable that John's natural fatherly affection could one night cross the line. Little JonBenét truly loved her father, and he loved her. In some ways, she was the closest substitute for Patsy, who John in his own way loved as much as he did JonBenét. The fear of death—of losing someone—is so intense and life-changing that it can drive people into doing things they would never ever normally do. As we've already seen with Patsy Ramsey, the threat of death and loss can literally drive a person crazy.

There are some signs that John wasn't doing well mentally in December 1996. A close family friend reportedly observed changes in John in the months immediately prior to the murder. The friend described a bizarre scene around Halloween where John was desperately stuffing handful after handful of jellybeans into his mouth, dropping many on the floor, and hyperactively picking them up while continuing to stuff himself. His behavior was striking—like an out-of-control kid who needed Ritalin. As Christmas approached John became increasingly distant—"there but not there"—and the friend had the distinct impression that he was protecting himself as though he were harboring a dark secret.

Jellybeans have a childish connotation—kid stuff—and one

mouthful after another tells us something primitive and powerful was going on in John Ramsey. Perhaps it was an even more special Christmas than we realized. Not only was John facing the pressures of inordinate success, but also it was nearing the five-year anniversary of the death of his daughter Beth. Christmas would always be linked with tragedy for him. Christmas 1996 was also an anniversary of Patsy's survival—two years, and waiting on the magic numbers five and ten.

The pressures on John pushed him toward childlike behavior. There seems to be a childish hunger in John, and it fits with the kind of perverse desperation that could lead to sexual abuse. John Ramsey, CEO, was excessively gratifying himself in a childish way on childish things. Sometimes actions can speak far louder than words. The actions surrounding the murder speak volumes. There was blood on JonBenét's panties and evidence of vaginal trauma.

Lastly, we shouldn't miss the anger in all of this—on the parts of everyone involved. Patsy is angry about her cancer, her husband's neglect, her declining beauty, and about being replaced by her daughter; and Patsy acts it out by encouraging JonBenét to have power over her father and, in a subtle way, degrade him. We see the same tendency in the ransom note. JonBenét, for her part, acts out her anger at all the turmoil over possibly losing her mother and being exploited. And John acts out his anger by turning to other women, through an affair or child abuse. This whole sordid sexual mess is much more about anger than sex.

MORE DENIAL

Could the child beauty pageants have been good for JonBenét? Good because they boosted her confidence? Good because they were just wholesome little dress-up games? Good because they helped her lose her fear of being in front of people and they taught her poise?

The rationalizations are endless. But I can assure you that if JonBenét had been in therapy as an adult she would have told her therapist—and perhaps herself for the first time—just how exploitative the whole environment really was.

Whether or not John Ramsey overtly sexually abused his daughter is one issue. But without a doubt, emotionally he and Patsy sexually abused their daughter—the extreme child beauty pageant participation is their confession.

Through their actions before the murder John and Patsy were revealing that, even though they would deny it in the smoothest possible argument, they could justify using their daughter—justify even attacking their daughter. They expressed incredible hostility toward their daughter while trying to put the best possible "spin" on it.

LOVING JONBENÉT TO DEATH

Patsy and JonBenét loved to sing the duet "Together," from the Broadway musical *Gypsy* about a stage mother who exploits her child. At the same time that she and JonBenét, with smiles on their faces, were *denying* the exploitation, their actions were *confirming* it. That's just how great our deeper mind's need to confess is—and our conscious mind's ability simultaneously to deny reality.

People control children in many subtle ways and one of the most tempting is to love them to death. One photographer noted an unusually close relationship between Patsy and JonBenét, which he interpreted as exceptionally loving, as the perfect mother-daughter relationship. When the mother has a potentially fatal illness, she can mold the child like putty—while making it appear that the child *freely chooses* to do whatever the situation called for.

Perhaps the most telling comment came from photographer Randy Simons, who told *People* magazine that Patsy once confided in him, "This is not just my daughter, this is my best friend." As endearing as this might sound on the surface, it points to Patsy's emotional immaturity. What does it say when a grown woman's best friend is a six-year-old?

What role did John play in this abnormally close mother-daughter relationship? Had he failed to become his wife's best friend? Had he unconsciously pushed Patsy toward JonBenét—and then repeated the process himself? Both Patsy and John Ramsey were using JonBenét as a third party to protect themselves from true intimacy.

REAPING WHAT YOU SOW

In August 1996 JonBenét wrote on her Sunburst USA International Beauty Pageant questionnaire that her father was "the nicest guy in the whole world"—and also the person she admired the most. She was just at the point in her emotional development to go through the very natural stage of wanting to "marry Daddy," just as young boys want to marry Mommy.

For JonBenét to use "guy" to describe her father suggests something outside a father-daughter relationship. I can't ever recall hearing a young girl describe her father as a guy. It's "nicest daddy" or "nicest person" or maybe "nicest man," but "guy" suggests ever so subtly something more. Like the "guy" she would marry one day—a much more common use of the word for a six-year-old. If Patsy wrote the quote instead of JonBenét, it suggests she was pushing JonBenét into a "guy-girl" relationship with John.

With all the attention focused on JonBenét's sexuality, surely the idea would have occurred to her deep down that her dreams indeed might come true and she could become the only girl in her daddy's life.

Her mother's serious illness would have fueled JonBenét's natural fantasies of supplanting her mother in her father's life. Her dream about having a baby and living in her mother's room was an exceptionally undisguised oedipal dream (see page 69). All of this could very easily have persuaded JonBenét to participate in some type of sex play with her father, especially since her mother and father had set things in motion by tacitly encouraging her premature sexuality.

A PERSONALITY PROFILE OF JOHN RAMSEY REVEALS:

- he was deeply traumatized over several major losses between 1992 and 1996.

- he was stressed by success.

- he was under great stress in December, 1996.

- he is gifted at blocking out painful emotions.

- he has a cold and ruthless side.

- he enabled JonBenét's seductiveness.

- he is inclined to act out sexually.

Chapter Twelve
John's Letter—Matching Bookends

Dear Paul,

I am writing this letter to tell you I am deeply hurt by how you have portrayed my daughter, JonBenét. We, as a family, have lost one of the most precious things in our lives, and it is difficult to imagine that we will ever have joy in our lives again.

What you have incorrectly portrayed is a very small part of JonBenét's life. It was an activity that she and her mother enjoyed doing together, and she was a very competitive spirit. There was much more to her life. She was very religious. Did very well in school. Loved to go to the beach, and all the other things a normal six-year-old normally enjoys.

You are young, and I can forgive you for what you have done." [Later, he adds that he hoped the young man would learn that others can be hurt by his actions.]

Sincerely yours,
John B. Ramsey

Largely overlooked in the investigation of JonBenét's murder is the fact that John Ramsey also wrote a letter that became public knowledge. Perhaps the most revealing thing about John's letter is what prompted John to write it: a local art exhibition in Boulder, following JonBenét's death, that was entitled "Daddy's Little Hooker."

A student artist named Paul had picked up on the messages in JonBenét's pageant/glamor pictures and blamed John for enabling the whole sex queen scenario. John, "incensed," wrote the artist a letter that "just happened to be made public" by Mike Bynum, a close friend of the Ramseys and a former state prosecutor.

Typical of the Ramseys' close friends, Bynum has remained loyal to John and Patsy. When asked by Dianne Sawyer during an interview on ABC if he had ever asked the Ramseys, "Did you do it?" Bynum replied, *"I never asked the question. I never would ask the question."* Earlier he had stated, "The Ramseys ... are absolutely incapable of murder and incapable of harming that child."

THE TRIGGER

What triggered John's letter? Is John just acting as any indignant father would, or did the artist strike a nerve, hit too close to home?

Considering the letter from the vantage point of John's almost certain complicity in the murder of his daughter, all sorts of possibilities emerge. First, the overall tone of the letter is one of *condemning someone for defaming JonBenét in such degrading sexual terms*—"deeply hurt by how you have portrayed JonBenét." The simplest decoding reveals that John Ramsey is so guilt-ridden that he must externalize his guilt—particularly over his sexual behavior—onto this young man named Paul. If nothing more, John—not Paul—had consistently portrayed JonBenét in degrading sexual terms every time he paid for her to compete in a pageant and have those pictures made. Paul didn't create those provocative pictures.

John himself gave another telling clue during a national television program when he protested the charges that he had abused his daughter, and explicitly stated "I didn't sexually abuse my daughter. *JonBen-I*—JonBenét and I—were close." This crucial slip-up suggests that at the exact moment he is most vociferously denying his guilt, his deeper mind is overriding his lie. In effect John is saying, "I really was far too close to her, so close that JonBenét and I were one." Surely if John Ramsey can lie to us about the murder of his daughter, he is far more capable of sexually abusing her and lying about that.

JONBENÉT THE THING

After stating that he is incensed about someone portraying JonBenét in a negative light, John writes, "We ...have lost one of the most precious things in our lives." *Is his use of the word "things" a confession that deep down he was using JonBenét as a thing, an object?* He added "precious" (things), but John is a master of cover-up, and his choice of words could be a subtle confession.

He uses "we" and "I" exactly as Patsy did in the ransom note. First, he tells us that he and Patsy treated JonBenét like a "thing." He has chosen to introduce Patsy early in his letter, when he mentions the loss of JonBenét. Since Patsy is most directly responsible for that loss, by immediately connecting himself to her ("we"), John reveals that he was involved in JonBenét's death as well. By emphasizing his and Patsy's painful loss, he is indirectly revealing one reason why they took JonBenét's life: Both he and Patsy were themselves victims of loss and death long before JonBenét died.

John goes on to say that he can't see the possibility of them ever having joy again, revealing point blank that he and Patsy ("we") are miserable over what they did and see little hope for the future.

JOHNS'S SECRET MISLEADING PORTRAYAL

"What you have incorrectly portrayed is a very small part of JonBenét's life." For the second time in three sentences John has used the word "portrayed." Ostensibly he's telling the young artist that there's a misleading portrayal going on and that it was a small part of someone's (JonBenét's) life. But read it a deeper way, listening for the big ideas and apply them to John—one of the basic rules of two-level communication. Take every word out of John's mouth as a part of him.

Secretly, John is saying that this *entire letter is an effort to create a misleading portrayal of what was really going on,* and that all he wants us to see is the smallest part of her life. The use of (only) a "very small part" of JonBenét's life on the heels of emphasizing a portrayal is really the same message. *When the deeper mind wants to get its message across, it repeats the same idea over and over*—here it is the idea of a cover-up. *"Portrayal is close to "betrayal."* Read in that light, John reminds us that he betrayed JonBenét and the truth.

If John Ramsey has been actively engaged in trying to portray himself and his wife in a certain misleading way—such as being fine upstanding citizens when they're not—wouldn't he feel guilty about it deep down and somehow try to confess to it? If he were guilty, his deeper mind would continue the same story—but with more blatant hints of a cover-up. *Also as is typical of the deeper mind, John would tell us what he's covering up—which is exactly what he does next.*

FAMILY COMPETITION: JONBENÉT AND PATSY

"It was an activity that she and her mother enjoyed doing together (and she was a very competitive spirit)." Outwardly John is talking about JonBene´t and Patsy enjoying their beauty pageants as mother and daughter. But since he brought up the idea, he is implying that JonBene´t also enjoys an activity related to the pageants with another parent—himself. The essence of the pageant is JonBene´t's seductiveness, a subject that John overtly connects to Patsy, but it's clear that John was very involved in it too. John Ramsey actively reinforced JonBene´t's pageant participation—which was nothing more than proving she was the most seductive (read sexual) six-year-old around, the one who could get the men.

He took great pride in JonBenét's competitiveness with her precocious sexuality: "... and she was a very competitive spirit." Notice the sequence of John's story. First, JonBenét and Patsy enjoyed doing an activity together, suggesting that Patsy was also competing in her own way. *But John only mentions JonBenét being competitive, implying that she was more competitive than Patsy and that JonBenét was the winner—* which is very revealing considering the kind of competitor Patsy was when it came to beauty contests. John is strongly hinting *that Patsy and JonBenét were desperately competing for him and that a major problem occurred when JonBenét won his affection.* Obviously John is suggesting that he enjoyed having women compete for him. To have JonBenét compete with Patsy in some real way would also have been a "good" way of expressing his anger at Patsy for putting him down, for getting sick, and for threatening to leave.

Once a Patsy/JonBenét/John triangle forms, JonBenét's intense competitive spirit takes on much more ominous meanings. For John to know how strong his daughter's competitive drive was, he would have to have experienced it himself.

JonBenét's participation in the "harmless beauty contests" suggests other triangles: JonBenét was constantly competing with other little girls for the judges' (father figures) attention. And John was enabling her to keep on competing.

John's deeper mind has a tremendous need to explain exactly what happened in that terrible final eruption between Patsy and JonBenét. *John is embellishing on exactly what did go on that last night.* Deep down he recognizes the intensity of JonBenét's competition with her mother, and he intuitively knows that this was a central reason Patsy exploded so quickly that night she killed JonBenét.

By spontaneously telling a story about JonBenét's sexuality and competitiveness and linking it to Patsy, John is strongly implying that "Yes," sexual abuse was going on that night. The story in John's letter fits precisely with the story in Patsy's ransom note. Patsy and John independently reveal what happened that night—and their stories match perfectly.

Look at the sequence once more. First, John gives three messages that a cover-up is going on ("portrayal" twice and "small part of JonBenét's life"), followed by this crucial sentence about intense pageant competition involving Patsy and JonBenét, and then followed by yet another perfect description of a cover-up, "There was much more to her life." Another clue that there was much more going on between JonBenét and John than meets the eye.

The sequence of ideas enables us to fill in the details. While it may seem like we are guessing, the deeper mind signals us that we are on the right track by placing matching bookend images of a cover-up ("small part" and"much more to her life") on either side of the story about competition.

John wrote this letter when JonBenét was called "Daddy's Little Hooker." His train of thought—along with his key slip of the tongue broadcast nationwide—strongly suggests that the artist had portrayed the scenario correctly, not only symbolically (John Ramsey sanctioning the pageants) but also literally.

MORE MEANING TO "JONBENÉT'S SMALL PART"

Looking back one sentence, the term *"small part"* (of JonBenét) now takes on a meaning that strikes another crucial and familiar note. In Patsy's ransom note, a "small foreign faction" or "small defect" could lead to catastrophe. John echoes this idea of a small part of someone, but he insists that it was unimportant—we know better, and so does he.

This "small part" of JonBenét most likely caused Patsy to explode the night of the murder, the same "small part" of JonBenét that he (and others) had experienced in a seductive way, the same "small part" of her that Patsy had gone to great lengths to nurture including bragging about it and pinning a lot of her hopes on it. JonBenét's "small" sexuality was not fully developed, but it had caused a big ripple to run through the Ramsey household.

On a more literal level, John is very likely alluding to a small body part of JonBenét's (her vagina). He had a tendency to be literal at moments, as when he referred to her as "a thing."

And John knew full well that small parts of people can have great impact. Like Patsy, John was constantly surrounded by the same pressure of knowing that the *slightest* change, the *slightest* part of someone being imperfect could spell real trouble.

John may have suggested the idea of a small foreign faction for Patsy's ransom note, alluding to her cancer. They had a shared perception of the constant stress of her cancer—and John had his own fears of cancer as well.

MORE COVER-UP: THE BEACH AND BEAUTY PAGEANTS

*"She was very religious. Did very well in school. Loved to go to the beach, and all the other things a **normal** six-year-old **normally** enjoys."*

Try as he might to portray himself as a normal, loving father, *John reveals just how impersonal and distant a father he often was.* Kids aren't religious. Kids love Bible stories, love singing or going to Sunday school, and occasionally love God and Jesus.

Adults are religious. Notice how *businesslike* John is. He doesn't have time to personally refer to JonBenét, even with so much as a "she." He just writes "did well in school, loved the beach." He is seemingly more interested in her *performance* than in JonBenét as a person—revealing in yet another way that indeed he could treat her like a "thing." And by avoiding "she" or "JonBenét", he depersonalizes her to reduce his guilt.

John idealizes his daughter in terms that he uses to idealize himself: church-goer, good student, good performer. He doesn't realize that he's giving us other clues.

John makes even stronger references to cover-ups and uses the **message marker** *"school" to instruct us to pay close attention.*

The beach seems at first an idea from a good, wholesome person, but *it implies an escape, a place where troubles are washed away, a place where no one can find your footprints, where there are no clues as to who has been there—an image of the ultimate cover-up.* Perhaps John was also thinking of footprints in the snow and the lack of footprints around his house the night of the murder. The snow preserves footprints, freezes them, but footprints wash away at the beach.

A SECOND MEANING TO "BEACH"

The beach also symbolizes a carefree existence, a getaway, where the normal pressures and rules of life don't exist. Where people run around partially clothed in various states of undress, often pushing the boundaries to the point of being skimpily clad, if clad at all. However hesitantly we apply this line of thought to JonBenét, we can envision a seductive little beauty queen at the beach—not the least because we have already seen her disrobe and strut around in a bathing suit during competition.

John Ramsey describes JonBenét as specifically enjoying two things—the *beauty pageants* and the *beach.* He links these two events to her "passion." If we understand his great need to confess, we can see how revealing these clues are. The skimpy, seductive clothing people wear in beauty contests and at the beach are amazingly similar—and they wear cover-ups over their outfits.

Once again we see how gifted the deeper intelligence is. Of the countless activities and pastimes little JonBenét enjoyed, John's deeper mind focuses on the beach, which fits so perfectly with beauty contests and provides a safe way of confessing, of cluing us in on the cover-up.

John tips us off to a cover-up by overselling how "normal" JonBenét's life was—at the exact place in the letter where he was revealing the clearest image of what was really going on. This hint underscores just how crucial a word "beach" and all that it implies is. "Normal" is a cover-up like "portrayal." John is trying hard to portray JonBenét and himself as "normal." His deeper mind has worked over-time to reveal that, and it elaborates by talking about "the beach"—the ultimate cover-up.

Since the invaluable message-laden word "beach" follows immediately the reference to "school," it confirms that we really need to go to "school" on what John Ramsey is saying in this part of his letter.

SECRET ANGER: MORE ACTING OUT

One other possible meaning of "beach" is a stretch but worth considering. "Beach" is very similar in sound and spelling to "bitch," and we can see why a beach might have negative connotations for John. Why the beach might be a bitch for John. The beach and beauty pageants would stand for the same thing in John's mind: the power that women, even little ones, had over him. Their seductiveness was too much for him to handle in his vulnerable state.

Patsy has called most of the shots during their marriage because of her far greater social skills. This leaves him weak and vulnerable, which fuels his hostility—which he only expresses indirectly. By his sexual abuse of JonBenét he both degrades her and reveals who had power over whom in the end. Child beauty pageants attack little girls' childhood innocence, telling them they should be more than what they are and pushing them into their sexuality long before they're ready. In a word, using them.

John's anger at women also fits with Patsy's put-downs of John in the ransom note. He was well aware of how she treated him, and now he was paying her back. He knew firsthand that a woman could be a "beach," and he was treating her like one. There were plenty of other reasons for him to be furious with women. Three had left him high and dry: His mother by dying of cancer, his first wife by divorcing him, and his daughter (Beth) by suddenly dying on him. Patsy had almost repeated the same thing with her own cancer. The more you love somebody the more they can hurt you—and by 1996 John Ramsey had a lot of unfinished business with women waiting on his victim JonBenét.

OBSESSION: HURTING A YOUNG PERSON

*"You are **young**, and I can forgive you for what you have done" (and he hoped the **young** artist would learn that others can be hurt by his actions).*

The idea of someone who is young is very much on John's mind—not this young artist but the young JonBenét. When John raises the subject of someone who has terribly defamed JonBenét, he is really talking about himself, and deep down he desperately wants forgiveness.

Three times, directly or indirectly (i.e., six-year-old JonBenét), John alludes to someone being young—and his preoccupation gives a big clue. Such an obsession is a message to look much deeper, to explore what "young" could really mean in this context. *"Young" is the most major confession in this letter.* It is the *buzzword* of sexual molestation—**pedophiles like young girls.**

Look at the sequence again. It starts with the preceding sentence (and even earlier). "Loved to go to the beach and all the other things a normal [young] six-year-old normally enjoys." *By emphasizing four ideas* and tying them together John is shouting: "Cover-up, cover-up! Beach—beach—pageants—sexuality! Normal young six-year-old, normal young six-year-old! (The one thing JonBenét wasn't.) Remember, young—young!

And somebody hurt a young person terribly, made them into a hooker—Daddy's Little Hooker. John Ramsey is not talking about the artist Paul, but about himself the father. That's who tried to turn JonBenét into a hooker. This is the powerful story he's telling in code.

Once again at the very moment John Ramsey is trying his very hardest to conceal what has been going on, his deeper mind is at its most revealing. You may think that John's repetitions are strictly coincidence, but if you do you are setting aside the phenomenal ability of the deeper mind to observe and reveal—in code—what's really going on.

"Young" is a subtle clue—but it is a subtle obsession. John has "youth" on his mind—in particular youths who either get hurt or hurt others. This is John's way of confessing that he can't get over hurting the young JonBenét—the one who hurt her needs forgiveness. He is also saying that JonBenét, with her seductiveness and enticement, hurt him and caused him to do something he regrets.

As much as we want to make JonBenét totally innocent, we can't. Adults pandered to her most primitive drives, but the drives were also hers—and she used them, however unaware, to hurt others.

THE LIE CONTINUES: FAILURE TO TAKE RESPONSIBILITY

Oddly John closes his letter with a question mark. He hopes someone has learned that they can hurt people with their actions, but he's not quite certain. Is this not a perfect picture of John Ramsey, who hasn't at all shown us that he's learned from his actions, since he continues to hurt others, and the memory of JonBenét by lying?

Above all John's saying quite plainly that he's a man who often *speaks through actions*, as he certainly did with JonBenét. He's also telling us in his own way that he's a poor communicator verbally—just as Patsy mentioned in the ransom note and as friends noticed.

John's letter doesn't contain the raw emotion and violent images of Patsy's ransom note, but it does contain subtly *seductive* images (being a "thing," enjoyable activities, competitive spirit, small body parts, beaches). *John's letter serves to highlight, by contrast to the ransom note, just how much pain Patsy was in.* But we must always keep in mind that he is more typically a person of action (as opposed to words) than she is, and that the ransom note was written at an overwhelming moment when they were "the two gentlemen" who were watching over JonBenét's dead body.

SIMILARITIES WITH PATSY'S RANSOM NOTE

John's letter is similar to Patsy's ransom note in some ways. Like Patsy, John uses message markers and repeats himself when he wants us to know what he really thinks. He alludes to pageants three times ("what you have portrayed," an activity, and competition) and to a beach once—four implied references to sexuality. He uses "portrayal" and "normal" twice along with three other ideas of a cover-up ("beach," "small part of JonBenét's life," and "much more to her life"). He uses "young" at least three times. To decode it once more, John Ramsey's preoccupation with covering up is a confession that a major one is going on in this letter. Behind it is his overwhelming guilt about what he has done to his **young** daughter JonBenét. By stressing "young" he is revealing that he is fully aware deep down that she was far too young to be involved with him in this way.

One last note. Overall we must take John's letter as a confession of just how competitive and controlling he really is, much like Patsy. Knowing that he's committed a heinous crime and knowing that he is lying to the young artist, John still has the audacity to publicly berate this young man for basically telling the truth.

Indeed, the Ramseys' public relations campaign has become vicious—they don't seem to care who they hurt in the process of covering up their shadow sides. John reveals in his letter that he is tremendously competitive and intends to play the hardest hardball possible. People called John's father "Czar"—like father, like son.

JOHN RAMSEY'S PUBLIC LETTER TO THE
YOUNG ARTIST SECRETLY REVEALS:

- John repeats four key ideas which reveal his true motives.

- John's confession to a cover-up.

- Strong hints John was sexually abusing young JonBenét.

- John blamed others for his faults.

- John's letter matches Patsy's ransom note story of child abuse.

- John saw JonBenét as a thing, an object he could control.

- John enjoyed Patsy and JonBenét competing for his attention.

- John was furious with women for hurting him greatly.

Chapter Thirteen
More Comments, More
Revelations

We must never forget that every second of their lives the
Ramseys are aware that "the other shoe could drop any day."
They are acutely aware of their guilt and of the reality that the
police are pursuing them. This means every comment that either of
them makes must be filtered through this reality. *When we filter their
remarks, we see them secretly responding to the police investigation (and
to their own guilt) at every turn.* In the various public comments the
Ramseys (particularly Patsy) have made since JonBenét's murder, they
make one confession after another.

Virtually every comment that Patsy or John make contain clues
from their deeper mind. First, they continually deny their crime, which
is their most obvious defense, but often they add a unique twist to these
various denials. When either of them speak beyond their denials, their
deeper mind is communicating the real story of the circumstances and
events surrounding JonBenét's death. They continually reveal new
information about their crime, and the more they talk, the more they
reveal. The deeper mind within each of them contains their conscience,
their soul, and it will have its say.

JOHN RAMSEY'S GUILT

At one point John called JonBenét's murder "nauseating." Shortly
after the murder he also stated publicly, "If we don't have the full
resources of all the law enforcement community on this case, I am going
to be very upset." But if he did commit the crime, we can see his comments in another light altogether. He himself is nauseated by the crime,
and he is also keenly aware that someone is not putting everything they
can into solving this murder—namely himself.

As hard as John is trying to cover up, he still slips up and—in his
own way—confesses. He either failed to destroy the practice ransom
note in the pad or, inadvertently, gave it to the police. His deeper mind
caught him and—through his action—said, "The person who owns this
pad (Patsy) is the same one who wrote the note." (Isn't the practice
note itself typical of Patsy's personality—to practice your performance
before going on stage?)

As I have mentioned, one of the most striking clues in the whole
investigation thus far was when John, vehemently attempting to deny

that he was sexually abusing JonBenét, made his striking slip of the tongue "JonBen-I" at the most crucial moment imaginable. While he was insisting on national TV that he had maintained the appropriate distance as her parent and wouldn't think of sexually abusing her, he wanted to say, "JonBenét and I were very close" but instead slipped up and said, *"JonBen-I."* When John's conscious mind wanted to keep the two of them clearly separate to reflect proper boundaries between them, his deeper mind confessed that a major boundary between them had been crossed. Given the circumstances, it's as striking a confession as the deeper mind can make. **The powerful deeper mind can override the conscious mind's attempts to conceal. In the end, this will be the Ramseys' undoing.**

PATSY PROFILES THE KILLER: A GUILT-RIDDEN WOMAN

Patsy's deeper mind has the same tendency to reveal the truth. In the months after the murder, she has been (not surprisingly) even more revealing than John has—and continues so every time she opens her mouth. Only days after JonBenét's murder, Patsy told the public in a very dramatic fashion, "There is a killer on the loose. I don't know if it's a *he or a she*, but if I were a resident of Boulder, I would tell my friends to keep *your babies* close to you."

In this seemingly simple comment, Patsy both confesses and gives a motive. Given that virtually everyone would think that such a killer was a male, her idea that the killer could be a woman is a subtle confession. Patsy implies that the killer wants to take women's babies away from them—like cancer took away Patsy's ability to have babies. "I don't know if it's a he or a she" also points to Patsy's sexual identity confusion and hints at her search for power in the face of powerlessness.

She certainly got right the part about the killer not being caught yet: especially when we consider this was the only homicide in Boulder in 1996. Imagine how much emotional effort such a constant charade takes. Many saw Patsy's theatrics for what they were—an overdone act by a woman quite familiar with the limelight—and how to use it.

Patsy continues to confess in one form or another as her deeper intelligence refuses to go along with the cover-up. Four months after the murder, she told everyone that two people were involved in this murder. She was so preoccupied with guilt, that she impulsively called *Larry King Live* to blame someone else (the paparazzi) for causing the death of a beautiful young princess. She revealed enough information in the lengthy ransom note to eventually get herself caught—if the authorities listen.

PATSY'S TIP-OFF: A BAD HEART

In her television appearance on May 1, 1997—the day after her police interrogation—Patsy, amidst her adamant denial, very subtly revealed that she was the murderer. *"I'm appalled* that anyone would think that John or I would be involved in such a *hideous, heinous* crime. Let me assure you that I did not kill JonBenét. I did not have anything to do with it. *I loved that child* with **my whole of my heart** and soul."

The most striking aspect to her comment is her subtle slip-up "my whole of my heart." You could tell she wanted to say "my whole heart" but something in her wouldn't let her. A more natural option would have been "**the** whole of my heart." But nobody says "my whole of my heart."

Read in a more literal way, "whole of my heart" is very close to "**hole** of my heart" or "hole in my heart." Patsy is really saying that she loved JonBenét imperfectly and that on the night of the murder she had a hole in her heart, all the love was temporarily gone. She uses "my" twice—my whole, my heart—to emphasize that she's quite aware deep down that it was her heart, and in one sense her heart alone, that was the problem. Her heart was the one with the hole in it.

Body language in combination with the encoded verbal language of the deeper mind sends a powerful message. *Patsy distinctly closed her eyes three times during the interview when she said: "I'm appalled," "hideous," and "I loved that child."* We can read someone closing their eyes as saying, "I really don't see it the way I'm telling you I do" (I'm lying) or "I don't want to see what I'm talking about."

When Patsy was saying she was appalled by the accusations, her closed eyes were saying she didn't really see it that way at all, that she knew full well she was guilty and why she was being questioned. When she was insisting she loved her child, her closed eyes were saying, "Don't believe me. In fact, I can't even bear to look at such a lie. I didn't love my child at the particular moment I took her life. Who do I think I'm fooling?"

She revealed the same thing when she said "hideous," dragging out the word and keeping her eyes closed for a prolonged period—by far the longest during this segment. She was really saying, *"Pay attention. Notice that I recognize that my crime was hideous beyond belief, which is why I emphasized it so—including shaking my head, closing my eyes,* and stringing it out by saying it so slowly. It was so hideous that I can't bear to look at it either, and I want you to see that this part of me exists."

Patsy is trying say that part of her really did love JonBenét and she simply lost control and did something she greatly regrets. Her closed eyes reveal that she can't look at her lie. If we think about *how close* "hideous" is to "hide" and "hidden," we can see more suggestions telling us to look for hidden clues in her words. The deeper mind shows us again that you can run, but you can't hide.

There is one last interesting aspect to Patsy Ramsey's denial at this particular time. She first was appalled that anyone would think that she or John could have murdered JonBenét, but when it came to the denial—she only referred to herself—she only felt the need to insist on her own innocence. Focusing exclusively on herself when it came right down to the specifics was Patsy's way of revealing that she held one of them primarily responsible for JonBenét's death.

CRAFTY TACTICS AND HOLDING A POSE

More than ten months after the murder, Patsy agreed to be interviewed privately near her Atlanta home and videotaped for the *Geraldo Rivera Show* with one reporter present—in other words, all the familiar control. Nonetheless, she couldn't stop her deeper intelligence from dropping revealing clues. First of all she appears far from being grief stricken and almost too happy when she reminisces about JonBenét— she appears to be enjoying herself. She tells a seemingly insignificant story about JonBenét having an incredible talent for standing on her head. She was really saying that everything was turned upside down in regard to JonBenét.

JonBenét was known for being able to hold a pose far longer than other beauty pageant contestants, and Patsy laughingly went on to comment on how long JonBenét would stand on her head. JonBenét could hold a pose for no telling how long—maybe thirty minutes or more. This seemingly inconsequential story was too coincidental—it fit too well with what we know reality to be. *Patsy and John Ramsey have turned the investigation of JonBenét on its head, and they intend to hold that pose as long as they can.* One thing's for sure—they both know it's a pose.

I LOVED HER TOO MUCH

Patsy revealed far more during the *Geraldo* show. All smiles, she told another anecdote about JonBenét, the one about when JonBenét asked her how much she loved her. *Right off Patsy addressed the question of her love for JonBenét—the major reality everyone was looking at.* Patsy says she told JonBenét that, along with her brother and her father, she loved JonBenét more than anything in the world. Then Patsy says that JonBenét corrected her by informing her that you're not supposed to love anyone that much—you're supposed to love Jesus more than anyone else.

Surrounded by her comfortable neighborhood, as always impeccably dressed, with the big smile and the nice jewelry, in the most casual relaxed fashion, Patsy made another hidden confession. *In response to being questioned by JonBenét herself about her love for*

JonBenét, Patsy indirectly confessed that she had made a mistake in loving JonBenét too much, something JonBenét had recognized. *This is the only time publically the beauty-queen perfect Patsy has even admitted doing anything wrong—which makes her comment even more significant.* Without consciously realizing the significance of her story, Patsy revealed one of the central underlying problems in her relationship with JonBenét—Patsy "loved" her too much. Patsy loved her to death by failing to give JonBenét her own life (just as we have seen Patsy didn't really have hers). The revelations of Patsy's deeper mind fit perfectly with reality, and consumed by guilt, Patsy must keep on confessing.

I Made Her My Idol

Patsy confesses that in the process of loving JonBenét too much, she failed to love God. She made an idol out of JonBenét—she failed God. Deep down Patsy knows she broke two of God's most sacred commandments (killing, failing to love your neighbor or loving someone else more than God), and she must confess.

If we simply follow the big ideas and the sequencing, we see a marvelously cohesive hidden story revealed by Patsy's deeper mind. *First her love for* JonBenét *is questioned (How much do you love me?)—followed by her declaration of excess love (more than anything in the whole world)—followed by a correction (that's too much)*—followed by the recognition she has failed to love God. This hidden story fits hand in glove with reality.

It also fits perfectly with Patsy's earlier comments about loving JonBenét with "the whole of my heart and soul." Patsy has come to realize that she loved JonBenét too much—she confesses that she should have saved part of her heart for others—including God.

Deserves Harsh Punishment

Patsy's conscience was bothering her badly. She calls it a hideous, heinous crime. She says that she fears the stress of the murder will cause her cancer to return. Sometimes a fear is a secret wish, particularly when someone is guilt ridden, and Patsy's fear is her way of saying that she deserves to have cancer. Patsy Ramsey has a powerful need to confess—to attempt to clear her conscience of the gnawing guilt, another "small, foreign faction" this is eating her alive.

The Killer Spills More Beans on Geraldo

Patsy can't make a completely casual comment because every second of her life her conscience wants to confess to clear itself of guilt and she also wants to confess to escape the constant police pursuit that terrifies her like a death sentence. So on the November show Patsy says, *"Geraldo should do an investigation on the murder. He should use John Douglas. Maybe the killers will spill the beans to a friend or behave differently so that someone knows who the killer is. Geraldo should encourage anyone with clues to come forward. Maybe it was a pedophile—there are fifty pedophiles living in Boulder. Or maybe it was a University of Colorado student who saw JonBenét riding her bike around the neighborhood."*

The big ideas and their sequence reveal hidden messages compatible with Patsy's earlier story. Patsy talks about the existence of hidden clues, the pressure the killer is under to "spill the beans," someone with clues coming forward encouraged by Geraldo. She's talking about herself spilling the beans to Geraldo (encouraged by him) at this very second because of the pressure she is under. Indirectly Patsy is revealing that she has been under pressure all along to leave clues and has done so.

Then she points to the immediate clues: one of fifty pedophiles, a college student, someone who saw JonBenét riding her bicycle. First Patsy tries to blame the crime on a pedophile, armed with the knowledge that there are fifty in Boulder. At the same time that she's presenting this familiar cover-up, she hints at an overlooked pedophile, namely John Ramsey, who actually was involved in the murder. A pedophile who gave JonBenét a bike on Christmas Day and was going to help her ride it. Patsy Ramsey is underscoring that sexual abuse had a lot to do with JonBenét's murder.

Next Patsy goes to the idea of a college student, which we can expand as follows: someone who is highly intelligent, who appears to be a casual bystander but is the culprit. She is describing Patsy (and John) Ramsey—highly intelligent people who are depending on their smarts to convince people they were innocent parties.

Following this she says the killer may be someone who saw JonBenét riding a bicycle, a clue that this innocent act is connected to the murder. JonBenét's bike riding symbolizes her growing independence, and Patsy's mind connected JonBenét being damaged with bike riding. Patsy probably doesn't appreciate that her mind has figured out what was behind her rage, but it has. *This is identical to the idea of loving JonBenét too much because when you love someone too much the most threatening thing they can do is "ride their bike"—separate from you, get a life of their own.*

How to Catch the Killer

"Geraldo should encourage anyone with clues to come forward." Patsy recommends that the police bring in John Douglas, the ex-FBI profiler. But Patsy's deeper intelligence didn't really mean John Douglas

himself who was on the Ramseys' payroll—it meant someone like John Douglas, someone who can find the secret profile that fits the killer. Her deeper mind is telling us that the profile is available. *She is saying to listen to the hidden profile her own deeper mind has already provided.*

GERALDO INTERVIEW ECHOES POLICE INTERVIEW: V FOR VICTORY

"Maybe the killer will spill the beans to a friend or behave differently so that someone knows who the killer is." These comments reflect Patsy herself spilling the beans to Geraldo, and they also harken back to the Ramseys' television appearance on May 1, 1997, after meeting with the Boulder police. As John and Patsy are sitting side by side, filling up the TV screen, Patsy prominently holds up two fingers and waves them in what looks like a **"V" for victory sign**—*unconsciously taking us back to the closing of the ransom note as she talks about the killers.*

Prompted by John, she says she has a strong hunch that two people are involved in this killing—the murderer and a confidant, someone the killer has told. Doesn't her hunch combined with her striking two-finger victory sign represent the two killers staring us in the face? Isn't this too coincidental not to be another confession? John and Patsy typically override their denials with a confession.

Earlier in the interview Patsy stated, *"There are at least two people on the face of the earth that KNOW who did this*—that is the killer and some other person that killer may have confided in. All we need is one phone call, the one phone call to this number that will help the authorities come to a conclusion to-to [stutter] this case." Patsy emphasized the word KNOW very distinctly—two people know and her stutter ["to-to"] is a secret message reminding us that we were looking at those two people. She is giving a powerful hint.

When she said "killer," the one time she used it during this segment of the Geraldo interview, **John Ramsey noticeably looks away from her and down,** the only time he can't face her or the American people. The word "killer" out of the killer's mouth is too much for even John. His body language reveals that deep down he knows who did it and that he doesn't want to look at her—or anyone to look at him.

A HOUSE OF CARDS IS JUST A PHONE CALL AWAY

Patsy is revealing how close the authorities are to breaking the case—one phone call. One communication from a knowledgeable person. (Later, John will tell us the same thing.) When one person familiar with the deeper mind's messages shows Patsy what she is really saying—approaches her the way she secretly recommends—she will break. In the ransom note Patsy leaves clues that John will be the first to break. But as time goes on, she changes her mind. Her conscience is eating at her.

When Patsy tries to talk about the authorities bringing a close "to—to—the case," her stuttering also reveals, through another slip that she really doesn't want the case to be closed because when it is, the noose will be around their necks. Both in the ransom note and in her comments after the murder, Patsy talks about two people being involved in JonBenét's murder. She implies that one of them was the primary culprit and the other went along primarily for the cover-up, but she is intentionally being somewhat misleading. She also repeatedly makes plain that both she and John were responsible.

MORE HINTS ON GERALDO: PATSY IS CLOSE TO CONFESSING

"I wish they would find the killer. On the other hand, it frightens me to think that **I may actually know the person.** *Maybe it is better that I don't know who it is right now."* Patsy is getting closer to the understandably frightening idea of confessing. She has moved from thinking that there are two people who *know* about this crime to her *knowing* the killer—and to the idea that right now it's better that she doesn't know, doesn't admit who did it. She still wants to continue the charade a while longer, but she's getting closer to confessing. Her choice of the words "right now" meaning that it won't be long now. "Right now" only lasts a moment and then "right" will have to stand on its own apart from "wrong." Deep down she is confronted every moment of her life with doing what is right, and doing right means telling the truth.

She confesses the same thing later when she says, *"I cried when I watched your last show and Cyril Wecht (the forensic coroner) said that all the evidence pointed toward me and that I should be arrested immediately. And your audience clapped. It was so hurtful ... Jane Stobie [an employee of John Ramsey] ... doesn't know what she is talking about when she tells those lies on your show."* Once again read the ideas: She broke down (cried)—all the evidence pointing toward her—many wanting her arrested immediately. Patsy is saying that she can't help but listen to what others are saying, that it is causing her to break down, and that secretly she herself is one of those people who want her arrested because she knows that all the evidence points toward her.

She tells a second time that she is beginning to crumble when she stresses how devastated—hurt—she is. Then her cover-up continues as she describes someone else, but secretly she is revealing who she is—someone who is telling lies on the *Geraldo* show.

ANOTHER STRIKING PICTURE: THE HALLOWEEN STORY

Another revealing comment Patsy made on Geraldo's show reveals that she is coming increasingly closer to that monster day when everyone knows that she killed JonBenét, "I like it best when I am sleeping. I feel like I am still with JonBenét. I feel safe when she is with me. When I wake up, everything is OK for a second, and then I remember what happened. This Halloween wasn't the same without JonBenét."

Of course Patsy likes it best when she can block murdering JonBenét out of her awareness, when she can pretend that JonBenét is still alive. Patsy has extraordinary powers of pretending and blocking out reality—as the entire cover-up demonstrates. Under those conditions, Patsy feels safe when she's covering up reality which is an interesting twist. It's not JonBenét who is safe, but Patsy. Patsy recognizes that in light of her guilt she is not at all safe and her preoccupation for her own safety is a subtle confession—otherwise she wouldn't have to worry about being safe. (And once again she reminds us that she had clung to JonBenét because she then had felt safe—from cancer.)

Patsy is finding it harder and harder to pretend because she is waking up and having to face what really happened. The Halloween right before the *Geraldo* show was a different Halloween than ever before—it was not like the pretend kind of Halloweens she enjoyed with JonBenét. This Halloween a real live monster lurked nearby ready to get her. She is coming to terms with the monster inside of her. *Halloween symbolizes masks, monsters, skeletons, death, deceit—trick or treat. Patsy reveals that she has been wearing a mask, and when she takes off her Miss America mask everyone will see death, destruction, deceit, and skeletons in the closet.* Patsy has played a most vicious game of trick or treat.

PREVIOUS HINTS: THE CLOCK IS RUNNING

Patsy Ramsey has been hinting all along that there was a waiting game going on, a game that would eventually end. In May, when negotiations with the police department over interviewing the Ramseys broke down, Patsy impulsively went public: *"I will sit with investigators **around the clock** if that's what you want. You'd think if they believed we were guilty they'd want to talk with us."*

Once again a striking image from her thoughts fits in with the story—waiting around the clock. First *we think of Patsy and her husband sitting there with JonBenét's body waiting for morning to come,* waiting until they could talk to investigators and start the charade.

Patsy is also thinking of the biological clock that she's sitting with—she knows that the time has already run out on one clock (her fertility), but she *doesn't know when the time is going to run out on her second and biggest biological clock (her life).*

She's also thinking about the clock running out on her and John's attempted cover-up. Deep down she knows the police have more than enough evidence, deep down she knows she has left a ton of hidden clues, and deep down she knows the clock on her conscience is running out and she (or maybe John first) will have to confess.

At the time she made this comment, though, Patsy was indicating that she wasn't ready to talk: She refers to the police as the people refusing to talk—as usual projecting her traits onto someone else. But her idea that the police surely would want to talk with guilty parties is not far from the guilty parties themselves wanting to talk with the police. Her guilt is bothering her more and more and she implies that one day soon she will want to talk. Her confession clock is running, and the pressure is building.

How much longer can she hold out? Will an arrest or an anniversary throw off her precarious balance? She is hanging by a thread, and as she revealed earlier it will take only one communication to break her.

Patsy's public comments repeatedly refer to a clock ticking. In her May interview she talked about the stress of the murder and said, *"It was hour by hour, day by day, week by week. I mean, there is no **rule book** written as to how you handle something like this ... it's just overwhelming."* Here she connects the idea of the clock running with a rule book. Patsy knows she has broken the rules, and she knows she won't get away with it.

Even as Patsy talks about others, she is really talking about herself. When she talks about the tabloids on television, she is speaking about a part of herself: *"These tabloid photographers have ruined our lives. They are printing false information. They stalk us. They stalk my child."* She knows that she herself has ruined her life, that she has been lying about it, and that her own conscience is stalking her.

Both she and John have said in no uncertain terms that they will find the killer. John once said, *"We'll find you. We will find you. I have that as a sole mission for the rest of my life."* Patsy vowed the same thing. Without realizing it, they are predicting their own fate—their consciences are after them, slowly determined to bring about justice. John said *"a" sole mission instead of "my" sole mission,* a tip-off since "a" is somewhat impersonal and implies that a part of him that he is not aware of will bring him down. That part of him is his soul, his conscience. The pilot within him is talking here, and deep down his soul is revealing that it is indeed on a *"soul mission."*

Is Patsy Ramsey Giving Us Further Warning?

On September 25, 1997, Patsy told Geraldo's investigator, Jennifer Kay, that she was terrified to come on camera and that she was certain the killers were still out there. She told of her fears that her life and her son Burke's life were in danger. The investigator was impressed with Patsy's insistence that the killers be found.

Patsy has made references to "joining JonBenét soon" in other comments. Friends have insisted that she was referring to fears that her cancer would return, and they do not feel that Patsy would commit suicide. But her comments on the *Geraldo* show may suggest that she is considering taking her son's life and her own life in one fell swoop. She may very well be considering it if the noose closes tighter around her. Her comments reveal that it is at least in the back of her mind. Wouldn't she be tempted to spare herself the shame she would very possibly never be able to tolerate and at the same time enact her rage on her other child—rationalizing that he wouldn't want to be around and have to deal with so much emotional pain?

Patsy revealed in the ransom note how cold-blooded she can be in a pinch: "Don't think that killing will be difficult." Patsy has already demonstrated that she is perfectly capable of taking her own child's life—and lying about it—and casting aspersions on friends. Someone as determined as Patsy is capable of almost anything.

PUBLIC COMMUNICATIONS FROM THE RAMSEYS REVEAL:

- Patsy repeatedly confesses to the crime.

- Patsy confesses to cover-up.

- Patsy knows the cover-up will eventually fail.

- Patsy is terribly guilty.

- Patsy is close to breaking.

- Patsy must confess to see JonBenét again.

- John is wracked with guilt.

- Patsy admits to being overly attached to JonBenét.

- Patsy reveals she is secretly a monster hiding behind a mask.

- Patsy's slip reveals she "had a hole in her heart" and failed JonBenét.

- Patsy gives police clues how to catch her—read between the lines.

Chapter Fourteen
Christmas Letter 1995:
The Manic Patsy

Twas a week before Christmas with a million things to do,
And wouldn't you know it, Mom came down with the flu!

Fortunately the gifts were all gotten and under the tree,
But the Christmas cards didn't make it — as you can well see!

So we'll take this opportunity to extend the Holiday Cheer
And be the first to wish you a Healthy & Happy New Year!

We've finally given in to the computerized form letter! What better way to keep the high-tech industry in business!? Speaking of business, John and Access are going great guns. Europe has been successfully conquered with offices in every country except Norway! Mexico & Canada opened too. (Can you believe this grew out of our garage on Northridge?) Anyway, John was rewarded by parent company, Lockheed-Martin, by being elected an officer of the company.

All work and no play makes John a dull boy, so he leaves plenty of time for the latter. This year John, John Andrew, and Melinda took the crew of the Miss America (our sailing sloop) to victories in the NOOD Races in Chicago and a 4th place division finish of the Chicago-Mackinac Island Race. Seventy-knot winds in the Mac race really made the finish line look pretty good! John Andrew is a freshman at CU here in Boulder, and Melinda is due to complete her Nursing Degree from MCG [Medical College of Georgia] in Augusta next June.

Burke is busy in his third grade year at a new school named High Peaks. It is a Core Knowledge school which accesses high academics and personal achievement. He loves it! He continues with Boy Scouting and the piano. This winter he is the tallest guy on his basketball team. Summer on Charlevoix was spent taking golf and sailing lessons each day. Burke is quite the sailor!

JonBenét too had a busy summer in Charlevoix. She was crowned Little Miss Charlevoix in a pageant in July and spent

the rest of the summer riding in convertibles in various home-town parades throughout Michigan. She performed a patriotic tap & song for her talent. She and Burke both won ribbons in several decorated bicycle contests. In October, JonBenét became Little Miss Colorado, she rode on the "Good Ship Lollipop" float during the Boulder Christmas parade. (Grandpa Paugh built the float!) She waved and sang all along the parade route! She also takes piano, violin, and drama classes. Busy little Pre-kindergartener! [sic.] (Busy Mom hauling her around!)

I continue to have good check-ups at NIH in Bethesda, MD. God has surely blessed me with energy and the ability to return to raising a family. I thank Him every morning when I wake up and see the sunrise reflecting on the Flatirons over Boulder. Please continue to keep us in your prayers.

Hope your Christmas was merry and here's to 1996! By the time you read this we'll be cheering on the Buffs at the Cotton Bowl in Dallas and then on to the Fiesta Bowl in Phoenix! Thanks to everyone who visited us in Colorado or Charlevoix this year. Please come see us in 1996! Love to you all!

The Ramseys

Important events never happen in a vacuum. There are always surrounding circumstances that contribute. That is especially true in the Ramseys' case. One of the best ways to get a handle on the context of their lives is to hear it straight from them. Patsy Ramsey's 1995 and 1996 family Christmas letters provide sterling opportunities to monitor her inner world and observe how her thinking is changing.

Patsy's 1996 letter (see Chapter 14) reveals her state of mind immediately prior to the murder. We can greatly profit by realizing that a Christmas letter, however "canned" it may seem, is still a form of spontaneous communication.

Although we will not look at these letters in the same detail as the ransom note, we still get a significant look at exactly what was on Patsy's mind in the weeks prior to the murder, and we can *compare it to her state of mind the year before in 1995.* Without question, there are some striking changes. In Chapter 19 we will look at her 1997 Christmas message—it too contains crucial communications.

The first thing we should establish is that Patsy Ramsey wrote all three Christmas letters. Throughout the first two letters, it is obvious that she wrote them—referring to herself in first person. She was also the author of the even more crucial 1997 Ramsey Christmas Message. Patsy was a journalism major and the writer in the family as well as the primary nurturer of the family—all of which points to her as the author of all the Christmas letters. And they all sound just like her.

The very first comment in the 1995 letter is a reference to Patsy's health, which has not been good—she has had the flu. Of course she is trying to explain that the lateness of the letter is due to her illness, but we see the same idea repeated at the end of the little poem that makes up the first paragraph, "... wish you a *Healthy* and Happy New Year!" A simple "snapshot" of the mind of Patsy Ramsey around Christmas 1995: She spontaneously mentions two health concerns—even *capitalizing* *"Healthy"* to tell us once more just how constantly it was the main subject on her mind.

The only overtly negative event in this letter is about her physical health (and one other subtle concern). Likewise, in the next letter we will find only one overt mention of an unfortunate event. It will become clear that all three events have great significance. They are instances where Patsy Ramsey—who is characteristically upbeat, to say the least—allows us to look behind her mask.

Right off the bat, we see another telltale sign of a Patsy Ramsey letter that links her to the ransom note. She ends the first five sentences (and six out of the first seven) in as dramatic a fashion as the English language allows—with exclamation points. **Unbelievably she uses seventeen exclamation points in the entire letter ending with two in a row (and four out of the last five sentences)**—*just as we saw her begin and end the ransom note in the same bold fashion. Even her punctuation reveals a Patsy Ramsey who does everything "bigger than all Texas." The same pattern continues in her 1996 letter—although with a significant change.*

THE BUSINESS AND PATSY'S GARAGE

The main body of the letter opens with a flourish and a focus on the magnificent business success John and Access Graphics are enjoying—"going great guns"—conquering Europe and opening offices in Canada and Mexico. John has even been made an officer in Lockheed-Martin. Then she makes a parenthetical comment about how, unbelievably, *this huge business grew out of something as small and insignificant as "our garage."* Here Patsy makes a definite link between the success of the business and her contribution to it—it started in *our* garage.

Since we can view a garage as another container or nest, a womb-like place where the business grew, it conjures up the same striking image of birth (and delivery) we see in her ransom note. In the simplest terms imaginable, *"our garage" is where their business was born. Is it any wonder that Patsy might be inclined to feminize the word "business" in the ransom note, making it "bussiness" since she plainly feels she had a part in it (see Chapter 2)?* And, furthermore, making it feminine because she saw the world in those terms at this particular time and desperately needed to create deep inside her the image of herself as a powerful, fertile woman. The very next sentence confirms that mothering was on Patsy's mind as she mentions the *parent* company rewarding John by making him an officer in the company. It is a picture of someone growing up in their corporation, like kids do in life. Now we can see a related concern that she hinted at a few sentences earlier: her idea of "keeping the high-tech industry in business," implying that it's an ongoing battle.

Reading between the lines ever so simply, since Patsy has already connected herself to the business, her secret concern is that she herself might go out of business—be useless as a mother, without question her primary business. This meaning is also strongly suggested by this being the only other overt hint in the letter of a negative event. Interestingly Patsy Ramsey identifies with the word "business" in more ways than one, as it applies to her other roles, particularly that of being a mother.

PATSY'S BYWORD—BUSY

This letter gives us another meaning of "business" to Patsy Ramsey. *Business meant being busy, conquering, "going great guns."* In short business meant power—and so did staying busy, which is why she was so obsessed with it.

"... week before Christmas with a million things to do"—the gifts, the decorations, the Christmas cards. John *going nonstop* with his business, taking in as many countries as he could squeeze into one year. Then John shifts from all work to play at the same breakneck speed, sailing *Miss America* to victories and medals in Chicago and Mackinac Island in seventy-knot winds! John's two children from his first marriage went along as crew as they took a break from school. (Melinda is on the verge of completing nursing school, another subtle reference to health.)

Their son, Burke, is also on the move: "Burke is *busy* in his third grade" with academics (another highbrow word for Patsy), personal achievement, Boy Scouting, piano, basketball, golf lessons, and sailing lessons. ("He loves it!")

And their daughter: "JonBenét too had a *busy* summer." Winning a pageant in Charlevoix, riding in a convertible in different hometown parades in Michigan, performing tap and song, winning ribbons in bicycle contests (along with Burke), winning another pageant (Little Miss Colorado), planning on competing nationally, riding on a "Good Ship Lollipop" float (her grandfather built) as a "little Miss Shirley Temple" waving to the crowds and singing all along the parade route, in addition to taking piano, violin, and drama classes. Patsy was this busy way before she had cancer, which only proves that she had been driven by fear for a long time—but now her fear has a more specific focus.

The next sentence reveals even more how much staying busy meant to her. *"God* has surely blessed me with *energy* and the ability to return to *raising my family.* I thank Him every morning when I wake up and see the sunshine reflecting on the Flatirons over Boulder." Unquestionably, Patsy was truly grateful to God for the fact that she was still living, but remember her deeper mind is sending an additional message here: Patsy equates God with energy. In other words she worships staying busy because it gives her a sense of power to overcome the terror of death hiding deep inside. Busyness was also her God.

Furthermore Patsy equates energy and staying busy with raising a family—with being a mother and a homemaker. Her feminine identity is tied up in busyness, which she capitalized in her letter: "Busy Mom." Femininity had been important to Patsy before as a way of overcoming her demons, but now it takes on far more importance. For Patsy to lose her ability to mother—to be busy raising her family—means certain death. As long as she can speed through life being Supermom, Patsy can't be stopped, which hints at what happened the worst Christmas night of her life—she was going at full speed and couldn't slow down enough to make a choice a better mother would have made.

After Patsy tells us her bottom line in this 1995 Christmas letter, she adds a "P.S." as she resumes her game plan of full-speed ahead. "By the time you get this" they would have been to the Cotton Bowl to cheer on the Colorado football team ("the Buffs"—are we not seeing Patsy Ramsey in the buff here?) and followed that by bestowing their energy on the two teams in the Fiesta Bowl. Then they would be waiting on everyone to visit them either in Colorado or Charlevoix, wherever you can find them—all culminating, in Patsy's usual flair, with four more exclamation points in the last five sentences.

As she ends the letter, Patsy is hinting that a lot of competition (two football games) is going on which she is emotionally invested in. "By the time you get this" implies strong competition will be going on that you might not be aware of. In a similar vein, Patsy is telling her friends, "It may take you a while to catch on that powerful rivalries are building within the Ramsey family."

Looking back at the letter, we see three competitive spirits in one boat—John, John Andrew, and Melinda—and the boat is traveling at incredible speed. Read: A threesome is involved in major competition which is greatly intensifying. An intense family competition involving a father, a son, and a daughter is another subtle version—a generic version—of the family triangle. Patsy by implication points to John, Patsy, and JonBenét which will become clearer in the 1996 Christmas letter.

Note how the paragraph ends with a two references to health (nursing and medical college) and two references to school (college and medical college). Two *message markers* advise us this is particularly important. *The decoded message is: The direct result of a powerful family triangle is* **"somebody is going to get hurt."** Patsy is sensing the rivalry brewing with her children which she tells us by another message marker and linking it to her children. "Burke is busy in 3rd grade at a new school High Peaks (a message marker and a striking sexual image). 3rd grade again suggests a threesome. More message markers abound (new school, Core Knowledge, high academics, sailing lessons) as competition spills out from Patsy's letter. Her deeper mind is emphasizing just how big an issue competition is with Patsy Ramsey: academics, personal achievement, basketball, size (tallest boy), golf, sailing, beauty pageants, bicycle contests and football games.

Think of all the possibilities. Burke and JonBenét compete with each other for each parent's attention. Burke competes with his father for his mother or his sister's favor. JonBenét competes with her mother for her brother or father's attention. Make no mistake about it, competition is another part of the Core Make-up of Patsy Ramsey, beauty queen. In 1995, she appears to be living through her husband and her children's games—but ill winds of competition are blowing through the Ramsey household. In the 1996 letter, Patsy Ramsey will make plain there is one particular threesome she has her eyes on which will result in great damage to one of its participants.

PATSY'S PICK ME UP—POWER

This simple Christmas letter continues to reveal even more messages from Patsy's deeper mind. The hyphen in the word "check-up" recalls the crucial accidental hyphen in "pick-up" in Patsy's ransom note and reveals an entirely new meaning to it: *Patsy was looking for a "pick-me-up" for the terrified, depressed state of mind that was causing her to constantly run at full speed.* One pick-me-up was the temporary thrill Patsy got from manipulating JonBenét into doing the "busy" work she herself could no longer do, even if it meant prostituting—using—her daughter.

Key words such as "core" or "knowledge" act like message markers and signal deeper meanings. Patsy used "Core Knowledge" (choosing words that are capitalized) in talking about her son, Burke, who was in a school by that description (she repeats this idea in her 1996 Christmas letter but in reference to JonBenét). Patsy is talking about her son's Core Knowledge experience, which hints at the masculine side of Patsy Ramsey—a major part of her personality.

Note her thoughts about Burke—in a school called High Peaks and tallest boy on the basketball team. The man who stands out. Just as "Burke is quite a sailor!" does in the last description of him. Patsy continues: Sailing boats at seventy-knots, mountains that rise above, businesses that conquer going great guns, football teams playing in bowl games, convertibles that contain beauty queens, beauty queens on floats waving and singing all along the parade route. The images are certainly about power, and largely masculine in nature, even more so considering the disguised phallic references in mountain peaks, floats, convertibles, lollipops, and routes.

Even the beauty queen images speak of dominance and victory—a boat named *Miss America*. In a not-so-subtle way Patsy is revealing that in her depths—at her core—she sees power in a masculine sort of way, and it's that power that stands between her and death. Her mother's words contribute strongly to Patsy's deep-seated belief: Be a beauty queen and overcome men, who only want to use you and will abandon you at the drop of a hat. Patsy is revealing why she had such an attraction to power and to coping in the way she did. Her mother taught her from early on, and Patsy picked up the banner in a mighty way.

When Patsy's cancer struck, she had already made up her mind as to the best way for her to handle stress: seek power and achievement. Be the tallest, the fastest, the smartest, the richest, and the most beautiful. All of these ideas were mixed together in Patsy's head, and deep down she saw herself as a dominant, even masculine, person—which is reflected in her making JonBenét's paragraph far and away the longest one in the letter. At times Patsy saw her husband as a "dull boy," so surely she got a great deal of satisfaction when he named his boat *Miss America*.

HINTS OF MOTHERLY CONCERNS

We see hints of Patsy's softer, more feminine side in this letter, particularly in her mentioning that JonBenét is a Pre-kindergartner—capitalized to let us know how big an issue it was for her. She underscores this by capitalizing her own role—Busy Mom hauling JonBenét around in her car (in this context another feminine symbol of a container, a powerful container)—to let us know how important being a mother and a woman was to her. She also misspells "kindergartner" adding an extra "e" (kindergartener). Was it Patsy's way of saying "E-gads"—revealing that she wanted to change the fact that JonBenét was growing up? Now the hint at the beginning of the letter that Patsy was struggling with the issue of going out of business—out of "busyness"—as a mother becomes even stronger.

When Patsy wrote her 1995 Christmas letter, she was feeling tremendous stress about many things in her life, including her health, her femininity, JonBenét growing up, and the inordinate success of John's business. The vastly underappreciated source of stress—caused by success—continued to drive Patsy as her 1996 Christmas letter reveals.

144

PATSY RAMSEY'S 1995 CHRISTMAS LETTER
SECRETLY REVEALS:

- Tension was building in Patsy.

- She was developing a powerful empty nest syndrome.

- Her empty nest syndrome reminded her of cancer.

- She constantly fears her cancer will return.

- She is covering up her pain with manic activity.

- She is obsessed with power.

- She is incredibly competitive.

- She senses a powerful competition growing between herself and JonBenét over John.

Chapter Fifteen
Christmas Letter 1996: Patsy's Premonition?

Dear Friends and Family.

It's been another busy year at the Ramsey household. Can't believe its almost over and time to start again!

Melinda (24) graduated from the Medical College of Georgia and is working in Pediatric ICU at Kennestone Hospital in Atlanta. John Andrew (20) is a Sophomore at the University of Colorado.

Burke is a busy fourth grader where he really shines in math and spelling. He played flag football this fall and is currently on a basketball binge! His little league team was #1. He's lost just about all of his baby teeth, so I'm sure we'll be seeing the orthodontist in 1997!

JonBenét is enjoying her first year in "real" school. Kindergarten in the Core Knowledge program is fast paced and five full days a week. She has already been moved ahead to first grade math. She continues to enjoy participating in talent and modeling pageants. She was named "America's Royale Tiny Miss" last summer and is Colorado's Little Miss Christmas. Her teacher says she is so outgoing that she will never have trouble delivering an oral book report!

John is always on the go traveling hither and yon. Access recently celebrated its one billion $$ mark in sales, so he's pretty happy! He and his crew were under way in the Port Huron to Mackinac Island yacht race in July, but had to pull out mid way due to lack of wind. (Can you believe that?) But, his real love is the new 'old looking' boat, Grand Season, which he spent months designing.

I spend most of my "free time" working in the school and doing volunteer work. The Charlevoix house was on the home tour in July and will likely appear in one of the Better Homes & Gardens publications in 1997. On a recent trip to NYC, my friend and I appeared amid the throng of fans on the TODAY show. Al Roker & Bryant actually talked to us and we were on camera for a few fleeting moments!

We are all enjoying continued good health and look forward to seeing you in 1997! One final note .... thank you to all

*my "friends" and my dear husband for surprising me with the
biggest, most outrageous 40th birthday bash I've ever had!
We'll be spending my acutual [sic] birthday on the Disney Big
Red Boat over the new year!*

Merry Christmas and much love,
The Ramseys

Once again Patsy begins her Christmas letter on a familiar note: "It's been another busy year at the Ramsey household." But unlike her 1995 letter (see Chapter 14), she does not end the sentence with an exclamation point. Patsy is ever so subtly revealing that something has slowed her down. She waits until the second sentence to close with her trademark exclamation signature: "Can't believe it's almost over and time to start again!"

There's a *clear difference* in the level of energy in this letter and the one Patsy wrote in 1995. The pace is still somewhat upbeat and frenetic, but it has slowed considerably. *Patsy uses only nine exclamation points in her 1996 letter, significantly fewer than the seventeen in the 1995 letter.* Also, the paragraphs are shorter (the first two are only two sentences each), as is the entire letter. And there is also a noticeable lack of emphasis on achievements as compared to the year before.

Patsy gives a subtle hint why—*time is running out.* In the very next sentence she makes three medical references: Melinda has not only graduated from *medical* college, but she's working in *Pediatric ICU* at a *hospital*—where sick and injured children are treated. Last year Patsy referred to the medical college as MCG but this year she is more overtly obsessed with medical treatment—specifically crisis medical treatment of damaged children. *She links this preoccupation with children being hurt—with children growing up (graduating)—with time running out.* These are the *first three ideas in the letter*—telling us they are the most important things on Patsy's mind. Certainly one suggestion is that time is running out for Patsy and causing her to think of hospitals and ICU— but for some reason she links it to damaged children. Hold this idea in your mind—and the striking sequence as well.

Patsy makes a hidden distortion in talking about Melinda: She doesn't say Melinda graduated in nursing but rather implies she is a doctor—trying to make a woman stand out more than she really deserves. Patsy follows her comments about Melinda with a comment about John Andrew, a sophomore in college, just as she did in her 1995 letter. She does not use an exclamation point in either comment, further indicating that she is somewhat down.

Patsy changes the order of her comments in her Christmas letter. In her 1995 letter she commented on John Andrew before Melinda; in the 1996 letter she comments on Melinda first. Also, she commented on John in the first paragraph of her 1995 letter, but she waits until the fifth paragraph in this year's letter, indicating perhaps a loss of status for some reason and that more important subjects are on her mind. By commenting on all four children before mentioning John, Patsy is revealing that the children now fill her deeper mind.

PATSY'S CHILDREN ARE CHANGING—FAST

"Burke is a busy fourth grader" recalls Patsy's usual preoccupation with being busy and also points to *Burke getting older*, moving along in school—another quiet reference to time. The fact that Patsy *mentioned both Melinda's and John Andrew's ages* in the previous paragraph now takes on more significance. *Patsy did not mention anyone's age in her 1995 letter, revealing how much more aging is on her mind in 1996.*

Patsy picks up the pace in her comments about her son. Burke is shining in math and spelling, playing flag football, and "on a basketball binge." What an unusual choice of words: binge. Patsy and her sisters tend to binge on food when they're stressed (both of her sisters are obese), and something inside Patsy in December 1996 is causing her to think of binging. She is under stress and very needy.

Patsy reveals what the immediate stress is after binging herself once more on Burke's achievements. "His Little League team was #1. Not only is Burke getting older, he's *lost* just about *all of his baby teeth,* (so I'm sure we'll be seeing the orthodontist in 1997)!" One of Patsy's two babies is growing up with barely any signs left of being a baby. *She deeply feels the loss of her son's childhood—a major loss for Patsy. Already she can smell the empty nest because she went through the "empty nest syndrome" in a much more powerful way when she lost her own cancerous "nest" to surgery.* She is thinking of her fourth grader in terms of his still being a baby with baby teeth—but she can already see down the road when he will leave the nest like Melinda—and John Andrew—have.

However Patsy is writing on an even more ominous note here— someone's *body is changing,* and they are *losing* something, it's the second reference to bodily damage in the first three paragraphs. A formerly stable, solid part of them is falling out, gone forever. Patsy is revealing how her mind works: She links the loss of childhood to bodily losses and time running out. It is only a baby step away in her mind from the loss of her babies to the loss of part of her body—and to the loss of her life.

This is the burden that Patsy is carrying in the back of her mind. **The normal loss a mother feels watching her babies grow up has been magnified dramatically in her mind because she sees everything in her life through the filter of her cancer and her terror it will return.** In her desperation, deep down she thinks, "Be number one or die."

In December 1996 when Patsy is thinking about losing her baby, she is looking into the future, 1997, and thinking about needing help in straightening something that's crooked (orthodontics). Does her brilliant deeper mind know that a deep sense of trauma within Patsy herself (something is crooked—defective) is going to cause a "crooked" event that will require a lot of attention in 1997? Now Patsy's earlier thought about a daughter of John Ramsey being connected to a Pediatric ICU (where we find children in crisis with acute physical problems) begins to take on a whole new possibility. She particularly underscores the importance of the ideas of damaged children and children growing up by using three characteristic *"important message markers"*: references to school (twice) and graduation.

Immediately after writing about a crooked event involving a child's body, Patsy shifts to—guess who—JonBenét (the deeper mind's ability to quietly make important linkages is astonishing).

We could stop at this point because we have the whole story of this letter right here—and the whole story of the JonBenét's murder. Patsy with her gifted deeper intelligence is looking at her cancer—her primary disturbance and motive—and telling us that time is running out on her. She is simultaneously experiencing JonBenét's going off to school in such a hypersensitive way that she can already see her graduating just like Melinda did. Since separation from JonBenét—her connection to life— means certain death, Patsy is terrified. She is furious with JonBenét about growing up—her anger at JonBenét is so great that she already knows she is going to damage her.

The first thing Patsy says is that JonBenét has now entered *"real" school,* emphasizing *"real"* with quotation marks. Patsy emphasizes that it's *five full days* a week, and that JonBenét is *progressing so fast* that she's already been moved ahead to first-grade math. The stress of separation is now *real* to Patsy.

At this point Patsy takes another manic break and binges on JonBenét's achievements—she is still into talent and modeling pageants, winning two of them including "America's Royale Tiny Miss." Then Patsy returns to what's eating at her—JonBenét is so communicative and outgoing that she "will never have any trouble delivering an oral book report."

Not only is Patsy watching JonBenét rapidly grow up before her eyes, perhaps she is saying that JonBenét already has enough to say to write a book and she could readily give an oral book report. Is Patsy so perceptive that she knows there is already enough information out about JonBenét that if something happens to *JonBenét* she will speak from the grave, the whole truth will emerge, and books will be written? (That may seem somewhat of a leap, but Patsy is unmistakably *connecting JonBenét to books*—books that have a lot to say.) JonBenét's behavior in pageants was so obvious that we can indeed read her like a book—her actions speak volumes.

And to make the connection obvious, as Patsy is writing about JonBenét growing up she uses the word **"delivering,"** still relating to children and Patsy's identity as a mother, *but this time the child will deliver without Patsy's help, the child will do it all on her own.*

Patsy overtly puts a positive spin on this idea, but if we read between the lines the words still connote loss and change. Added up the ideas clearly stand out: Not only is Burke losing any remnants of his being a baby, but JonBenét is now in "real" school, five full days a week, moving so fast she's getting promoted and learning how to talk really well.

Like she did in her 1995 letter, Patsy mentions the idea of "Core Knowledge" in 1996, but now she's talking about JonBenét rather than Burke. In her 1995 letter she was dealing with her "core masculine side," with nonstop achievements to prove herself to the world. But here she deals with her "core feminine side" and it's all about paradise lost, children growing up, and body parts falling out.

The deeper mind draws our attention to particularly important knowledge, tells us it will have a certain character, and then proceeds to back up its claims. Here in these two letters, we can clearly see a difference in a "masculine" and a "feminine" letter, and how each fits perfectly with basic gender issues and symbols.

JOHN ALSO IS CHANGING

Subtly, but very powerfully, the tension continues to build in Patsy, and finally she gets to John in the pecking order. She has moved him from first place in her 1995 letter to fifth place in 1996, suggesting that he and Patsy are further apart. And the very first reference to him is about how he's often away: "always on the go, traveling hither and yon." Once again Patsy is thinking about separation—and now it's John who is far away. A second reference hints that John has moved away from her emotionally, too.

In her typical fashion Patsy follows this possible downer with another momentary victory when she reveals that John's company has passed the $1 billion mark in sales. In one of the most striking sequences in this letter, Patsy follows John's sterling business accomplishment by a story of a sailing competition he had to pull out of because of a lack of wind. *The huge sales are followed by the wind being out of the sails.* Patsy emphasizes this story with a "Can you believe that?"

Patsy goes from a story of incredible success, beyond the Ramseys' wildest dreams, immediately to a story about retreat and impotence. From sailing along in seventy-knot winds to dead air only one year later, it's a striking analogy of how Patsy saw what happened in her world in

1996: incredible success, two children who are growing up at about seventy-knots a year, and a husband who is gone much of the time. Success followed by pain. Having spent the last ten years of my life closely studying the effects of success on people, I can assure you that the greater the success, the greater the "natural" urge to back off.

Only a few companies reach a billion dollars in sales, and in John and Patsy's mind it would have been a significant milestone—and also a millstone around their neck. *The central message from the deeper mind is that one minute Patsy thinks about real success and the very next she thinks about retreat and failure.* And for Patsy incredible success comes directly on top of an acute reminder of her mortality, her two children are growing up and eventually won't need her. Patsy's right brain unmistakably describes in vivid terms the natural reaction at such times—a strong urge to get her boat out of the water, to leave the contest, and to develop the misperception of having lost her power.

John's New Boat and Patsy's Premonition?

Could Patsy be unconsciously predicting that in 1997 the wind indeed would go out of the Ramsey family's sails—John Ramsey and his entire crew? Did Patsy know deep down that the Ramsey family's life, as they knew it, was on the verge of becoming dead in the water.

That is exactly what happened, and it hints at Patsy's deeper awareness that bad winds—winds of death ("dead air")—were getting ready to blow through the Ramsey household. Even more unbelievably, Patsy reveals exactly *how* it's going to happen. "Can you believe" reflects on her awareness that the deeper story she is getting ready to tell is beyond belief—prepare yourself.

Patsy next says that John's real love is another boat. **A new "old looking" boat** called *Grand Season* (which he spent months designing). The wind has gone out of their sails, but now a grand season is upon them. *The sequence is so striking that it suggests stronger than ever that Patsy had a premonition that a season unlike any they had ever seen was just ahead.* It was a new boat but it was old looking, perhaps Patsy's way of revealing that all of this had to do with aging and that it was to occur because of something John had been up to with the "real love" of his life.

Patsy Ramsey seems to be saying rather plainly that John Ramsey had another love. *Was it JonBenét? It was a new boat, not an old one. A young girl and not an old one—but one made to look old.* Does this not describe JonBenét perfectly, the JonBenét Patsy and John created. Step by step, Patsy's 1996 Christmas letter seems to point to a sexual abuse scenario leading to the murder of JonBenét. She is telling the whole story of the last night of JonBenét's life—and last year—1996. Following his great success John Ramsey has suddenly run into dead air sailing his old boat *Miss America, which Patsy doesn't even call by name in this letter.* In other words, the old boat that was named for Patsy is dead in the water, and John has to withdraw from the race. In the context of what was to happen, the symbols beg to be read: Success (and other major pressures) caused John and Patsy to turn away from each other—their marriage was temporarily stalled. Intimacy was severely lacking, nothing was happening between them—an incredibly common occurrence following success.

Another powerful motivation to turn away from each other was that—Miss America was dead in the water, referring to Patsy's cancer, a death threat that hangs over her head and has made her an ineffective woman. A boat is often another powerful feminine symbol of a container as testified to by the fact that boats usually carry female names.

So John turns to "his real love," a new love that he has been designing, strongly suggesting that John has had designs on little JonBenét. Even though the police reportedly think John demonstrates no real evidence of being a pedophile, undeniably he had a major role in "designing" seductive little JonBenét—he enabled it every step of the way. Enabling is often easy to overlook, just as the police are apparently doing in assigning all of JonBenét's precocious sexuality to Patsy. But here Patsy reveals that secretly John had a huge hand in the process and was encouraging it for months, as the letter says.

Patsy's right brain, gifted storyteller that it is, is not finished, and her letter continues by saying that after John's great success, he's impotent—he can't move his boat. A boat can also be a masculine symbol, and in this light John's boat is dead in the water. Whether or not he was literally impotent we don't know, but when a man turns away from a woman (and particularly to a child), the woman will see him as impotent—and he is really. And if the woman encourages the child to become seductive toward men, her father included, then the woman is bringing her man down.

Now the enabling shoe is on Patsy's foot as she not only encouraged a role in JonBenét, but also encouraged one in her husband. Patsy gave JonBenét a premature push toward adult sexuality and brought her husband down all in one fell swoop—another subtle outlet for her tremendous anger. It was Patsy Ramsey herself who also took the wind out of John Ramsey's sails—just as deep down she felt all the wind had been taken out of hers.

This powerfully condensed sequence in Patsy's 1996 Christmas letter strongly suggests that in an impotent state John had found another love, that indeed he was sexually abusing JonBenét. All the pressure (unexpected success, the possible loss of Patsy, the recent loss of his daughter Elizabeth and his father, plus his own health concerns) had gotten to him. He then turned away from his old boat *Miss America* (Patsy) and toward his new—but made to look old boat *Grand*

Season (JonBenét). As a result the race was over.

Patsy is saying that John quit in mid-race, just as she did. In addition she is saying that in the face of success, John became impotent—figuratively and possibly literally. Patsy's story illustrates the powerful effect the threat of death, *including success*, can have on human beings—what goes up, must come down.

DEEPER INTUITION

Is the human mind really so capable deep down that it not only can see an emotional hurricane coming, but also describe what is behind it? All of us are familiar with people having an intuitive sense of an ominous event. My study of the O.J. Simpson case led me to the strong conclusion that O.J. knew deep down that he was building up to a catastrophic event for a long time before he murdered Nicole—and so did Nicole.

Patsy's deeper mind has the same capability. And if John Ramsey was sexually abusing JonBenét, without question Patsy Ramsey knew it in the back of her mind. The rage in her would have kept building, even if she had partially orchestrated the whole scenario.

This 1996 Christmas letter, written only weeks before the murder, gives great credence to the apparent message in the ransom note that Patsy went over the edge when she caught John molesting JonBenét. She reveals in the Christmas letter that subliminally she had known the abuse was going on and saw it would lead to a certain cataclysm. By saying in the story that *more than one person* was trying to sail John's impotent boat reveals that she helped unfold the whole JonBenét scenario.

PATSY SEES THE FUTURE: NATIONAL ATTENTION

In the letter's final two paragraphs Patsy continues the same deeper story—one that hangs together and eerily foreshadows the catastrophe on the very day the letter celebrates, Christmas. Patsy moves more directly to the subject of herself and says something that is becoming increasingly obvious—she has no "free time"—meaning that she is not a free person. By putting "free time" in quotes Patsy is once again demonstrating that she's a prisoner to compulsive busyness—working in the school, volunteer work, and nonstop activity. Of course she wants us to think—as she thinks consciously—that all of this is grand and glorious. But Patsy is not a free woman—she is a prisoner to appearances, to performance, to image. And she may be predicting that one day she will literally be a prisoner.

How will Patsy handle her pain, besides continuing her addiction to action? She says she is going to find another stage. First she tells that her Charlevoix home was on the home tour and will likely appear in a national magazine—in 1997. It's an unmistakable message that her femininity, symbolized in her home, is still prominent and sought after.

Then she tells that she and a friend appeared on the TODAY show and that the hosts (Al Roker and Bryant Gumbel) actually talked to them. In other words, she stood out from the crowd.

Putting the whole sequence together, Patsy hints at a Ramsey family catastrophe related to John and his real love, then talks about not being free—implying that she's a prisoner of sorts, and then talks about the future and being in national magazines and on national television. Is this not precisely what happened? John had his new love and she had her national attention, although it really didn't make her free.

If Patsy knew that someday she was going to explode as she did, it would be natural for her to accurately perceive deep down where it would all lead. Being the natural dramatist that she is, she could see the national media awaiting her.

After drawing our attention to the idea of a grand season, Patsy's deeper mind seems to be describing the entire future scenario in striking detail, demonstrating once again that the human mind deep down can see quite clearly into the future—based exclusively on what it knows about us and those around us.

ONE FINAL NOTE—AGING IS BEHIND THE LOSS OF CONTROL

So that everyone knows what's behind all of this at the deepest level of her mind, Patsy tells once more of a "few fleeting moments" and "enjoying continued good health." Her health concerns are driving her crazy because she thinks life is slipping away from her.

Lest anyone miss the message, Patsy adds *"one final note." "Note" is a particularly important word, a verbal highlighter as message marker* like "hence" (conclusion) and "letter" in Patsy's ransom note. The final note in Patsy's 1996 Christmas letter is that *Patsy Ramsey is turning forty.* Patsy is aging—and it's not just *any* birthday. Think about what turning forty means and how "losing" both your kids in the same year exacerbates it. Having her kids grow up seems like death to a desperately possessive woman like Patsy.

Turning forty had another special meaning for her as well—so special that, despite trying to hide her fear behind an outrageous birthday bash that occurred early, it was still the **biggest fortieth birthday party she had ever had.** *As Patsy saw it, she had already had several other fortieth birthday parties with which to compare it.* Thus in the back of her mind she was an old, worn-out, used-up woman with no wind whatsoever left in her sails, just one step away from the grave. She could already feel that cold earth enclosing her, and there was only one answer: keep moving, another party, another trip, another ride on a boat, construct another fantasy. This time it's on the Disney "Big Red Boat," where she says she will be spending her actual birthday.

But what is a fortieth birthday party really about,•and why might it be so outrageous? Forty is a familiar symbol of age in our society, of youth being gone forever. Of all our birthdays, forty is the one most symbolically connected with aging, the one that means you are "over the hill."

In trying vainly to hold back Father Time, people do flamboyant things at fortieth birthday parties, even having sexual productions with strippers and transvestites. It's a time to be wild and free, outside the boundaries—all in an effort to deny that there really are any boundaries such as time and ultimately the end of time. Patsy embraces that idea, bragging on it in her letter, that, yes, something outrageous went on at her party. *And revealing that in the face of a stressful event she, too, would sanction being outside the boundaries.*

DID PATSY EVEN PREDICT THE DAY SHE WOULD EXPLODE?

Patsy suggests that a major event—this wild, partially sexual event that she described as a *bash*, as an *out-rage*—occurs early. Just the mention of "early" leads directly to Patsy's ransom note that suggests another bash occurring early—a perpetrator bashed in JonBenét's head, a bash also certainly associated with a sexual event.

Patsy's deepest motivation for murdering JonBenét was basically to ward off her terror of aging, loss and death. Her assault on JonBenét was really a manic flight from the pressure of time that was closing in on her—another "birthday bash" occurring on the biggest Birthday of the year. In 1996 Patsy Ramsey was obsessed with *birthdays* to ward off *death days,* and her use of the word "birthday" twice just ten words apart demonstrates her continued preoccupation with this idea.

Further revealing just how much she dislikes aging and this particular birthday because of what it symbolizes, Patsy—normally phenomenally meticulous about her spelling—misspells the word "actual" (birthday), writing instead **"acutual" (birthday) as in "acute." In her mind deep down she was now in an acute condition because of aging.** This dovetails perfectly with her crucial slip in her 1995 Christmas letter when she felt so strongly about JonBenét growing up that she misspelled (damaged) the word "kindergartner." These slips are too powerful to be coincidental. Once again Patsy Ramsey is revealing *that slips are a hallmark of her communication*—another characteristic signature of a Patsy Ramsey letter—which points again to her *ransom note.*

By telling that her birthday party was premature and that it wasn't really her birthday, Patsy is also fine-tuning her story. She is linking a major event—a bash, an outrage—with something false, occurring on a birthday that wasn't really her birthday. This is a reference not only to the flamboyant party that occurred on December 25, 1996, as a cover-up for Patsy's pain, but also that it would occur on someone's else's special day, not hers. Could Patsy look into the future so clearly in 1996 that she knew the very day she was going to explode—on the biggest Birthday of the year and not her day? (Perhaps Patsy is just saying that a "big party bash" is coming soon and on whatever day it occurs she will experience it as a huge victory over death—like a wild fortieth birthday party.)

Having a transvestite at Patsy's party also implies "cover-up," somebody appearing one way and being another. Surely Patsy is thinking about the transvestite when she calls her party "outrageous." It's another way of shouting that a big event is going to occur and there will be something terribly false about it, something that will require looking beyond appearances. And once again that major event will have everything to do with sexual identity—Patsy's in particular.

BIG RED BOAT—ONE LAST RIDE

But Patsy is not through yet—she says she is going on the Disney "Big Red Boat" over the new year. It's such a simple, almost childish, name—unlike *Miss America* and *Grand Season*—not one you would particularly want to draw attention to unless it had other meanings, which it does.

First of all Patsy seems to see that the next year, if it unfolds as she suspects it will, is going to be unbelievable beyond any fantasy Disney could create, suggesting that her fantasies of national attention will come true. And using a sexual suggestion she says that she will experience all this attention in an exhibitionistic phallic sort of way (Big Red Boat)—which recalls the early picture of Patsy in her showgirl outfit that is ten layers deep in phallic symbols.

But "Big Red Boat" also symbolizes blood (a lot of it), and passion, and red eyes filled with tears—and also being figuratively at sea, where the Ramseys still find themselves. It is also another subtle feminine picture of a container, so this whole story is about a woman who has lost her moorings, whose boat has been at sea now for some time and is about to capsize. Patsy knows that her boat will eventually have to come back to shore—and she will have to come down to earth. In this last thought of escapism, Patsy seems to be revealing that indeed her deeper mind sees everything, including the future. First we find Patsy Ramsey the beauty queen in a pinch, trying to make-believe her way out. As my friend said earlier, under stress real beauty queens have an incredible ability to create their own reality (see Chapter 10), but their deeper minds, like everyone else's, are more gifted still at telling the truth. Patsy Ramsey knows deep down that one day the fantasy will be over: "Over the new year" will come to an end, and she will then get back to reality.

But when Patsy signs off her last public communication before her horrendous event, her boat is leaving the from shore—and she is still stuck on the boat. When Patsy will quit floating and come back to the real world, only time will tell. Intuitively she knew she had a long journey coming up and it would be "exhausting," as her ransom note confirms.

Summary

Patsy's own thoughts reveal a cohesive hidden story that fits hand in glove with what we already know about her life in 1996: She experienced other blows to her feminine identity: Her children were growing up and not needing her, her husband was pulling away, and she had continued powerful concerns about health. To Patsy turning forty and her children growing up meant she was about to die. Knowing that John was sexually abusing JonBenét added tremendous fuel to the fire. As a result of his overwhelming pressures, Patsy Ramsey knew that one day soon her rage would erupt and JonBenét would be damaged.

Patsy's 1995 (see Chapter 14) and 1996 Christmas letters reveal the important subjects that were really on her mind deep down, the wounds in her psyche that enslaved her, and the deeper mind's ability to tell a logical in-depth story. If the future came to pass as Patsy suggested it would in 1996, it would confirm that our deeper mind is fully as gifted as the breakthrough to the deeper intelligence claims it is.

BETWEEN THE LINES, PATSY RAMSEY'S
1996 CHRISTMAS LETTER REVEALS:

• Patsy is thinking about damaged children.

• Patsy is still thinking of time running out on her.

• Patsy empty nest syndrome is much worse.

• Patsy is secretly depressed.

• Her fortieth birthday devastated her—the final nail in the coffin.

• John Ramsey's real love is a "new old looking boat"—JonBenét.

• Patsy predicts the murder of JonBenét.

• The murder will attract national attention.

• She will attempt a cover-up.

• Patsy frequently makes crucial slips in letters—one of her trademarks.

Chapter Sixteen
JonBenét's Murder:
Possible Scenarios

W hat exactly happened the last day of JonBenét's life? How could a day of such promise—Christmas Day—end up in dis- aster? The evidence overwhelmingly points toward an unplanned event where a series of "unrelated" actions cascaded, one upon another, until there was an unexpected breakdown—a violent earthquake that permanently shook an all-American family—as well as our national image of what such families represent.

Neither Patsy nor John would have planned such a killing—in their own home, with no suspects anywhere near, on a sacred night, with a light pristine blanket of snow on the ground, in a town that up until that point in 1996 had experienced no other murder. Not to mention the overwhelming evidence that they both truly loved JonBenét, however imperfectly.

The family enjoyed a festive Christmas morning at home and attended a party at Priscilla and Fleet White's house that night. Between 9 p.m. and 9:15 p.m. the Ramseys left the party with Burke and an exhausted JonBenét to drop off presents at two friends' homes located on the twelve-block ride home. First they stopped by Roxanne and Stuart Walker's house for ten minutes. Reports vary whether JonBenét and Burke got out of the car, but Roxanne Walker did notice a cute sleepy JonBenét. The Ramseys then left to make one last stop, apparently at the home of Susan and Glen Stine. This time Burke and JonBenét definitely didn't get out of the car, and the visit was extremely brief. The Stines also noticed a sleepy JonBenét in the back seat of the car. Reportedly the Ramseys drove straight home. (One report had Patsy leaving the Whites without John, but both arriving home around the same time.) They both described putting Burke and JonBenét to bed.

John and Patsy also would have been tired, and they were planning to get up early the next morning to pack for a trip. This was by no means the night for a premeditated murder. The absence of immediate motive, alibis, and the mere energy to carry out a well-conceived sce- nario indicates that this was not a well thought out murder. JonBenét died because of an unplanned catastrophe.

Patsy's ransom note gives striking clues such as "sudden execu- tion" and "beheading" that point toward an unexpected event and an impulsive act. And the autopsy on JonBenét's "damaged" body suggests a rage killing with a severe brain injury coming first and then asphyxiation. Most likely Patsy impulsively struck JonBenét in the head with a heavy object, immediately rendering her unconscious.

What could possibly have thrown Patsy Ramsey into such an uncontrollable rage that Christmas night 1996. What was "the straw that broke the camel's back"? What are the deeper reasons behind Patsy's rage. *As John said in his own profile of the killer, there was a recent stress and a triggering event.* The terror that haunted Patsy Ramsey (see Chapter 6) provided her deep, underlying, powerful primary motive to kill JonBenét, and something JonBenét did that Christmas night incensed an emotionally vulnerable, extremely tired Patsy. JonBenét may well have set Patsy off single-handedly without John's involvement.

On Christmas afternoon Patsy made a disguised reference to JonBenét being hurt when she commented to Shirley Brady, JonBenét's former nanny, about John clearing the snow off the sidewalk and, by implication, making it safe for JonBenét to ride her new bike. This ordinarily casual thought is quite significant because Patsy had it on the very day she would damage JonBenét's body beyond repair. At some level Patsy knew that her anger at JonBenét was growing—as the striking hints in her 1996 Christmas letter also suggest.

BATTLE OVER BED-WETTING?

If we were to survey parents on what their children most commonly do to trigger the parent's anger, it's safe to say that it's some repetitive problem—as in, "I've told you a thousand times not to do that!" Whatever a child does that "pushes your buttons" as a parent is not only an immediate irritation but also usually reflects a larger power struggle.

What was the power struggle between this "perfect mother" and "perfect daughter," as the photographer described them? It has to be a struggle over something that really struck a nerve in Patsy.

Bed-wetting, called *enuresis,* has been raised as a strong possibility. JonBenét had wet herself that night, as the autopsy reflected in her empty bladder and the urine stains on her clothes reveal.

What would the common act of enuresis mean to Patsy Ramsey's psyche, and what aspect of it could have set her off to act so violently toward JonBenét? Patsy was, at times, prim-and-proper beyond belief, a trait she hid behind a relaxed and casual public demeanor, exactly the kind of demeanor that an accomplished beauty queen can emulate at will. But whenever being "casual" was not important to the overall effect, Patsy didn't hesitate to make JonBenét as "perfect" and over-dressed as possible. For instance, she made JonBenét wear dressy clothes for pictures taken at a birthday party where all the other kids were casually dressed. Just as Patsy repainted the living room *five* times in one week to make sure she approved of the color in varying patterns of daylight.   Patsy Ramsey was an obsessed perfectionist, extremely attuned to externals.

Bed-wetting is never a pleasant event: not to sight, touch, or smell—or to schedule, for that matter. It's always unplanned and happens on the child's biological schedule, certainly not the parents' personal or logistical one. And for an obsessively well-groomed parent who was accustomed to being in control, such a breach would have been especially distasteful. Patsy disliked it enough that before the housekeeper got there, she would strip JonBenét's bed and put the soiled sheets in the wash.

For a "perfect" parent with a "perfect" child, *any* flaw would take on far more import—perhaps the first sign of a chink in Patsy's perfect armor—particularly if that chink came at a time when Patsy's distressed volcanic life had no more room for chinks, even from her beloved child. Patsy was so preoccupied with enuresis and with JonBenét wetting her pants that she frequently insisted that JonBenét use the bathroom before going anywhere. Patsy had to have been getting increasingly frustrated with JonBenét's enuresis because it was reportedly becoming increasingly frequent the last few months of 1996.

PERFECT AUTOMATONS

A photo of Patsy with her two children and her mother taken not long before JonBenét died shows the four of them dressed to the nines and posed in exaggerated, stiff automaton fashion—like toy soldiers with their arms down at their sides, except for JonBenét who is saluting. The picture is a pose within a pose and offers its own commentary on the whole family: It's a confession that all of them were exaggerated "posers." It's as if they're saying, "Our posturing makes us appear that we're so perfect we're not human."

Although the picture was the photographer's (Judith Phillips) idea, she had to have been picking up on the family trait of posing to even suggest it. Little JonBenét, dutiful child that she was, *saluted on her own*—revealing that she had become excessively compliant with adults and hinting how she often related to both parents.

Writer Frank Deford saw the same quality in Patsy at the Miss America pageant in 1977 when he was a judge. His notes reveal the same impression of her way back then: "too much of an automaton" (too much of a non-person, in other words).

Statistics show that a significant percentage of kids from age six to six-and-a-half still wet the bed, but such behavior is far from automatic—it's a way children wordlessly express themselves. JonBenét didn't have many outlets for self-expression since she was confined to a life in Camelot and had to constantly pose and make-believe. And pose she could—as one professional photographer noted, JonBenét could hold a pose far longer than most kids her age could even dream of.

BEYOND BED-WETTING—SOILING

Recently it was revealed that during the last three months or so of her life JonBenét was not only wetting her bed, but she had also begun soiling herself at night—defecating in her underwear. At one point JonBenét even soiled the blanket on her bed, even though she had been toilet trained for years.

This rare phenomenon called *encopresis,* indicates a significant disturbance both within the child and within the family. *Encopresis strongly suggests something extraordinarily faulty in JonBenét's relationships with Patsy and John. JonBenét's brother, Burke, had demonstrated encopresis several years earlier—to the point of smearing his feces on the bathroom wall, also strongly suggesting something deeply disturbing going on in the Ramsey household.*

JONBENÉT EXPRESSES HERSELF

Given JonBenét's overall compliant personality, one that had been carefully groomed, it's safe to assume that JonBenét had to express many of her frustrations indirectly, just as her parents do. Not only did her mother make it hard for JonBenét to be an individual, but JonBenét also had a hard time separating from such a kind and loving mother—again especially since the whole idea of separation reminded JonBenét of how easily (far more so than her school friends) she could lose her mother to death. (Patsy was diagnosed with cancer right before JonBenét's third birthday).

JonBenét's enuresis and encopresis under such conditions could easily be subconscious signs of hostility: A literal way of JonBenét saying, "I'm angry about what's happening to me." *Encopresis and enuresis occurring simultaneously mean the bed-wetting is, at this point, largely psychological* and the acts reflect significant rage in JonBenét.

This could also be JonBenét's way of exerting control when she didn't feel she had any. JonBenét was clearly speaking up through her enuresis and encopresis and revealing that behind her winsome, carefree persona she was a desperately troubled little girl.

FAMILY SECRETS AND MESSAGES FROM JONBENÉT

Last but not least, bed-wetting and soiling combined could have been JonBenét's way of saying that she didn't like the little "family secret" she was being forced to keep about herself and her father—a disguised message to "stay away from my me and my bed."

In a child like JonBenét, who possessed inordinate skills of denial honed through months of posing, her excretory symptoms could have been her cry for help, one of the few tip-offs (along with her excessive visits to the doctor) that she was suffering abuse. Enuresis can represent not only anger but also anxiety—another hallmark of sexual abuse.

Many kids can keep secrets for years—for decades—tolerating sexual abuse with little or no outward sign. Marilyn Van Derbur Alter, a former Miss America, was severely sexually abused by her father. Hiding her pain, she smiled all the way to the crown. It wasn't until later in her adult life that she consciously dealt with her "secret." Beforehand, all that the public saw was what Marilyn wanted them to see, and she protected her father the whole way through. Beauty queens are especially talented at misdirection, at hiding.

Was JonBenét protecting her father, the person she admired most in the world? The only adult person who would really be left in her life if something happened to Mother? JonBenét had any number of reasons to keep smiling and stay in denial—which makes her excretory symptoms extremely significant.

JonBenét made *twenty-seven* trips to the doctor in just *three* years. JonBenét's pediatrician, Dr. Francesco Beuff, claims this is not an excessive number, but most if not all other pediatricians would see visits this frequent as a red flag since most young children average three or four doctor visits a year.

Dr. Beuff performed several vaginal exams on JonBenét but evidently did not find overt evidence of sexual abuse. Dr. Beuff, however has been publicly criticized by one of his former nurses who said there were several complaints from patients about him doing unnecessary vaginal exams on young girls. Perhaps he tends to overlook sexual abuse in light of his own behavior?

Enuresis, encopresis, and physical symptoms all have to do with the body and could easily have been JonBenét's way of saying, "Something is going on with my body that I don't like"— letting her body speak when she couldn't. Even if some of the visits may have been prompted by Patsy's overprotectiveness, in light of the final event Patsy's preoccupation with harm coming to JonBenét takes on new significance—she was protesting too much.

Twenty-seven doctor visits in three years is a strong message JonBenét is sending from her grave. So is the fact that in the last few months of her life, she started having encopresis along with enuresis, and *both were getting worse.* JonBenét was becoming increasingly tense—something ominous was going on at home. Patsy was making it worse by ignoring JonBenét's cry for help, never seeking therapy for her and not even informing her pediatrician about the soiling. But deep down Patsy Ramsey knew what JonBenét was saying. Signals like these are one of the reasons family secrets really aren't secrets at all.

THE PERFECT WORLD: OVER IN A MILLISECOND

The last night JonBenét was alive, Patsy was dead tired, having worked herself to the bone, having just thrown a huge Christmas party with more than forty personal gifts for family friends, and having bent over backward to make sure her beautiful, perfect daughter had everything she wanted, particularly that day ... and now JonBenét has wet her bed again—obviously she didn't go to the bathroom before bedtime as Patsy had told her to do. Patsy was thinking about changing JonBenét's clothes, having to put the smelly soiled clothes in the wash, moving her to the other twin bed, having to strip both beds in the morning—and smelling that sickening bitter urine smell you can never quite get rid of. Patsy had warned her a hundred times—the little ingrate!

The enuresis also made Patsy increasingly aware in the back of her mind that JonBenét was actually *a separate person* from her—*the same idea symbolized by JonBenét's first bicycle without training wheels that Patsy and John had given her early that Christmas day*. Patsy didn't want anything to do with separateness because it reminded her of her utter terror—of death, the ultimate separation. Patsy wanted to continue the myth that she and JonBenét were not only perfect but *perfect for each other: "best friends,"* as she once said. But here was a child, soaked with urine, in a wet bed—a vivid, ugly, smelly reminder that Camelot was dying and that things would only get worse as JonBenét learned and grew—*assuming* that Patsy would live to see it, which in the back of her mind she seriously doubted.

Only two days before, the day of Patsy's big Christmas party, JonBenét had asserted her independence twice in one day—over a dress she didn't want to wear and over someone she didn't want to visit when she needed to be out of her busy mother's way. Patsy had to put JonBenét in her place twice—in one day. Patsy knew this headstrong independence was only going to get worse.

Imagine Patsy shouting at JonBenét that night above the smelly wetness—and JonBenét having the gall, *the gall*, to talk back: "Daddy wouldn't fuss at me like that. I want my Daddy. I'm not going to change clothes." That did it. Daddy better than Mommy? JonBenét has unwittingly struck her mother's nerve of nerves sending her over the edge into a white hot rage. Patsy picks up a nearby heavy security flashlight and blindly lashes out at JonBenét. This is one possible scenario—*but I don't think that's what happened.* For one reason, JonBenét was most likely killed before midnight which would be too early for a normal bed-wetting event. For another reason, the police found clean sheets on JonBenét's bed. Even if Patsy Ramsey had changed the sheets though, there are other far more compelling scenarios.

A More Likely Scenario: Sexual Abuse

Very possibly on that Christmas night the Ramseys will never forget, they arrived home from the party and delivering gifts, JonBenét ate a pineapple snack, and a bone-tired Patsy changed JonBenét's black velvet tights for a white pair of long underwear. Normally Patsy would have made JonBenét completely change clothes before bedtime, but when JonBenét's body was discovered she was still wearing the Christmas blouse she had on the night before at the party. Perhaps JonBenét had requested to sleep in her Christmas blouse with its big star and sequins on the front. Almost certainly it was brand new as the housekeeper had never seen it before.

Patsy had wanted JonBenét to wear a red turtleneck to the party, but JonBenét had insisted on wearing this particular blouse—and she could have made the same request at bedtime as attached as she was to the blouse. Patsy would be inclined to grant this special request on Christmas night. Or maybe JonBenét was just too tired to want to change it—and Patsy, exhausted herself, agreed. And for some reason JonBenét didn't undo her two ponytails, normally something she didn't sleep in. (Months after the crime, Patsy will reveal the child's prayer she said with JonBenét at bedtime that night: "Now I lay me down to sleep, I pray the Lord my soul to keep. *If I should die before I wake,* I pray the Lord my soul to take." Whether it really occurred is one matter, but surely it is a hidden confession.)

Both John and Patsy later claim the last time they saw JonBenét alive was when she had just gone to bed at 10 p.m.—interestingly both claim to be the last person to see her. John (as he reported) put Burke to bed while Patsy was taking care of JonBenét, and then together they retire to their third-floor bedroom. Patsy fell quickly asleep, but John was restless yet he did not take his sleeping pill (Melatonin) as he frequently does because he had something else on his mind. After a few minutes, thinking Patsy was asleep, John quietly left their bedroom to pay JonBenét another late-night visit.

On a day of celebration and excess, perhaps having a little too much to drink at the party, he visits JonBenét before she is fast asleep to get one more special pleasure to top off the day—secretly looking for comfort from the deep down unsettling day. Since he really did have to get up early and also wanted some sleep himself, he didn't wait quite as long as he normally did before visiting JonBenét.

A short time after John left, Patsy, still keyed up by the events of the day and the impending trip, awakens—to an empty bed. Puzzled because John is usually sound asleep from his sleeping pill, she gets up to check on JonBenét. Perhaps a concern about John and JonBenét's intimacy popped into her mind, but characteristically as a sexually naive person she brushed them off.

Taking the huge flashlight (made of indestructible airplane

aluminum) that was handy, Patsy made her way down the stairs to the second floor and JonBenét's room. Patsy planned to use the flashlight to look in on JonBenét without turning on the overhead lights and awakening her, but as she approached the bedroom door she heard John talking to JonBenét. Stopping just outside the room, she couldn't believe her ears.

Perhaps Patsy overheard the typical pitch of a sexual abuser: "I'm doing this because I love you. This is our secret. Don't tell anyone. If you tell, your mother will get very upset because she doesn't like us to have secrets. Don't do this with anyone else. This is our secret. You know how much I love you." Or perhaps Patsy heard JonBenét in some discomfort say, "You're hurting me" because, as the evidence shows, JonBenét was irritated enough vaginally to bleed. Whatever she saw or heard, it sent Patsy Ramsey into orbit.

After listening for a few moments, she suddenly entered the only door to JonBenét's darkened room, and focused the flashlight on JonBenét's twin beds, and got a full view of John in bed with JonBenét in a severely compromised position.

Now all the awareness that Patsy had been blocking slams full force into her consciousness. Maybe, too, for a split second her mind flashed back to a time she had forgotten about when she was a child and a man was in her room—she can't make out his face, but she can remember the terror and the smells.

Realizing he'd been caught dead to rights, John immediately distanced himself from JonBenét—stepping to the other side of the room and keeping his distance from Patsy as well. Patsy turned on the lights in the room as she reflexively moved to protect JonBenét and simultaneously enraged screamed incoherently at John. JonBenét, confused and increasingly frightened by her mother's rage, started to cry. As Patsy continued to lose control, JonBenét tried to break away to comfort her father and escape her temporarily deranged mother. Patsy refused to let JonBenét go, holding onto her ever more tightly. John made a move toward her, but Patsy's threatening tone held him at bay.

JonBenét panicked, at one point screaming in utter terror when her mother took a swipe at John with the flashlight. Patsy wrestled JonBenét to the floor in an attempt to prevent her running to John. Still holding the flashlight in her right hand, she grabbed JonBenét's face and neck with her left hand to gain control. JonBenét persisted screaming, and Patsy totally overwhelmed goes over the edge screaming, "I told you to be quiet!"

With one quick powerful blow, fueled by her rage, Patsy bashed in JonBenét's skull—and it's all over. Patsy and John look at each other with JonBenét lying limp between them. In one brief snap of her mind, Patsy destroyed her own flesh and blood.

As tired and vulnerable and hurting as Patsy was Christmas night

1996, it wouldn't have taken much to push her over the edge into a killing rage. In fact Patsy confesses this in her ransom note by repeating the central idea of "the *slightest wrongdoing* and you're in trouble." Patsy revealed that some "slight thing" had set her off and she overreacted badly. She had lost control for the briefest time in her otherwise secretly over-controlled life: Her life as the perfect mother of the perfect child, with the perfect husband, was over in a millisecond.

AUTOPSY SUGGESTS SCENARIO

All the facts from the autopsy fit together best in the sexual abuse scenario described above. JonBenét was bashed along the whole right side of her head, from just above her right eye to the back of her head. It was a powerful blow from an elongated blunt object that didn't break her skin. Her body had some abrasions, mostly on the right side of her face—below her right ear and on her chin—as well as one on the left lower part of her neck and on her back.

Her facial abrasions might be explained by someone holding JonBenét's face down with one hand since she was a small child. The abrasions on her back and neck may be rug burns, although sources close to the investigation say detectives feel the pattern of the abrasions *does not* suggest rug burns. Patsy may have acted alone and dragged JonBenét's body across the wall-to-wall carpets in her bedroom and down the stairs, but the garlands found in JonBenét's hair are similar to the garlands on the banister and suggest that her body was carried down the stairs. JonBenét weighed only forty-seven pounds and was not large for her age. The ligature around her neck caused additional skin abrasions and left a prominent furrow.

Her panties were lightly stained with blood. The autopsy revealed a small amount of dried blood in her vagina and two types of vaginal lesions: hyperemia (vascular congestion with interstitial chronic inflammation microscopically) indicative of a chronic vaginitis but also seen with acute trauma, and abrasions—epithelial erosion—of the hymen and vaginal wall, which suggests some type of acute trauma.

I reviewed the coroner's autopsy report and accompanying police affidavits with Dr. Robert M. Brissie, an experienced chief coroner and medical examiner for two large cities—previously Charleston, South Carolina, currently Birmingham, Alabama. Dr. Brissie, who is also Professor of Pathology and Director of the Division of Forensic Pathology at the UAB Medical Center and has taught detective courses in police academies, qualified his comments because of not having access to the photographs and the slides made during the autopsy.

Dr. Brissie concurred that the cause of death was strangulation with the head injury occurring shortly before. He was definite that the report strongly indicated sexual abuse with blunt trauma penetration but not by an adult penis, which would have caused more tearing. (A pediatric gynecologist specializing in sexual abuse reviewed the same report and strongly agreed that JonBenét had been sexually abused.) Dr. Brissie said that "only a minuscule possibility exists that a woman abused the child unless it was staged." The fact that the abuse was discovered incidentally and not prominently displayed strongly points away from staging—as does the fact that the coroner, Dr. John Meyer, found no blood on the exterior pubic area next to the bloody panties. Dr. Meyer felt that *someone had wiped the area with a cloth to hide the bleeding*—and stated that the vaginal injury was consistent with digital penetration. On the other hand, Dr. Brissie said that urine could have washed away the blood.

Numerous traces of dark fibers in the vagina suggest many possibilities to Dr. Brissie including the clothing of the abuser and the black velvet tights JonBenét had on earlier. Dark fibers along with dark hair were also found on the outside of her blouse. A birefringent foreign material—possibly talcum powder—was also found in the vagina.

Dr. Brissie saw numerous possibilities for the abrasions—from trying to bring the child under control to a sex game (which he doubted) followed by an assault if JonBenét threatened to tell. *But his instincts linked chaos with sexual abuse in light of the two assaults apparently following closely after sexual abuse.* In an extreme family crisis things get out of hand and family members can fall all over one another—which led him to wonder if anyone had observed bruises or abrasions on the parents.

Dr. Brissie reported rarely seeing the degree of bruising around the neck and the petechial hemorrhages around the eyes with ligature strangulation (even though textbooks report it). These findings were more consistent *in his experience* with strangulation by other means when the pressure on the neck varies and the blood flow is not constantly cut off. *He wondered if whoever strangled JonBenét with the ligature had difficulty completing the task, stopping and starting before she died.*

Given the ransom note with the child's body found in the home, Dr. Brissie immediately stated that almost certainly the killer had to be a family member who knew the child.

LOOKING BACK

There are several reasons to lean toward a sexual abuse story. First it provides the powerful trigger needed to set off the killer—**Patsy Ramsey who is normally very controlled and particularly controls her anger, needed an exceptionally overwhelming and unexpected event because as a former beauty queen she was adept at handling crises.**

As the housekeeper noticed, Patsy could handle JonBenét's bed-wetting and demonstrated no signs of undue frustration about it. And Patsy was familiar with JonBenét's bed-wetting—it would not have been an exceptionally overwhelming or unexpected event on Christmas night 1996.

But sexual abuse is altogether another story for Patsy, and few things would catch her more off guard than finding her husband sexually involved with their young daughter. It would be a double blow for Patsy: She would have been jilted for the first time in her life for another woman and at such a vulnerable moment, and she would have been replaced by someone she had given her life to and given life to—by a daughter who was more than her best friend.

For a grown woman and former beauty queen as highly competitive as Patsy, one who was always used to winning, losing out to a child would be an unspeakable insult. Patsy was the oldest of three very competitive sisters and accustomed to being top dog. Plus her self-esteem and feminine identity were secretly at an all-time low on Christmas night 1996: She was fat, forty, and being "put out to pasture."

The hidden competition between same-sex parent and child for the parent of the opposite sex has the potential to create incredible rage that few other family issues do. Add to Patsy's competition with JonBenét her deep-seated competition with John and resentment over his power, and John's sexual abuse of JonBenét would strike directly at Patsy's core—the emotional equivalent of plunging a knife into her.

As Patsy revealed Christmas afternoon, JonBenét was planning on being alone with her father riding her new bike, something that caused the slightest suggestion of anger in Patsy—JonBenét could get hurt. But it's Patsy's ransom note (see Chapter 3) that tells the story in Patsy's own thoughts—it's a marvelous description conveying the depths of her pain. In the note she keeps emphasizing an "early" or unexpected event that took place followed by the word "delivery" being obliterated in a chaotic black cross-out. Catching her husband with her daughter destroyed Patsy to the core of her feminine identity. Patsy also uses the word "pick-up" in her ransom note—suggesting that she has just been replaced by a prostitute who is also her daughter—and John has turned JonBenét into a pick-up.

"You're not the only fat cat" and "don't underestimate" me in the ransom note along with "don't think killing will be difficult" are the words of an angry, hurt competitor who will not take it lying down.

Beyond the extraordinary clues Patsy gives in the ransom note that sexual abuse was the trigger that enraged her enough to kill *JonBenét*, Patsy says in her 1996 Christmas letter (see Chapter 15) that John's real love was a "young 'old looking' boat." John's unbelievable slip-up ("JonBen-I") on a nationally televised program and his own letter confessing his cover-up (see Chapter 12) now stand out even more.

John and Patsy's deeper minds and the corroborative autopsy findings scream sexual abuse. Other sources of information also point to sexual abuse as the trigger that sent Patsy into a killing rage the night JonBenét died.

OUTSIDE STORIES—FURTHER CONFIRMATION?

The scenario of sexual abuse fits in many ways with information given to the police by Diane Hallis, a former secretary at John's company, Access Graphics. Hallis reported talking to an anonymous woman who called the office shortly after the crime (and who sounded credible) claiming to be the friend of a woman having an affair with one of John Ramsey's attorneys. The caller claimed that her friend had learned through her paramour that Patsy had admitted to killing JonBenét because she had found out John was sexually abusing her. Hallis passed a lie detector test in regard to her story.

On one hand it's doubtful that either Patsy or John would tell any attorney such a story, even if it were true. But Patsy has a tendency to tell everything, and the fact that the story seems to fit so perfectly with Patsy's ransom note suggests that it should be taken seriously.

Another interesting fact adds even more weight to this possibility. Laurie Wagner, *formerly a vice president at Access Graphics, repeatedly called The Globe to persuade them to not run Hallis's story—surely Wagner was calling at John Ramsey's behest, something very unusual for him. This tells just how bothered John was by the mere mention of sexual abuse, seemingly more so than being called a murderer. He overreacted and went out of his way to deny the allegations of sexual abuse on two previous occasions, on television and then in a letter to an artist that one of John's friends made public* (see Chapter 12). John's reactions are so mercurial and extreme that they suggest he is agitated by more than just allegations of sexual abuse—he is also agitated because he knows his sexual abuse led to the death of his daughter.

Melody Ann Stanton, who lives across the street less than 100 feet away from the Ramseys, came forward and testified that around midnight the night of the murder, she was awakened by a girl's long, blood-curdling scream coming from the Ramseys' house. She instantly thought of JonBenét—and abruptly awakened her husband who hadn't heard the scream but did hear a distinct sound of metal crashing against cement immediately after she woke him. There was nothing but silence after that.

A Boulder reporter who has visited the neighborhood several times told me that it seems unlikely that Melody Ann Stanton heard what she thought she did. The Stantons' house is not only across the street but quite a ways up from the Ramseys' house. The reporter said he could barely hear a powerful security alarm that had accidentally gone off inside the Ramseys' house one afternoon when he was standing in front of the Stantons'. Nevertheless, sounds carry in the dry Colorado air, and in the quietness of night it is possible a high-pitched scream could be heard. Certainly Melody Ann Stanton is a credible witness and a reluctant one—and like Diane Hallis's story, hers seems to fit in an eerie way.

Behind the Explosion

Patsy's ransom note not only reveals the immediate trigger behind JonBenét's murder, but it also reveals the deeper motive. As FBI profilers constantly stress, killers inflict on their victims their own deep down pain. *Whatever the immediate trigger for Patsy Ramsey's rage, it was one which made Patsy Ramsey inordinately helpless—one that most reminded her of the helplessness of being a cancer victim.* This is another reason to suspect sexual abuse over bed-wetting.

Patsy was secretly looking for a *big victory*, a victory over helplessness—and she was looking for a victim to experience her helplessness, which is why she encouraged JonBenét to play the role that she did. Patsy was looking for an enemy she could defeat. JonBenét was her rival who would have displaced her, but "defeating" JonBenét would give Patsy a temporary sense of power in the face of her ultimate powerlessness.

Tormented by the fear of her cancer returning, Patsy pushed JonBenét into becoming a highly sexual, seductive little girl—for adults (particularly those who judged the contests). Temporarily Patsy identifies with JonBenét's success, but it's not long before JonBenét turns her charms on her father, continuing the role that has been built into in her. Through a combination of circumstances including Patsy's own frigidity, John is particularly vulnerable—and the rest of the story unfolds in a logical way ending in JonBenét's murder.

A maxim in medicine says to go where the money is—pursue the most logical alternative first. Dr. Brissie, the coroner, said that crimes like this come down to money, sex, passion, drugs, insanity, or a combination of these motives, and as a psychiatrist, I would add to Dr. Brissie's list—the fear that drives the desperation or addiction.

In the back of her mind Patsy constantly carried the fear that at any second she could "deviate" and everything would collapse; her life would be over. She had lived with death for a long time—not consciously, but more like having a pressure cooker simmering on a back burner forgotten about until it exploded. The entire ransom note Patsy wrote reeks of cancer, of the potential for sudden catastrophe. And this terror finally overwhelmed a most vulnerable Patsy Ramsey on Christmas night 1996.

Life and death were very much on Patsy's mind that day in her

Christmas phone call to her Atlanta nanny, Shirley Brady. Patsy spontaneously said to Shirley, "I told you the good Lord won't let me die!"

The afternoon before she murdered JonBenét, Patsy was thinking about her own death, about JonBenét's growing independence, and about John clearing the sidewalk so JonBenét could safely ride her new bike. JonBenét never actually went out riding that Christmas afternoon—she was in bed because she didn't feel well. Was Patsy encouraging a sickly JonBenét and showing us again that she was having a hard time separating?

When someone is tired every stress is magnified, and when someone is exhausted stress is exponentially magnified. Almost everyone reaches a point once in a while when "it wouldn't take much to push them over the edge." Christmas night 1996, Patsy Ramsey went over the edge.

For months, for years: Patsy has stored up rage she can't express because it was unseemly to the pose of a beauty queen. She can never let anyone see her sweat, or lose control, or be afraid, or get angry—or most of all *be human*. She naturally thinks that her recovery from cancer depends on her behavior, and she has become even more perfect—or continues to try to. As a beauty queen she has even less leeway than most cancer victims to express herself—particularly to express her anger, which is a first cousin to fear. "Don't talk about it" is Patsy's motto, just as she has taught her kids. Patsy essentially refused to discern her illness with her kids.

Since Patsy doesn't talk much about her pain, her actions must speak for her. During an interview with the *Colorado Women's News* back in 1994, Patsy revealed, *"Facing cancer is so difficult because you're facing your own mortality. It's like someone pointing a gun at your face."* Deep down Patsy was obsessed with her own beautiful *face* constantly being on the verge of being destroyed. Was it then really an accident, when overcome by a blue streak of rage in a crisis, that she lashed out at the *face* of JonBenét?

WHY JONBENÉT AND NOT JOHN?

"Why did Patsy kill JonBenét when it was John's fault?" Patsy's ransom note gives an answer. Patsy's utter terror of cancer consumes her—and she has never recovered from the ovarian cancer's assault on her identity as a woman. Every single thought in the note links to cancer and the terror of death.

Four powerful forces—all symbolic of death—were coming together. Her continual reminders of cancer, her fortieth birthday, her impending empty nest syndrome, and phenomenal financial success coalesced to create an unshakable belief in her mind: "She dies, she dies, she dies, she dies." Patsy repeatedly says in the ransom note she was as good as dead—"99% chance of dying."

Characteristic of the way Patsy handles pain—by competing—she says she couldn't let "fat cats" go on living when she couldn't, particularly another fat cat woman because it was the loss of her feminine identity that Patsy felt so acutely. She got lost in her terror of death and struck out at JonBenét, who symbolized life and victory.

On one level Patsy didn't mean to kill JonBenét, but on another level she knew exactly what she was doing. When she killed JonBenét, she killed John, too, as well as the entire family in many ways. On that destructive level of her mind truly "killing wasn't that difficult."

And there she stood Christmas night 1996, weapon in hand, looking at her daughter's head bashed in—as though she had just found the body lying there, as though some stranger, some unknown person, had done this. What is she going to do now?

THINKING QUICKLY

We get a hint from a man named V. J. LaCour, who's intimately acquainted with beauty pageants and who told *Time* magazine, "Beauty contestants are quick thinkers. They have to be. They have to know how to alter a long-practiced routine if someone just ahead of them has [done the unexpected]."

Patsy was long accustomed to thinking quickly and had the reputation of being quite bright. Despite her horror at what she'd done, she had to think quickly.

And so did John. Suddenly he and Patsy had to go from being temporary enemies to blood brothers. Confused, frightened, enormously grieved, he stands there looking at his wife and a still-breathing but unconscious JonBenét. (The autopsy revealed the bleeding in her head which indicates she was still alive at the time of the second assault.)

Surely John and Patsy were in panic mode. But if any two people ever were prepared to handle such a situation, it would be a beauty-queen cancer survivor and a former military pilot who had recently lost both a father, another daughter, and (nearly) a wife.

A SECOND CRISIS

At this point the cover-up begins. Surely John and Patsy were engulfed in shock, the phrase in Patsy's ransom note "two gentlemen watching over your daughter" describe exactly what they did for at least a few minutes. The first issue was whether or not JonBenét was going to wake up from the blow to the head, and the second was whether or not to get her medical help. They had both witnessed the severity of the blow (which the autopsy revealed caused extensive damage). Patsy must have had the thought, "I've killed her." Dr. Brissie said that Patsy would have felt JonBenét's skull cave in when she hit her—Patsy would have known better than John how severe the injury was, but he too probably thought that Patsy had killed JonBenét.

A brief assessment would have led Patsy and John to the conclusion that JonBenét's body was damaged beyond repair. But since they weren't physicians, they had no real way of knowing that JonBenét would have died with or without medical treatment (as the autopsy revealed). Nor could they have known for a fact that she would have been permanently brain damaged—if by some miracle she had lived following emergency medical treatment.

What they did know was that no credible story would explain such a violent head injury to the authorities. And unquestionably both of them would have realized quickly how much they stood to lose if they "came clean" and told the authorities the truth.

Even if John had let Patsy take the full consequences, the biggest part of his life would be over: At a minimum he would forever be known as the husband of the woman who murdered her beautiful child. The story would make headlines in newspapers, magazines, and on television around the world.

What a tailor-made story for the media to pounce on: "Beauty Queen Wife of Business Magnate Slays Beauty Queen Daughter on Christmas Night." He would never be able to look anyone in the eye again. His trophy wife would be gone—in jail—and still none of the punishment could bring back JonBenét. He would be completely ashamed: No longer would people idealize him as they had for so many years. No more John Ramsey, CEO, millionaire, board member of Lockheed-Martin. His career would be over instantaneously.

That is what would have happened even if John Ramsey were *totally uninvolved* in the murder—but if the whole truth implicated him, particularly in some sexual way, John knew he was as good as dead too. Not only would he be shamed beyond belief, but a sympathetic jury along with Patsy's crafty attorney could make it worse on him than on her. (The courts call it *proximate cause* meaning if you caused someone to lose control and commit a crime, you can be found even more guilty than the perpetrator.) And when all was said and done he would be almost all alone: His older daughter gone, his father gone, his mother gone years ago because of cancer, JonBenét now gone, his wife almost a goner to cancer, and now absolutely gone if she's caught with jail time for both—plus his career and his status gone. Everything he had worked so hard for, gone in one fell swoop like a house of cards—and nothing but shame and raw grief staring him in the face. He had to find a way, any way, to deflect the guilt and the hatred that was sure to follow.

Too, "the Southern gentleman" had long been a part of his makeup—the hero, the strong silent type, coming to the aid of a damsel in distress. John's Southern charm went with the Southern common sense Patsy mentioned in her ransom note. How willing he would have been to assume such a role in order to redeem himself—if, indeed, he had been caught in a compromising situation with JonBenét.

Patsy knew well her role of being rescued and just when to play it. It fit perfectly her tendency toward magical thinking, as she revealed at JonBenét's memorial service when, sobbing in tears, she dramatically told her babysitter and another friend, Pamela Griffin, to "fix it," a hidden confession that she had "broken" something. Undoubtedly one of the things Patsy told a guilt-ridden John Ramsey that Christmas night was, "Fix it."

Logic and the facts suggest that John and Patsy didn't plan to kill JonBenét on Christmas night 1996, and only one of them inflicted the initial injury. But the way things happened after that reveals there was more to JonBenét's death than a simple "accidental" rage murder. If one of them had "simply" killed their child, they wouldn't have protected one another, and the truth would soon have won out over their elaborate cover-up.

JonBenét Isn't Moving

When Patsy and John saw that JonBenét was not awakening, they had to decide what to do next. Should they now rush her to the hospital, reputations be damned, and get her help? They chose instead to commit a "second murder," moving from Patsy's rage killing to a premeditated killing.

Who had the coolest head at the time? Patsy the beauty queen had probably gone from rage to shock to incredible grief in thirty quick seconds. John had most likely gone more slowly from anxiety and shame to shock and disbelief. Whatever their individual reactions, together they made a fairly quick decision. The lack of swelling in JonBenét's brain and the pineapple found in her proximal small intestine during the autopsy along with Patsy's ransom note referring to "tomorrow" and with John Ramsey's public statement that JonBenét died on December 25th (confirmed by the tombstone having the same date) all point toward JonBenét being killed close to midnight. It also suggests that one or both of them never went to bed, and that even if the murder took place after midnight, it still seemed like Christmas night to both of them.

Since JonBenét arrived home right after 9:30 p.m., she most likely had her pineapple snack around then. It would have taken around two to three hours for her stomach to empty (which it was) and three hours (and a maximum of four) for her proximal small intestine (the first part, right after the stomach) to be completely empty—which means that she was strangled as early as 11:40 p.m., maybe even a little earlier having eaten a small amount on an empty stomach. (It is possible but highly improbable that she had a snack in the middle of the night and was killed later.) This means her head injury likely occurred well before midnight, which probably explains why Patsy and John insist JonBenét died on December 25th. Both of them also want to see the head injury as the death blow and want to deny the strangulation, the second part of their heinous crime.

To kill JonBenét before the pineapple left her small intestine and before her brain began to swell means that Patsy and John couldn't have taken very long to make their fateful decision—probably less than thirty minutes. They made a clear choice: We will not attempt to get her help. We will end her life now.

Impulsiveness itself is a sign of inordinate shame on the part of the killer, and two people involved in the cover-up suggests two people who are deeply ashamed. Only inordinate shame that comes from direct personal involvement in the murder would cause both Patsy and John to proceed further with their cover-up and refuse to get their daughter medical care. One final reason they acted quickly, at least unconsciously, is that they were afraid JonBenét might wake up, and then they couldn't have killed her. "Sudden execution" in the ransom note hints at their sudden decision.

Both Patsy and John lied to the police when they said they had not given JonBenét a pineapple snack before bedtime. It was one of JonBenét's favorite foods, and pineapple was present in the Ramsey house and not at the Whites' Christmas party. The autopsy findings prove unequivocally that she ate the pineapple at home and had time to eat it before she was murdered. Patsy and John report their last contact with her was at 10 p.m., which allows ample time for her to have a snack.

Why would Patsy and John lie about something as trivial as having given JonBenét some fruit? Maybe they just wanted to give an appearance of distance from JonBenét after they got home. Maybe they simply had a story and were sticking to it. Maybe it was another subtle confession, telling us that they not only were liars but that they were certainly not comforters that night. Most likely it was part of their cover-up and their plan to deny anything pleasurable took place after they got home—another subtle clue about sexual abuse. Whenever a lie occurs, it's probably part of their cover-up.

Patsy and John also lied to the police about who saw JonBenét alive last. Patsy told the first two officers on the scene at 5:52 a.m. that she was the last one to see JonBenét and that was at 10 p.m. the previous night. Sometime after 8 a.m., John told Detective Linda Arndt that he had been the last one to see JonBenét, again at 10 p.m. the night before.

Since Patsy talked to the police earlier in the day and closer to the time she and John last conferred, John may have been the one who forgot their planned cover-up story. His making the mistake rather than

Patsy also fits better with the cover-up. Logically Patsy and John would want to distance John from JonBenét and the true story—of sexual abuse and the murder. Patsy and John's basic plan seemed to be: Keep the story from coming out, and stay away from anything to do with sexual abuse.

Drawing on his vast experience, Dr. Brissie sees Patsy and John trying desperately to avoid being interviewed to prevent inconsistencies from surfacing in the hands of skilled interviewers. He considers their avoidant behavior as almost prima facie evidence. Almost immediately after the murder they have trouble keeping their story straight. They are revealing how easily they would break in the right hands.

PATSY'S CHOICE?

Patsy's disguised confession letter (a.k.a. her ransom note) suggests ever so slightly that at some point—most likely right after the head injury—John Ramsey tried to "grow a brain" and find some way out, but whatever his plan was it was unacceptable to Patsy.

Patsy unquestionably realized that her life as she knew it was over unless she or John could come up with a plan. She would forever be a pariah who killed her own daughter, would continually be mentioned in the same breath with Susan Smith—if, in fact, Patsy didn't completely replace Smith in public consciousness. And perfectionist that she was, forever image-conscious, she could not tolerate that reality for a second.

Neither could Patsy allow a damaged JonBenét to live. Patsy Ramsey, beauty queen, could not bear for the rest of her life to look at JonBenét's "remains"—a brain-damaged child, her beautiful face distorted with a paralysis making her look like a premature stroke victim, a ghastly parody of her former self. Her guilt would be overwhelming knowing she herself had damaged JonBenét.

Even more so, bodily damage of any kind was completely unacceptable to Patsy. Her perfectionist nature would barely let her tolerate a room painted the wrong color for twenty-four hours, much less a flawed child—once the epitome of beauty—for a lifetime.

Most importantly, a brain-damaged JonBenét with a *crooked face* would be a constant reminder of Patsy's greatest terror, the cancer that had ravaged her own beautiful body. This last terror was so great that it ruled Patsy's life. It's why a mother who just bashed in her child's skull could also refuse to get the child medical help. This is also why, as awful as it sounds, one of Patsy's and John's greatest fears was that JonBenét might wake up.

Perhaps Patsy let John know in no uncertain terms that they had to do something with JonBenét's body—which meant that they had to first *have* a body, a corpse, rather than a living, breathing human being. If

Patsy was the one pushing for the "second murder," however they reasoned it out, it seems that she finally got through to John. Patsy's ransom note hints that deep down she was the more "cold-blooded" of the two at the time ("don't think that killing will be difficult") and in many ways the most threatened.

Imagine the bargaining that went on between them. If Patsy had any leverage to use against John, knew of any skeletons in his closet, this would have been the time to bring them up—as her threats in her ransom note suggest. In light of the probable sexual abuse—murder scenario, Patsy didn't have to threaten John very much—he was as big a part of the tragedy as she was.

Even though John, as a Southern gentleman, would have been inclined to rescue damsel-in-distress Patsy and would have had particular difficulty turning over his loved one to the police, nevertheless he could not have refused JonBenét medical help unless he had another powerful motive. The fact that John chose to protect Patsy above getting JonBenét help speaks volumes about his guilt and is one of the most compelling factors that points to his sexually molesting JonBenét.

When their daughter's hopelessly damaged body confronted them with the reality that Camelot was over, these two competitive marketing geniuses shifted into a different gear. They both knew the game plan instinctively: Cut your losses. Face the bottom line. And there *was* the bottom line, directly in front of them.

How could they salvage such a damaged ship while somehow preserving what they'd spent a lifetime building? How could they preserve their dignity—and JonBenét's, of course, because this would wreck her reputation too?

Once Patsy and John made their choice to refuse JonBenét a doctor, they had to decide what to do with her. The first step in the tragedy had come spontaneously. The second step involved some desperate forethought. The signature S.B.T.C. on the ransom note suggests one possibility that we have already covered. In the biggest crisis of her life, Patsy Ramsey may well have spiritualized the whole event. And John may have been more than willing to go along with Patsy's "spiritual inclinations" for his own reasons. Very simply JonBenét had to die for him to cover it up and keep on living—which ironically has a symbolically spiritual meaning. Whatever happened, the Ramseys still had to come up with a cover-up.

DESPERATE DECISIONS

Perhaps one or both of the Ramseys had seen the popular movie *Ransom*. Even if they hadn't seen the movie, both of them would have recalled the story of family friend Bill McReynolds who had played Santa Claus at the Ramsey family Christmas party for three years. On the day after Christmas in 1974, McReynolds' then nine-year-old daughter had been kidnaped along with a friend and shortly after released unharmed. Later McReynolds' wife Janet adapted the incident into a highly acclaimed play in which a young girl was kidnaped and murdered, her body discovered in a basement. Both the true story and the fictionalized version of McReynolds' daughter provided some suggestions about what to do with the unconscious JonBenét.

It wouldn't have taken the Ramseys long to realize just how few their options were though. They had to make JonBenét's death look like a crime that had occurred in their own home. They couldn't dispose of the body anywhere else since they could all too easily get caught.

Then too JonBenét's older brother was upstairs asleep and could awaken any time. A staged "accident" was out of the question—the only plausible scenario was a crime.

Eventually, with a still-alive JonBenét, perhaps John came up with a plan he and Patsy agreed on—however hard it was to swallow: They would have to finish off JonBenét and make it look like a crime. Only a kidnaping gone awry or a child molestation/murder would make any sense to the authorities and, by extension, the public. The story of Bill McReynolds' daughter loomed larger and larger—perhaps along with the recent movie *Ransom*—which might have led them to come up with a kidnaping ploy to throw the police off the track. Their wealth made the kidnaping idea seem more plausible.

But who was going to bring JonBenét to the end of her suffering? And how? Who thought of strangling her, and who carried it out?

I cannot imagine any mother killing her child twice within one hour when any other option presented itself—particularly if the mother felt that someone else had caused the murder in the first place. John probably finished off his daughter because he would feel terribly guilty for his part in the first assault and would be much more inclined to carry out a heinous act as a form of self-punishment. Also having John finish the job would give Patsy one more hold on him. Then they were in it together equally.

The haunting reminder in Patsy's ransom note, "It is up to you now, John," implies both threat and sympathy as reasons for John's cooperation. The two sentences preceding that sentence appear to warn John not to *underestimate* Patsy, which also suggests that Patsy holds something very powerful over John, powerful enough that she could insult him and call him a "fat cat."

Patsy is far more in control of their relationship than it may appear. She is a master at getting John to do what she wants, as evidenced by her mother's comment about the way they both saw John and his money—something they could control and use. Perhaps Patsy talked John into going along with her and finishing what she couldn't.

One last obvious clue as to who did the final deed is John's reputation as a cold person. He was better than Patsy at splitting off his anger and, as a pilot, blocking out his emotions.

No matter which of them strangled JonBenét, both Patsy and John had to justify their actions in some way. After the funeral Patsy told several friends, "JonBenét's better off in heaven." She may have uttered those very words standing over JonBenét's dead body. Almost certainly they would have told themselves that she was better off dead than living with severe brain damage and that no purpose would be served by their confessing to murdering her—it wouldn't bring her back.

The sequence of JonBenét's physical assaults—along with what we know about Patsy and John Ramsey—suggests this was a two-person murder: Patsy in a fit of rage lashed out, inflicting JonBenét's head injury, and John finished off their daughter with strangulation. A "co-murder" also suggests a reason both of them have held it together this long—secretly each blames the other.

The Accomplice

Even if John had not been directly involved in the murder, once he had gone along with the cover-up, he was an accomplice. Now they were both in it for however it played out: "In for a penny, in for a pound," as the British say. Maybe all John Ramsey did was help Patsy cover it up, but the rope as weapon seems mechanical, like something an engineer would carry out.

John's hobby was sailing, and ropes would have been much more familiar to him than to Patsy. Moreover a garrote is the kind of technique a military pilot with survival training would be familiar with. Certainly it was a familiar form of execution terrorists in the Philippines used when John served there while he was in the navy. Moreover, rope identical to that used in the murder was found in a store two blocks from Access Graphics. Since the rope was somewhat thin, it is perfectly conceivable that the part not used to strangle JonBenét was cut into small pieces and flushed away.

Whether it was Patsy or John or both of them who caused JonBenét to breathe her last, it is a moment neither one of them will ever forget. The dried mucus on JonBenét's right sleeve suggests she was strangled from behind while she lay unconscious, face down with her right arm underneath her. The autopsy findings also suggest that she urinated on herself while in that position because only the front of her long underwear was urine stained. Perhaps JonBenét was strangled face-down because her parents could not face what they were doing. As Dr. Brissie suggested whoever strangled her had a hard time carrying it out emotionally—another reason to think it was someone who also loved her.

Scattered clues suggest other details about JonBenét's murder. Significant evidence suggests JonBenét was first assaulted upstairs, probably in her bedroom. The remnants of green garland in her hair were likely caused by her father carrying her down the small back staircase when she was unconscious or dead and her hair accidently touching the garland wrapped around the banister.

A killer unfamiliar with the house almost certainly wouldn't have used the back staircase. The journey from JonBenét's bedroom to the basement, down a back stairway through an extremely large house with a confusing layout (because of all the additions the Ramseys had done) would have been a difficult task for anyone unfamiliar with the house— particularly at night.

Where did Patsy and John strangle JonBenét? They might have done it downstairs to avoid Burke seeing them if he got up and stumbled into JonBenét's bedroom. And most likely the equipment they needed was downstairs. Also they might want to do it in an unfamiliar, out-of-the-way place, to later minimize their memories of the event. The unfinished windowless basement room where the body was found fit the deed—dreary, cold, out of the way, and hidden—like the Ramseys wanted to hide their deed.

They selected the basement room for another reason as well—the door was partially stuck and very difficult to open, which caused the police to overlook the body at first, although they did find a nearby open window, which was certainly staged to make it appear the killer had come from outside.

Recent Corroborating Evidence

Recently a next-door neighbor of the Ramseys, Scott Gibbons, has validated that *at least one of the Ramseys was up around midnight on the night of the murder.* He can see the Ramseys' kitchen from his side window, although he can't see clearly what's going on in the room because of baffling on the Ramseys' windows. That night he saw low lights in the kitchen he had never seen before—all he could tell was that someone was up and didn't want to be open about it. He interpreted that as someone not wanting to awaken others, but it just as easily it could have been someone who didn't want to be seen specifically by him, but who needed to come in and out of the kitchen.

Concealed activity in the kitchen around the time another neighbor, Melody Ann Stanton, heard a girl scream strongly suggests that something unusual was going on in the Ramsey house around midnight Christmas Day 1996. The only inconspicuous way from JonBenét's upstairs bedroom to the basement—where her body was found—is through the kitchen.

The fact that the police found the possible murder weapon (a heavy black flashlight) and Patsy's notebook with paper used for the ransom note in the kitchen suggests that it was the hub of activity the night of

JonBenét's death. In a bizarre family ritual, Patsy very likely may have sat at the kitchen table to write her ransom note.

CLUES HIDDEN BETWEEN THE LINES OF PATSY'S RANSOM NOTE AND CHRISTMAS LETTERS SUGGEST POSSIBLE SCENARIOS:

- JonBenét may have enraged Patsy because of bed-wetting, but that is unlikely.

- The autopsy and Patsy's ransom note point toward sexual abuse.

- Finding John abusing JonBenét that night was the most likely trigger for Patsy's rage killing.

- Patsy hit JonBenét in the head with a blunt instrument, knocking her unconscious.

- John strangled the unconscious JonBenét to kill her.

- Patsy holds something over John's head.

- JonBenét was "accidently" killed because she had become Patsy's rival.

Chapter Seventeen
The Ramseys and the Crime Scene

Other clues uncovered in the investigation of JonBenét's murder also point to a Patsy Ramsey rage killing. The attempted staging of the crime—with the ligature around JonBenét's neck and the rope tied to her right wrist—just doesn't hang together. The rope around her right wrist is extremely loose and didn't leave any mark, clearly indicating it was added after the murder (and the rope had slipped completely off the left wrist).

Distinct findings suggesting sexual abuse. JonBenét had on a pair of long white underwear (urine stained) over a pair of white panties with printed rosebuds and an elastic waistband with the words "Wednesday" on it. Only the panties were blood stained. The autopsy revealed significant trauma of the vagina, which implies ongoing sexual abuse as well as sexual abuse the night JonBenét died. The abuser would have been excited enough sexually to cause JonBenét to bleed.

Three findings during the autopsy—abrasions of both the hymen and vaginal wall along with a bruise on the outside of the vagina (labia majora)—are all located on the right side of JonBenét's body and suggest digital penetration by a right-handed person lying next to JonBenét's right side or possibly penetration with a foreign object. (The foreign material in the vagina, very likely talcum, could have been used with either.) The crime scene reveals that the killer was trying to cover up the sexual abuse. In light of several previous hints of sexual abuse from both Patsy and John's communications, the vaginal findings revealed by the autopsy must be seen as far more than coincidental.

Thus the autopsy and crime scene point toward both a rage killing and sexual molestation. Some people have suggested that Patsy sexually abused JonBenét as a part of the crime scene staging, but hiding clues is not typical of staging.

READING THE CRIME SCENE

Even though John disturbed the crime scene, the information that is available can still be applied to both Patsy and John Ramsey. Both Patsy's ransom note and the crime scene were creations from Patsy and John's minds, and elements of the cover-up can represent various self-portraits of the murderer and her accomplice.

Take for example the garrote. Surely the rope represents the bondage that both Patsy and John continue to feel. A slow torturing death suggested by the garrote points perfectly to how Patsy experiences her cancer. The rope also suggests "life hanging by a thread." Taping JonBenét's mouth shut means that they wanted to shut her up, which says that she had secrets to tell—just as they do. It symbolizes their ongoing refusal to talk.

Wiping down JonBenét's body suggests Patsy and John not only were trying to cover their tracks but also wanted to clean her up and wash away their guilt as well. The reported lack of sticky residue on the duct tape removed from JonBenét's mouth suggests that Patsy had washed her daughter's face before the tape was applied, perhaps cleaning her up for her "presentation" to the world.

The sudden, blunt-trauma blow to the head reflects the sudden blow Patsy had received from her cancer—and even the sudden traumas John had recently experienced with the deaths of his oldest daughter and father. The twin insults of a head injury and strangulation point toward a killer who has experienced more than one trauma or two killers who have each experienced their own trauma or traumas.

When the coroner examined JonBenét's body at 8 p.m. some twenty hours after the murder, he found her arms extended up over her head in rigor mortis. The position calls to mind the image of a crucifix. Indeed the evidence is compelling that JonBenét was a type of sacrifice for Patsy and John Ramsey, and they unconsciously revealed that in their selection of her body position.

One final note of irony: When the coroner arrived at the Ramseys' house he found not only a blanket covering JonBenét's body on the floor but also a Colorado Avalanche sweatshirt. Indeed an avalanche had hit young JonBenét, just like it had hit her mother and father earlier.

LINKING THE CRIME SCENE AND THE RANSOM NOTE

The suitcase, with a blanket and Dr. Seuss book inside, found near the window, has all the earmarks of both a phony, immature cover-up and a mother's touch. It is exactly what a child who is threatening to run away would take, when in reality they never get past the door. And it is also what a mother who felt she had neglected her child would do.

But a far more important message links the crime scene to the ransom note. A suitcase is a container, something we gather our belongings in, like a big purse—another feminine symbol. The killer reveals—this time in show and tell—that the whole crime is about femininity. The suitcase is largely empty, just like Patsy Ramsey's body has been emptied of her femininity.

The suitcase containing the child's book also symbolizes a womb holding a baby. Patsy has temporarily restored her damaged femininity.

The blanket suggests the cover-up itself, which briefly gives Patsy comfort but in reality is just a fantasy—another tale from Dr. Seuss. All in all the suitcase is another confession that screams "cover-up." **Thinking she was covering her tracks, Patsy Ramsey left all her trademark symbols as clues.**

The Ramsey family was planning to leave on a trip the day after Christmas 1996, and perhaps that was why JonBenét's suitcase was so readily available. An empty suitcase illustrates a dream that never came to pass, a journey that was never made, a life that was never lived. The Dr. Seuss book and the suitcase also point us back to Patsy's 1996 Christmas letter that indirectly links a trip to fantasyland (Disneyland) to a huge "birthday bash." Patsy is revealing ever so subtly that she knew all along the trip itself was a fantasy that would never occur because another event—a bash, would thrust Patsy Ramsey into the limelight, would supercede it. (The *Dr. Seuss book could also have been a substitute gift* from a guilt-ridden Patsy—for the trip to Disneyland JonBenét would never take.) Thus **Patsy linked the crime scene to both her ransom note and her 1996 Christmas letter** written shortly before she murdered JonBenét.

A MOTHER'S FINAL TOUCH

Just as the deeper mind can cause the body to move in certain ways to communicate distinct messages *(body language)*, it can also cause someone to do certain things to communicate through *action language* that uses props. The crime scene suggests yet another action and another prop at the crime scene.

The autopsy revealed a *red heart* on JonBenét's *left* palm—either an ink doodle or a killer's signature. Assuming it was Patsy's signature, what would the red heart say? Patsy was a part-time artist, and the palm is a very subtle symbol of a container—it's where we hold things.

A heart left by the killer could be saying "you have my heart in your hand." An apology of sorts—a mother saying that after all was said and done, she had really loved her child. But she's also saying that she had held JonBenét in the palm of her hand and loved her too much, loved her in a controlling suffocating way.

Drawing a heart on JonBenét's palm also could have been one last way Patsy made clear *that one of the central causes of this crime was that she hadn't allowed JonBenét to have her own life,* that she had destroyed JonBenét because she was really trying to destroy herself, and at the same time cover it up, as a closed palm would signify. Drawing on JonBenét's left palm (and not her right) could be another way Patsy was revealing that her deed wasn't right but rather deviant and hidden. Patsy could be making another subtle confession that indeed she had written the ransom note with *her left hand* as the police suspect.

The fact that a red heart drawn on JonBenét's palm has all these potential messages that fit Patsy Ramsey so remarkably well suggests that this was her final signature. It also fits well with Patsy's impulsive nature and her constant need to be connected to her child, which would be greatly magnified at such a moment of final separation. Patsy would desperately want to have one last connection with her daughter, to demonstrate one last special kindness. You can hear her thinking, "What's the harm in it? If they prove it's my drawing, I can say I did it before she died."

One of Patsy's friends recently revealed that Patsy often drew a heart in JonBenét's palm and told her, "While you're asleep you have my heart in your hand and you don't have to be scared." Someone who knows the Ramseys well said that *JonBenét herself never made such drawings on her palm*—only Patsy did. All of this strongly confirms that Patsy's deeper mind was working overtime to communicate the truth about JonBenét's murder.

Apparently two blankets were discovered in the basement room of the Ramsey's house, one covering JonBenét's body and one under her body. Combined with the suitcase that contained JonBenét's special items, this last symbol now even more powerfully suggests a mother's touch. A mother who symbolically wanted to do everything she possibly could for her deceased child.

Also, the room where JonBenét's body was found was particularly bleak—the only unfinished room in the house and was to become a wine cellar—with a concrete floor, a lightbulb hanging from the ceiling, and paint cans and other supplies on the floor. Patsy would have had the strongest urge to soften and feminize the room—such as adding blankets. The blankets also suggest protection and cover-up. The excessive number found at the crime scene emphasize that—and also resonates with Patsy's excessive mothering.

After strangling JonBenét to death, Patsy and John moved into their ransom note mode and conceived their cover-up story of Patsy finding JonBenét missing. Even though claiming a kidnapper had done it was another stretch, they had little choice. The fact that Patsy found the note reveals that they wanted to cast Patsy in the victim role as much as possible to draw attention away from her—but the person who found the note is the one who wrote it.

ONE LAST CHRISTMAS PERFORMANCE

Once the police arrived to investigate JonBenét's disappearance, they searched the entire house but didn't apply the necessary force to open the stuck door to the unfinished room where JonBenét's body was hidden. The Ramseys had to feign panic for seven hours, all the while knowing that their daughter's body was downstairs. Doesn't that alone tell a lot about their ability to hold a pose? They couldn't appear to believe that their daughter's body might actually be in the house as that would immediately point the finger at them.

They must have been pleased to see that their first goal had been accomplished—they had hidden the body well enough so the police wouldn't be the first to find it. When JonBenét's body went undiscovered, Patsy and John had some breathing room, and the stage was set for them to move into their martyr role, which they claimed in a hurry. Now they played the victims to the hilt. How lucky they were in one sense because if the body had been found quickly, they would have been immediate suspects—but now they had an opportunity to build their case. How unlucky Patsy and John were in another sense because if they had been suspected right away and interrogated appropriately, we would never have gotten to see how absolutely cruel and devious they can be.

One other "fortunate" aspect of the police's failure was that it allowed John to discover the body and disrupt the crime scene and cast doubt on any trace evidence found on the body. John loved to read murder mysteries and particularly loved gamesmanship—which as we have seen, he could carry out with the coldhearted best of them.

Once Patsy and John had killed JonBenét, it was as natural as ducks taking to water for them to come up with a scheme to defeat the police—not only to save their own skins, but also to distract themselves. To substitute *a game for their pain* as they had both been doing for years. Patsy's junior version of the "Miss America" game, took her mind off her cancer. An investigative journalist who observed the Ramseys up close for months after the murder—probably more than anyone—told me that Patsy had the type of mind that would do well in prison. She was remarkably good at distracting herself with projects. John shared Patsy's ability to create self-serving distractions.

Patsy could be just as calculating as John when confronted with an immediate goal, and together they came up with the plan to mislead the police. They planned for Patsy to find the note and John to find JonBenét's body. As a worst-case scenario, if the police had been first to find the body, John and Patsy were still prepared to go along with the cover-up. But John was hoping to—and indeed did—beat them to the punch by grabbing JonBenét's body and moving it, simultaneously disrupting the crime scene and providing ample reason that trace evidence from him would be found on JonBenét's body. This leads us to think he had moved JonBenét's body earlier.

After the police had made their search that morning, John called his bank and also made one call to Atlanta to arrange to get $118,000 in cash. Earlier, right after calling the police, John and Patsy had called two sets of friends—Fleet and Priscilla White and John and Barbara Fernie—who had immediately come over to the Ramseys' house. John Fernie was to go to the bank later and make sure the ransom money was available. The Ramseys' minister, Rol Hoverstock, was also contacted and he had come to the house as well. What fine props these people made for John and Patsy's game, and how desperately they must have secretly needed these props to take the pressure off and to inadvertently embellish the kidnaping myth. The positive reinforcement the friends gave the police for the kidnapping story was invaluable to the Ramseys.

Without finding JonBenét's body, the Boulder police fell for John and Patsy's game hook, line, and sinker. Dreamtown, U.S.A.—right next to "Rocky Mountain High"—with a murder rate of one (if that), a wealthy influential citizen's exclusive home, the day after Christmas, no body, appropriately distraught parents with a ransom note, surrounded by a believable cast of characters who themselves believed the charade. Unconsciously, at least, the Ramseys must have protected themselves from the police officers' intuition by quickly assembling friends who sincerely bought into the cover-up.

By late morning things were going so well for John and Patsy that two victim-assistance counselors had arrived at their house, adding the finishing touches to their cover-up. Patsy and John were officially declared victims.

John's behavior earlier that morning had undeniably established that he did not want the police to find the body right off, if at all. After coming up empty-handed in his initial search of the Ramseys' house, one officer told John, "Look around and see if she [JonBenét] is hiding." John then proceeded to search the home the first time with his friend, Fleet White, who later told his wife that upon coming to the jammed door and the room where the body was, John had said, "Oh, don't worry about it. We'll try harder later [if we need to]."

After the counselors left, the Ramseys sat around for several hours wringing their hands, being comforted by their friends, and waiting on the phone to ring. The investigation had come to such a lull that all of the police except Officer Linda Ardnt had left. Finally she suggested that John Ramsey "look around the house and see if you see anything out of place, anything missing."

THE SECOND PART OF THE PLAN SUCCEEDS

Taking his two friends with him (Fleet White and John Fernie) to search the house, John couldn't stand it anymore—as Fleet reportedly observed in retrospect—and went straight to the room where the body was, revealing what kind of pressure he was under. Quickly he approached the stuck door to the room in the basement and pushed his way in. Fleet was right behind him. Taking full advantage of his fortuitous opportunity of beating the police to the punch, John grabbed JonBenét's body and totally disrupted the crime scene.

Appearing hysterical, ripping the tape from his daughter's mouth (or perhaps it was already off), John rushed upstairs with her body and laid it on the floor in front of everyone. He had carried it like you would a doll, with his two hands around the waist—most likely because of rigor mortis having set in. An investigator at the scene told *Vanity Fair* that, strangely, John didn't cry at all until he put the body down. He began moaning as he looked around at his audience.

But now Patsy had her stage, and she, too, could let go of all that tension—moving into her martyr and victim role—as she fell on top of JonBenét's body, rolling on the floor, screaming and crying in agony. (Was she repeating in ways the scuffle that had gone on between JonBenét and her right before the head injury—making another indirect confession?) But that outburst wasn't all pretense—it had to have been a shocking moment to see her daughter's body once again. Exhausted already by Christmas, incomparably more so by the emotional upheaval from murdering her beauty-queen daughter the night before, all her dreams now gone, knowing her marriage would never be the same, knowing she would be a major suspect, her public image forever damaged, having just lost the daughter she loved even more than she hated—never to see her again, having to concoct a ransom note while trying to fake her handwriting, waiting the rest of the night to call the police, having had no sleep, having had some time to reflect on the shocking murder, and having to carry out the pretense for seven interminable hours—how close to the edge Patsy must have come. Rolling on the floor in a half-mad frenzy was in many ways a true expression of her state of mind. Perhaps her spiritual plan—S.B.T.C.—was still in place, too.

PATSY LAZARUS

Quickly Patsy rose to her knees and screamed out, *"Jesus, you raised Lazarus from the dead. Please raise my baby!"* Whether spontaneous or planned (as was most likely), Patsy's words still came out of her own mind and reveal her inner world. Seeing John carrying JonBenét's body up from the basement could have triggered the image of Lazarus coming out of the grave.

Lazarus is in many ways a picture of Patsy herself. Lazarus was as dead as a man could get, wrapped like a mummy, and in the grave four days and already beginning to smell when Jesus performed his miracle—details familiar to Patsy. Not only is Patsy revealing her cover-up smells, but she also identifies with Lazarus. She is as good as dead in her mind from her cancer, so much so that she can feel the grave around her—and like Lazarus, can see two surviving sisters standing by her grave.

But now Patsy has been raised from the dead, spared for the

moment from the destruction of cancer, but only barely. Like Lazarus she was saved from death, but also like Lazarus—whose name was always linked with death—she was constantly reminded of death, so powerful was her experience. Lazarus is an ever-present symbol of both life and death—the two issues constantly confronting Patsy.

In Patsy's brief desperate cry there was a second death, a second person who died—in Patsy's terms the baby JonBenét. Jesus has raised somebody from the dead before, and now she wants him to do it again. But Patsy is still talking about herself, too. Jesus, she believes, has prevented her from dying once when she faced cancer, but now with JonBenét—her baby—growing up she has faced death and the loss of her femininity a second time. And again in her mind she is as good as dead. At this most crucial of moments, Patsy once more thinks in terms of *babies. Babies represent life and Patsy puts it plainer here than anywhere—her baby is dead, meaning her ability to have babies is dead, and, therefore, she is dead. (And "please raise my baby" also means "please raise my dead womb—me—from the grave.")*

It is perfectly normal for Patsy to be thinking about JonBenét being "her baby" at such a moment, but her deeper mind is helping her choose words that reveal hidden truths. Patsy's reference to "babies" at such a critical juncture is much more than coincidence—it is manipulative, and how like Patsy to become manipulative in a crisis. Patsy Ramsey, Christian extraordinaire, has just sent her daughter reeling into eternity at her own hands, long before Jesus called JonBenét's name, and she says to Jesus, "Fix it. Undo it. Pretend it didn't happen. Go along with the cover-up, if you don't mind—Jesus, old buddy, old pal."

But seeing through Patsy's guile and subterfuge, the whole scenario becomes a revelation about death, Patsy's two deaths. Patsy Lazarus had already been in the grave once and now she was going back because all her babies are dying—growing up—and all the babies inside of her have died, too. One more subtle but powerful confession.

Every time Patsy opens her mouth it's babies, babies everywhere. From Burke losing "all of his *baby* teeth" in her 1996 Christmas letter to "Jesus, please raise *my baby* from the dead" at the crime scene to "Mothers you'd better keep *your babies* close to you" pleading on television right after the murder to her 1997 Christmas message (as we will see in Chapter 19). Patsy constantly reminds us that she lost her way because she had lost her core feminine identity—her ability to deliver babies. She was obsessed with babies—life and giving life—to work off her deeper obsession with death which is why she was so vulnerable to JonBenét leaving the nest.

At such a primitive moment, when Patsy for the first and only time publicly comes face to face with her dead daughter, she confirms by linking baby JonBenét to death and to Jesus that in Patsy's mind the baby JonBenét momentarily became a baby Jesus who sacrificed her life for her mother (and father). Isn't that what Patsy and John Ramsey are still asking her to do? By not telling the truth about what happened to JonBenét—what they did to her—they are asking her to continue to sacrifice for them, to carry their lies and bear their shame. One day, as Patsy has predicted, one (or maybe both) of them will honor the memory of JonBenét's name with the truth.

Once the ball got rolling, John and Patsy had to keep up appearances—something they're continuing to do. The fact that John could carry his dead daughter's body may have been a confession of its own that he had carried her dead or almost-dead body before—many people simply can't pick up a dead body. And Patsy touched JonBenét's body too.

If indeed Patsy was still hoping against hope that God would raise JonBenét from the dead when she fell on top of her dead body, she must have felt a sinking feeling in the pit of her stomach when it didn't happen. She had to come face to face with reality when God said he wouldn't undo what she had done.

PATSY SAW IT COMING

Christmas Day 1996 was filled with separation anxiety for both John and Patsy. That day reminded them not only of what they had, but also what they could lose. And as strange as the outcome of that day was, even stranger is the fact that Patsy seemed to know it was coming—she even told about it in her Christmas letter she wrote two weeks prior. There was going to be a birthday bash like she had never had before.

Does Patsy know John's behavior patterns well enough to recognize that his bizarre bonding with JonBenét reflected the crazy separation terror alive at his core? And did she suspect that Christmas would stir up that terror by reminding him of his daughter Beth he had lost to death—and did she suspect he might try something with JonBenét Christmas night before their trip the following day?

I have witnessed the phenomenal ability of our deeper mind up close for nearly a quarter of a century, and yet I have never seen someone's deeper mind predict the future down to the exact day, as Patsy Ramsey's mind did in her 1996 Christmas letter. Deep down we are geniuses, and Patsy knew her husband's behavior patterns better than he did. She must have known that Christmas would stir him up like nothing else—with her birthday just around the corner and his right behind it along with an upcoming anniversary of his daughter Elizabeth's fatal car accident on January 8th. Deep down Patsy knew Decembers and Januarys were rough for John and that he dreaded them.

Patsy and John faced one more death threat in December 1996. John had experienced a prostate problem and had been sufficiently worried to fly to the Mayo Clinic to have it checked out. Typical of the way John dealt with such separation and death threats, he didn't talk about it. Apparently nothing serious was found, but Patsy learned about John's trip after the fact and began crying while telling a friend how frustrated she was that she hadn't known beforehand. And typically John never hugged or touched Patsy after returning from the trip, once more demonstrating how he dealt with separation—"it never occurred." But John did indeed notice all these separations or possible separations deep down.

THE MOTIVES

Even if Patsy killed JonBenét over another immediate issue besides sexual molestation, we know the real reason she killed JonBenét. We know she had a powerful reason to take JonBenét's life—and several other motives in addition to her main one.

When we look past Patsy's social climbing and behind her charisma, we find a mountain of pain—which has been there quite some time and continues to grow. Plain but not so simple, Patsy is terrified every moment of her life—awake or asleep—by the specter of cancer destroying her. It hung over her like the blackest cloud imaginable. It drives her crazy, as it literally did for a brief few seconds the night of December 25, 1996, and she had to destroy JonBenét before she herself was destroyed.

In many ways the worst part of Patsy and John Ramsey's behavior is the cover-up. John is consumed deep down by his own terror of death that continues to haunt him. And as he and Patsy reached levels of success they never imagined, their terror of loss and death grew in proportion to their good fortune. In the back of their minds, they were waiting for the other shoe to drop.

Patsy's ransom note makes plain that the final straw—whatever it might be—was only the tip of the iceberg. The central part of the story is the trauma Patsy and John were living with before the murder and continue to live with. The real story is how Patsy and John got to the night of December 25, 1996, and how their lives had been shaped by powerful forces largely outside their own consciousness.

MORE SIGNS OF GUILT

Many times it's in looking back over events that clues leap out. Such was the case for Patrol Officer Richard French who first answered the Ramseys' 911 call reporting that JonBenét was missing. As he told *Vanity Fair*, several impressions of the Ramseys stood out upon reflection. Initially he was struck by how differently the two were reacting— John cool and contained, while Patsy was sitting in a chair sobbing.

Strikingly unusual was Patsy's preoccupation with the policeman—*she followed his every move with splayed fingers over her face in a childish attempt to hide her interest.* Later Officer French would recall how the Ramseys in the greatest crisis of their lives together made no effort to console each other. There was no physical contact between them, and rarely did they even look at or speak to one another. Even for a couple as unaffectionate as they were, this highly unusual behavior strongly suggests that something powerful was going on between them. As much as Patsy and John wanted to conceal it, they were alienated from each other.

After initially talking to the police that morning, the Ramseys made numerous phone calls to friends around the country, apparently in a panic and reaching out for support—yet another sign that they greatly feared they were in trouble. Three days later at the first memorial service for JonBenét, Patsy and John continued to subtly reflect the alienation between them: While Patsy was inside the church falling apart emotionally, John was out in the parking lot chatting with friends.

READING BETWEEN THE LINES, THE CRIME SCENE AND THE RAMSEYS' BEHAVIOR REVEALS:

- **Torture strangulation staged to hide the real story.**

- **Patsy Ramsey's secret good-bye gifts to JonBenét.**

- **Patsy Ramsey linked crime scene with her ransom note.**

- **Patsy Ramsey was terrified of first policeman on scene.**

- **The Ramseys hid JonBenét's body so John could discover it.**

- **The Ramseys were alienated from each other.**

Chapter Eighteen
John Ramsey Profiles the Killer

O n July 23, 1997, nearly seven months after the murder, John Ramsey released his own profile of the murderer to the media:

JonBenét's killer may have been suffering from some stress in the weeks and months preceding the crime;

A triggering event such as a job crisis or crisis in a personal relationship may have caused this individual to vent anger, perhaps at a female close to him or perhaps at me personally;

Since the murder, this individual may rabidly read news reports of the investigation, listen to talk radio shows oriented to coverage of the murder;

He has possibly increased his consumption of alcohol or drugs;

He may have even turned to religion;

He may be rigid, nervous and preoccupied in casual conversation;

He may have tried to appear very cooperative with the authorities if he was contacted during the course of the investigation;

He may have quickly constructed an alibi for his whereabouts the night JonBenét was killed and may have repeated it several times to key individuals around him as if rehearsing them in the answer;

The killer is someone who may have previously been in my home.

John Ramsey ends with:
One key phone call and the killer can be brought to justice.
Other than trying to brainwash us into thinking the killer was unquestionably a male, note how well the profile fits Patsy Ramsey.

First she had two major ongoing stresses in her life for months prior to the murder, and, indeed, there was a triggering event the night of the murder that caused the killer to direct her aggression both toward John Ramsey personally and toward a female close to her, namely JonBenét.

Without question Patsy Ramsey has continually listened to various media reports as she has told us by calling Larry King's show and during an interview on Geraldo's show. Patsy has been unable to stop herself from listening. (Likewise John Ramsey's public statements and efforts to manipulate media stories ahead of time indicate how closely he is paying attention.) In light of her stress, Patsy Ramsey has returned to one of her drugs of choice, nicotine, and started smoking again. (We don't know about her alcohol use.)

Unquestionably Patsy has turned even more to her religion as we can see from her 1997 Christmas letter and her comments to others. Recall her telling Nedra as she impulsively called Larry King, "God will give me the words." A person who knew Patsy well saw her two months after the murder and noted that she looked like a ghost. (Of course, her grief is twofold in light of her dual role as the mother-killer.) And of course the Ramseys have tried to appear cooperative with the authorities, all the while undermining the investigation.

Constructing an alibi, repeating it, and rehearsing it describe precisely what Patsy and John Ramsey have done. Rehearsing is so typical of Patsy—remember the practice ransom note and the years on stage. Constructing an alibi is along the same lines as a portrayal or putting a spin on things that John made reference to in his letter to the artist. Both Patsy and John are superb spin doctors. And indeed the killer has been in John Ramsey's house—he slept in the same bed with her. Without question John is trying to reinforce the notion the killer knew JonBenét. Reportedly this was particularly aimed at his former good friend Fleet White.

PROFILE OF SECOND KILLER: A MAJOR CLUE

The profile seems to fit Patsy much better than John, which suggests that this is another unconscious tip-off by the Ramseys about the identity of the primary killer. But John (and Patsy) has a powerful force working against the cover-up—his own conscience. As he said in the profile, "... to lose our child in such a *vile* and *brutal* manner ... The person who did this crime is an *evil person* beyond imagination. He must be brought to justice and prevented from **stopping** *the life of another young child* who offers so much to the future of the world."

There is that special word again in John Ramsey's secret code—"young child." But now we see an even more valuable clue—the awkward expression "prevented from stopping the life of another." *A much more common phrase would have been "prevented from taking the life of another" (or "ending the life of another").* But *"stopping"* makes sense when we think of common expressions—someone stopping breathing or someone's heart stopping. **Somebody had to stop JonBenét from breathing**. That's the way John and Patsy would have looked at it.

This unusual choice of the word "stopping" is almost certainly a confession on John Ramsey's part that he was the one who actually stopped her from breathing—particularly emphasized by connecting it with the loaded description "young child," which was previously a confession of its own. *By connecting these two key ideas, we are really looking at a double confession as John Ramsey secretly reveals the two ways he harmed JonBenét—sexual abuse followed by strangulation.* Given the deeper mind's sensitivity to guilt, this was one secret too powerful for John to keep to himself.

This is John's own profile of the killer, and, without realizing it, he has accurately profiled both killers. Perhaps John didn't actually write all of this profile himself, but we can believe he wrote this last paragraph—the hidden messages are simply too strong to be coincidental. And he would have had final approval over the letter, which makes it his. In addition, John Ramsey was so controlling—and the letter is such a confession, including the extreme guilt implied in the first paragraph ("vile," "brutal," and "evil beyond imagination")—that I believe he wrote the whole thing himself.

John is continually growing more uneasy with the cover-up, "Over the past seven months, I have grown increasingly frustrated as the investigating authorities *have limited their investigation."* Simply consider the idea, and we can see that John is also talking about himself. Deep down he wants to cooperate and to stop limiting the investigation. *Like Patsy, he knows that the case is just one communication—"one phone call"—away from being broken.*

OTHER POSSIBILITIES

Of course there are other possibilities as to how the murder could have unfolded. Patsy could have become more enraged over JonBenét's bed-wetting and soiling because deep down she also felt JonBenét was a threat to her. This would have intensified the power struggle over bed-wetting alone. But Patsy had handled the stress of bed-wetting for years and hadn't lost control. Although the bed-wetting was getting worse, extreme anger wasn't typical of Patsy.

Some people have hypothesized that John alone committed the murder and that he was used to giving orders and manipulated Patsy into going along with the cover-up. But logic tells us that Patsy was no shrinking wallflower and loved her daughter too much to cover it up.

The abrasions on JonBenét's body suggest a battle with Patsy rather than John, who could more easily overpower her. John also lacks the powerful motives that Patsy had, other than possibly JonBenét being on the verge of revealing his sexual abuse—but she almost certainly loved her daddy too much for that. Threats weren't part of JonBenét yet, mainly she was about compliance.

And most of all the ransom note and Patsy's other communications not only underscore the powerful traumas stirring inside of her, but at times are disguised confessions (a woman killer, a hole in my heart, I loved her too much, etc.). Most impressively, the ransom note offers the psychological profile including a description *of the exact moment Patsy lost it*—when JonBenét was seemingly prostituted by John Ramsey. My experience is that the deeper mind usually gets things right and sees what's really going on in phenomenal ways. I cannot think of another real possibility. For Patsy to be talking about herself and telling us she lost control that night because she had come to the sudden realization that she herself had used JonBenét doesn't hang together. The hidden psychological profile in the ransom note explains exactly what happened like nothing else does.

The ransom note specifically challenges the theory that Patsy acted alone, telling us that John's behavior set her off. Additionally the ransom note refers to two killers: "we," "small group," and "two gentlemen watching over your daughter." *Logically, to carry out the entire "double murder" by herself seems too great a psychological task for Patsy Ramsey.*

Such a theory asks even more of a woman who already is asking the near impossible from herself. To directly assault her daughter once and carry out the cover-up with an accomplice is difficult enough. Think about hitting your daughter in a rage, then having to assault her again yourself that same night after denying her medical attention, drag her down the stairs, create an unfamiliar garrote and use it, stage a sexual abuse, and then come up with a ransom note.

The Ramseys together immediately reached out for their friends after they called the police, which reveals that their natural reaction under stress is to ask for help. It emphasizes that Patsy would have immediately reached out to John to do something after her first assault on JonBenét.

On the other hand, perhaps Patsy was ruthless enough to carry out the entire "double murder." Maybe she was cruel enough and ashamed enough to go ahead and finish off JonBenét. The brief time lapse between the two assaults also could point to one killer who is profoundly ashamed and frightened and who out of desperation acts quickly. If that is the case, I would expect that Patsy had something on John to force his hand, to get him to go along. Without that John certainly wouldn't have been nearly as motivated to cover-up for Patsy. For one reason, how could he ever trust her alone with Burke again if she so easily lost control? And the fact that there were two severe injuries itself suggests two killers. I don't think either of them could have directly inflicted two fatal blows in one night on their own daughter.

In the final analysis the ransom note is the most powerful evidence that clarifies who the murderer is because it provides the motive and describes the murder scene. And it dovetails with another impressive communication, Patsy's 1996 Christmas letter (see Chapter 15).

There is also something about the "integrity" of this crime that speaks of both a very impulsive person (Patsy) and a cold, calculating person (John). John simply seems more coldhearted on a daily basis than Patsy and more capable of carrying out the second part of the crime. Likewise the cover-up itself points to two people in a very basic way.

LOOSE ENDS

At least thirteen reasons point to a sexual-abuse trigger for Patsy Ramsey's rage:

1. **the crime scene and autopsy reveal sexual abuse.**

2. **the ransom note teaches it.**

3. **the enuresis theory is by default, and Patsy Ramsey had handled the bed-wetting for years.**

4. **the 1996 Christmas letter hints at sexual abuse.**

5. **John Ramsey's major slip-up (JonBen-I).**

6. **John Ramsey's excessive sensitivity to the subject—mentioning it on national television and writing a public letter to the artist.**

7. **John Ramsey's letter to the artist contains clues of a cover-up and a hidden confession.**

8. **John Ramsey's repeated efforts to prevent Diane Hallis from telling her story about sexual abuse.**

9. **JonBenét's soiling along with chronic bed-wetting—both of which were escalating.**

10. **John Ramsey's history of acting out sexually when under stress.**

11. **Patsy Ramsey had something on John Ramsey to encourage his participation in a cover-up.**

12. **the obvious alienation between Patsy and John hours after the murder.**

13. **Patsy Ramsey would have cracked by now unless she could somehow shift the blame to John.**

One other theory about the murder is that Burke did it. This is the least likely of all the possibilities. Among other reasons, if the Ramseys were so interested in protecting Burke they wouldn't have immediately let him go off with friends as they did. If Burke were involved, John and Patsy would have controlled him as they always try to control everything.

Some evidence in JonBenét's murder don't seem to fit—as is the case with any crime. The abrasions on her body haven't been completely understood. Why JonBenét didn't change out of her blouse before bed and why the Ramseys would lie about giving their daughter a bedtime snack are also puzzles. But the big pieces fall into place in a sexual-abuse scenario and so do the repeated hidden confessions of both Patsy and John Ramsey.

STRANGE FAMILIES

Despite all our analysis thus far, this murder still seems incredibly strange and vicious. How two people as highly motivated and image conscious as Patsy and John Ramsey could carry out essentially two murders and a ruthless cover-up begs us to keep looking deeper. The place to start may be with the speculation that a stun gun was used on JonBenét.

The point-like pattern of the abrasions caused Detective Lou Smit to consider the idea of a stun gun. Now we are told that, by and large, this theory has been ruled out, but simply the consideration provokes some interesting ideas, and maybe Lou Smit was picking up on more than he realized. The crime itself is so stunning that it evokes the image of a stun gun. How would a stun gun fit Patsy Ramsey—and her relationship with JonBenét?

A stun gun resonates with Patsy Ramsey's core personality in striking ways. She uses power and dominance as a way of coping with her pain and self-doubt. A stun gun fits with her emphasis on externals, a perfect match for her famous Las Vegas showgirl picture with all its disguised power symbols. Patsy's whole life is designed around being stunning—as a beauty queen, as the mother of a beauty queen, and as the perfect person and mother with her perfectly stunning home. Just like the stunning name JonBenét with the stunning accent. Just like the stunning exclamation points at the beginning and end of her letters, including the ransom note. Just as she herself was stunned by cancer.

And when people are stunned, they "shoot back"—they shoot other people if they are so inclined. We have already seen subtle but significant evidence of raw, cold-blooded power and hostility from Patsy and her mother toward JonBenét, John Ramsey, and others.

MEANNESS

Jane Stobie, the former manager at Access Graphics, told *Vanity Fair* that another female employee described Patsy Ramsey's family as **"the meanest people I've ever met."** Patsy's two sisters have gained a phenomenal amount of weight, reportedly in part to express ongoing hostility at their father who greatly dislikes their obesity. And Patsy would have the same simmering anger somewhere in her, waiting for an outlet.

A stun gun would fit her demeanor—capable of brief powerful outbursts of anger amidst an innocuous external appearance. Anger she could direct at the female body of JonBenét precisely because being a female had caused Patsy's cancer and the terror that engulfed her. Anger that would stun a nation—and certainly stun a husband.

There is one last hint linking Patsy Ramsey with a stun-gun mentality—her sister Polly and her mother. Recall the report of how the two of them stunned other employees in John's business by talking about young Burke Ramsey's stunning genitals. Polly also shocked others, particularly men, with her sex talk—once again showing us that the women in Patsy Ramsey's family were secretly about power and not primarily sex. A stun gun is a perfect metaphor for the dark side of the Paugh family.

Think again about Patsy's mother's stunning comments to a stranger that men are nothing but sex-craved maniacs who just use women and that women are so weak and needy that they must go along. What about Patsy's father, Don Paugh? Nedra Paugh saw Don as sexually obsessed—she saw all men that way.

And recently an unimpeachable source told me of interviewing a woman who knew Don well and described his interaction with her as blatantly sexual—and he was in his seventies. Although Paugh was often quiet and reserved, the woman reported that at one point Paugh overtly stared at her body in a sexual way and tried to hold her hand. It is hard to imagine this was a one-time thing.

Reportedly, Paugh could be ruthless in similar ways. Several Access

Graphics employees referred to Don Paugh as *"The Hatchet Man."*

EXTREME

The pattern seems clear. Patsy Ramsey's family can be summed up the same way Patsy can—*extreme*—as in extremely aggressive, extremely crude at moments, and appearing extremely sexual.

Certainly Nedra was extreme in her desire for her daughters to be Miss America. For two sisters to have been contestants in the Miss America pageant is extremely rare. Patsy's father had his own extreme tendencies. Patsy's sisters picked up on the family trait and both are extremely overweight, with Pamela demonstrating a particularly extreme swing from being Miss West Virginia to becoming obese.

Patsy herself was obviously extreme in her pursuit of becoming Miss America. Is it any wonder that when Patsy Ramsey reached the darkest and most impulsive moment of her life that she was extreme— in a crude aggressive way? She reflected her family's shadow side like she never had before.

Are we surprised that in the face of such crudeness and aggressiveness Patsy Ramsey became the family hero who wore the mantle of gentility? Can we not understand why she had to shut down sexually in a family that often expressed such a crude sexuality? Her sister is reportedly keeping men off balance with her talk about oral sex, and Patsy's friends are shocked by Patsy's extreme naivete about such matters. Can't we see how Patsy herself might have expressed her own crude sexuality with just the slightest patina of respectability by subtly forcing JonBenét into a sensuality far beyond her years? And as Patsy did so, simultaneously did she not have a huge blind spot to her actions because that was part of being the hero child whose sexuality stayed submerged lest it overpower her, like it did others around her?

And when a crime unfolds that reflects not only Patsy Ramsey's own unique stresses but also the milieu that shaped her life—the forces that were part of her fiber however deep she had buried them—we discover a crude sexual event that Patsy can simultaneously attribute to someone else.

We are closer to the truth about Patsy Ramsey's part in the murder of JonBenét. Her destructive actions reflected her family's abusive patterns in striking ways—toward JonBenét, toward many of those around her that she tried to implicate for her own misdeed, and toward the world in general as she continues to shock everyone. In its darkest hour, the human heart isn't pretty, but it is what it is.

A journalist who observed Patsy Ramsey up close and personal for several months after the murder got a good look at her shadow side. He was struck by Patsy's self absorption and described her as someone "who wouldn't hold the door open for little old ladies but, instead, wait on someone to hold the door open for her." He witnessed her shaking Burke in anger on at least one occasion.

More importantly he was struck by her inattentiveness to Burke. On the heels of losing JonBenét, you would expect Patsy to be at her most protective of Burke, but that wasn't the case. She allowed him to freely roam the streets of Charlevoix and to go out alone in a motorized rubber boat, over a quarter mile from home and out of sight. Even though it was a safe resort town, Patsy's behavior seemed excessive to the observer, and never once did he see Patsy doting on Burke or making sure he was warm. This left the impression that Burke was more like a thing to Patsy.

ANOTHER LOOK AT JOHN'S DYSFUNCTION

A closer look at John reveals a similar picture of "extremes." Beginning in his adolescence, adults noted John's extreme ambition. Attending engineering school, serving as a navy pilot, earning a master's degree, and starting his own company in his basement and sticking with his plan all speaks of John's determination.

His father, "Czar" Ramsey was exceptionally strong willed. Behind the father's iron fist was extreme separation anxiety, which he passed on to his son. Very shortly after John's mother died of cancer, his father married John's ex-mother in law, Irene Pasch. Isn't that turning a cold heart to the grief process? Perhaps James Ramsey was simultaneously covering over the separation/death terror that would have continued to haunt him from his repeated bombing missions during World War II.

Reportedly John resented his father's marriage feeling that his former mother-in-law had manipulated his father at a weak moment. His father was speaking volumes about a lack of boundaries: His wife barely in the grave and he latches on to the first relationship he can find—and with someone who is almost a family member to boot. It speaks of impulsiveness and fear. But it was no secret that James didn't deal well with emotional issues and had an inordinate capacity to block out emotions—traits that John shares.

Looking back further into John's past, he was reportedly intimidated by his father, which John would have experienced as a cold heart. In addition, the family moved from Omaha to Michigan when John was at the crucial age of thirteen, unquestionably a major separation trauma that almost certainly was covered over emotionally. Later John had to deal with his mother's cancer and death and his father's almost immediate remarriage.

COLDNESS AND GUILT

While Patsy was going through her tremendous battle with cancer,

John was often emotionally unavailable, which reveals how poorly he had dealt with his previous separation traumas. Friends were struck by Patsy's flying alone to NIH in Bethesda, Maryland for chemotherapy when her prognosis was so poor and her condition so weak—particularly at a time when emotional support can be so crucial. Routinely Patsy would return home from four days of intravenous chemotherapy and her blood count would drop so low that she would have to be hospitalized in Boulder for five days.

Each time Patsy would head back to Bethesda alone, until her friends finally pushed her mother into accompanying her. John somewhere along the line had developed a cold heart—reportedly just like his father's. (*Vanity Fair* quoted a Ramsey friend who remembered James Ramsey as *"very cold, like John was with everybody."*) In 1993 when Patsy got sick, John would not have been over losing his daughter and father the year before, but long before that he could be exceptionally cold—as his reputation testifies. Unquestionably he continues to be coldhearted after JonBenét's murder.

Former Access Graphics employee Jeff Merrick knew John Ramsey for nearly twenty-six years and worked for him for several years. Others had warned him not to trust John Ramsey, but Merrick continued on as the dutiful, loyal company man until, suddenly, he was replaced by one of Don Paugh's cronies and transferred to another job. The position was phased out one month before JonBenét's murder, and John Ramsey told Merrick there was nothing he could do.

Not long afterward Merrick was named by John Ramsey as a possible suspect in JonBenét's murder because of the firing, which Merrick had protested to Lockheed-Martin. (One detective asked Merrick, "How come John Ramsey keeps throwing out your name?") From solid employee and trusting friend to being unemployed and falsely accused of murdering JonBenét—all in one month. This seems to substantiate the prevailing view that John didn't have any real friends—only "throwaway friends," as the police call them, who John turned on after the murder in one way or another.

Like Patsy, John seemed to treat Burke in a cold detached fashion. The same observer who commented on Patsy's coldness toward Burke, said that Burke seemed like a "thing" to John as well. This resonates with loyal neighbor Joe Barnhill's impression of John at JonBenét's memorial service in Boulder: John was so cold that it seemed as if he were giving a company talk.

It's not a real pretty picture when we look behind the scenes at John Ramsey's life. It's certainly not the myth he wants us to believe. We find evidence in John of the dysfunction and extreme character traits that we see in his family—both good and bad: extremely motivated, extremely controlling, extremely coldhearted, extremely ruthless, and extremely avoidant. Like father, like son. John's dysfunction, like

Patsy's, erupted from deep within him on Christmas night 1996.

Perhaps all of this explains why JonBenét could be so unbelievably compliant—particularly in public. She was renowned for holding a photographic pose, sitting in a chair at John's office for several hours waiting on her parents, and in the extremely posed family photo spontaneously saluting like a dutiful child— totally submissive to the will of her mother (and grandmother).

Surely, this reflects a child who had been stunned at moments by both parents in their own way, by the hidden forces within John and Patsy Ramsey that had stunned them when they themselves were young. It doesn't take many such shocks to keep a kid in line. JonBenét had already begun to incorporate the family traits of extremism.

SELF-DESTRUCTIVE

There is one last aspect of John Ramsey's life we must not overlook—his self- destructiveness. *At the pinnacle of his business success, John contributed to the explosion that resulted in JonBenét's death as much as Patsy. He brought himself down.* As much as Patsy, out of her weakness, wanted to dethrone him, she could not have done it without his help.

An incident involving his oldest son, John Andrew, that occurred after the murder perhaps typifies what John Ramsey himself was dealing with during the summer of 1997. A writer who was covering the Ramsey murder story was having a drink in a local bar in Charlevoix while the Ramseys were vacationing there. At some point John Andrew came into the bar and shortly thereafter approached the writer and rather quickly began berating him. The writer attempted to pacify John Andrew, but he would have no part of it. Finally John Andrew, obviously intoxicated, became more intimidating, eventually getting in the writer's face and yelling, "Hit me, hit me, go ahead and hit me." The writer simply walked away.

The huge scene John Andrew caused reflected not only his frustration and anger, but also made him look so bad that surely he did want someone to hit him—to punish him like his two dead sisters (Beth and JonBenét) had been punished.

John Ramsey had the same tendency, and in the face of enormous guilt and fear, he was saying through his behavior, "Hit me, hit me." And so Patsy did: Not only did she hit JonBenét Christmas night 1996, but she also hit John Ramsey where he hurt the most.

ENDNOTE

With all said and done, though, it's still very hard for us to comprehend how parents could strangle their own daughter—whether she was unconscious and near death or not. Both have undoubtedly been consumed with guilt. John tells us in his letter to the artist that they would never have any joy again, and Patsy told her friend Pamela Griffin (who told Geraldo), "How can I ever be happy another day of my life?" When a reporter asked her what the worst time of day was for her now, she said, "All the time." At least Patsy and John are telling the truth about one thing: There's no joy in the Ramsey household now.

JOHN RAMSEY'S PROFILE OF KILLER SECRETLY REVEALS:

- **Patsy Ramsey matches the profile of the killer.**

- **John admits to being the second killer—who "stopped" JonBenét from breathing.**

- **Sexual abuse set Patsy off.**

ADDITIONAL INFORMATION REVEALS

- **At pinnacle of success John Ramsey brought himself down.**

- **13 reasons to suspect John was sexually abusing JonBenét.**

- **Patsy's family had a vicious side and enjoyed shocking people. (Her father was known as the "Hatchet Man.")**

- **John's father was a person of extremes—cold, rigid, and secretly afraid.**

Chapter Nineteen
Christmas Message 1997: After the Murder

With the Christmas season upon us and the anniversary of JonBenét's death approaching, we are filled with many emotions. We, as a family, miss JonBenét's presence among us as we see the lights, hear the music, and recall celebrations of Christmases past. We miss her every day—not just today.

On the one hand, we feel like Christmas should be canceled. Where is there joy? Our Christmas is forever tainted with the tragedy of her death. And yet the message rings clear. **Had there been no birth of Christ, there would be no hope of eternal life, and hence, no hope of ever being with our loved ones again.**

As the day of the birth of our Lord and Savior approaches, we thank all across the nation and around the world for your continued prayer of concern and support. It is those prayers that sustain us. We ask that as you gather with your families and loved ones this Christmas, be joyful in the celebration of the birthday of Christ, knowing that this is truly the reason of the season. We must continue to celebrate the birth of Christ for our hope of life together ever after.

Thank you for all you meant to her and mean to us.

With blessing and prayer for a Joyful Holiday and the Grace of God's ever present love for the New Year,

John, Patsy, John Andrew, Melinda, and Burke

Patsy Ramsey cannot *stop* confessing. If we had any doubts that she was the author of the ransom note, she has written another letter—a letter that perfectly matches the ransom note—and this time put her name on it.

As the one-year anniversary of JonBenét's death approached, the Ramsey family released a letter to the public. It was designed to be a communication thanking the public for their support, and it was basically a public relations move—or so the Ramseys believed.

But Patsy's hidden messages further corroborate her confession in the ransom note. People who know the Ramseys tell us without question that Patsy Ramsey wrote this letter. They refer particularly to the frequent "religious" sections of the letter, the key sections of the letter that have Patsy's unique stamp on them at so many levels.

The Boulder authorities still believe that the "ransom" note is the most solid evidence they have. District Attorney Alex Hunter recently told *The New Yorker* magazine that if the handwriting and the linguistics experts agree that Patsy Ramsey wrote the note, he might have enough "soft evidence" to charge her as an accessory. Reportedly he said, "If the linguistics experts say she wrote it, we may have something." What Hunter seems to be lacking is an emphasis on the "psycho" part of "psycholinguistics." The experts he has reportedly contacted are not specialists in psychology but rather in linguistics.

But even if Hunter gets affirmation from his current experts, he says he would still be puzzled as to who is the principal, and he is still looking for a smoking gun. *The fact that the idea of a smoking gun is linked with a discussion about psycholinguistics suggests that Hunter's own deeper intuition is trying to tell him that the smoking gun is there in the note—if only he can understand the hidden messages.*

This is where the breakthrough to the deeper mind and to psycholinguistics comes in. Indeed, if both the deeper mind of the killer and the author of the Christmas letter were clearly communicating hidden messages, we should be able to decode them and find a consistent, logical story. This is exactly the case when we read between the lines. If we understand the language of the psyche we see how the *ideas on the mind of the killer are the same ideas on Patsy's mind in her 1997 Christmas letter.* These deeper thought patterns in both letters uniquely fit her and not John.

A comparison with the contributions of other experts enables us to appreciate the messages from Patsy's deeper mind. The more contributions we have from different fields, the stronger the case.

OTHER EXPERTS

Hunter is consulting handwriting experts and linguistics experts. Thus far the linguists who focus on style with an emphasis on linguistic tendencies (including similar words, phrases, errors and syntax) have noted certain similarities in the ransom note and the 1997 Christmas letter. They have particularly commented on the striking use of the somewhat unusual word *"hence."* Additionally, they have noticed that in her Christmas letter, Patsy Ramsey frequently uses the word *"we"* (eight times), often beginning a sentence with it (four times). She used "we" in the ransom note seven times, and three of those to begin a sentence. People have also noticed that Patsy often repeats words such as "hope."

On a whole other level of communication the deeper mind repeats ideas using different words and sequences of ideas—to tell an elaborate in-depth story. The key to the deeper mind's language is to remember who it is looking at, at all times. If we keep in mind that subliminal perception/observation is constantly going on, we can break the coded messages.

It's not as complicated as it sounds. We already know some things about Patsy Ramsey: She has had a tremendous battle with cancer that she still fears, her daughter has been killed and the police are investigating her, and she has a guilty conscience. Patsy's deeper mind is constantly looking at her fear, the police, and her conscience.

ANOTHER CANCER LETTER

Reading between the lines, the ransom note from beginning to end speaks of cancer. So does Patsy's 1997 Christmas letter, although it contains an important twist that was not available to Patsy when she wrote the ransom note.

Remember to first pay attention to the ideas and not to the person to whom they appear to be connected. Listen: Something is upon us, anniversary of a death, death approaching, filled with emotions, missing someone among us, Christmases past, Christmas that is canceled or missed, no joy, tainted Christmas, tragedy of her death, no birth (no life), no hope of life, no hope of ever being with loved ones, the day approaches, concern, sustain, our hope, ever after.

Patsy includes all these obvious ideas of despair (and attempted repair) in the first two paragraphs of her letter. Of course she is talking about JonBenét, but don't miss that she is also secretly observing and talking about herself, and—from the outset—we see familiar ideas that link to cancer. Just like the ransom note, the *Christmas letter builds up to a key sentence* that ties together all of her secret thoughts about cancer and unmistakably reveals that Patsy's terror of cancer and death was indeed behind her loss of control. Look at her train of thought in the first sentence.

"With the Christmas season upon us and the anniversary of JonBenét's death approaching, we are filled with many emotions." The big ideas here are: time (Christmas) is upon us, *the* anniversary of approaching death, filled with emotions. Remember that these ideas are from Patsy Ramsey's mind and in the back of her mind she is constantly looking at her cancer. See how clearly the words fit with cancer.

Cancer is experienced as something that "came upon" someone, covered them over as it becomes a dominant issue in their lives, an issue in which they had no choice. It also hints at something that is moving—growing—and coming to a climax. But there's more that is coming toward Patsy Ramsey—an anniversary.

Cancer patients think of anniversaries in terms of survival—one year, two years, and hopefully five and ten years. After you have cancer, an anniversary date of your survival becomes "the anniversary" in your mind, taking precedence far beyond all others. Every single day, at least in the back of their minds, cancer patients think of time. Holidays also become special anniversaries for patients, vivid reminders of togetherness, of another Christmas with the family, but also of the potential: A year from now they might not be here—this could be their last Christmas.

Notice what *type of anniversary* Patsy Ramsey is talking about—the anniversary of "death approaching." Simply take out one word ("JonBenét") and see how the thought perfectly fits Patsy. This is the thought of a cancer patient if ever there was one. Somebody with as poor a prognosis as Patsy's always thinks of cancer as an approaching death. Patsy has repeatedly told us in the last year that she greatly fears her cancer will return. *Death approaching is still how Patsy Ramsey sees the world deep down.*

One sentence into the letter, and the first three major ideas all fit in a powerful convincing way with cancer. Knowing that the mind communicates consistently on two levels at the same time and that we tend to block out more painful perceptions of the world, logically we can see that Patsy had rather think consciously about JonBenét's death which is less painful than thinking about her own.

This also gives us another hint about her motive. By taking the life of JonBenét, she now had a death that she could deal with in a sense, a death that someone else had to experience and that gave Patsy a measure of being in control. In a strange but logical twist to reality, killing JonBenét took Patsy's mind off her cancer—and gave her the big stage she's been searching for her whole life. And anytime she wants to—as her letter indicates—she can focus on JonBenét's suffering and claim her stage. Not an immediately bad trade-off for "approaching death." The temptation when you're in Patsy Ramsey's boat is to desperately make any deal you can.

TWIN TERRORS: THE POLICE AND HER CONSCIENCE

The three main ideas in the first sentence fit two other realities Patsy is looking at in the back of her mind. As the anniversary of JonBenét's death was nearing, she sees the police coming down upon her as yet another type of approaching death. Here "approaching death" suggests that Patsy knows the police have the goods on her and could somehow bring about a conviction. She may be hinting that they should become more aggressive.

Simultaneously Patsy is looking at her own guilty conscience, and the same messages fit perfectly. Deep down she knows what she deserves, and "approaching death" suggests that she knows the end is not far off.

What would you expect her reaction to be under such stressful circumstances? Read the next idea in this light: "... filled with many emotions." Under such circumstances, could any words be truer? When we consider that deep down she is always looking at her cancer, once more she is telling us that being a cancer patient constantly filled her with emotions, and thus the night she killed JonBenét she was at her breaking point. When we apply the same idea to the other two realities of the police pursuit and her conscience pursuing her, Patsy is once again telling us that she is near a breaking point.

In this seemingly very coherent letter about JonBenét, Patsy is also talking on a deeper level about herself—just like in the ransom note when she constantly focused on the death of JonBenét but was also referring to herself.

One principle of decoding is that every word out of the person's mouth must be taken as a part of them. In the very first sentence we find these powerfully perceptive messages from the brilliant deeper mind of Patsy Ramsey. But these morbid thoughts don't stop here.

"We, as a family, miss JonBenét's presence among us as we see the lights, hear the music, and recall celebrations of Christmases past. We miss her every day—not just today."

Notice how frequently Patsy uses the word *"miss"* directly or by implication. She stresses that missing someone goes on and on, implying that it is the center of her life every day, and she thinks of Christmases that are over, that she can't go back to.

Patsy is also subtly telling us again that in the back of her mind she realizes that the days of her cover-up are limited. Her dramatic performance last Christmas was a celebration in its own way as she "celebrated"—focused on—JonBenét's death, but she realizes the public and the police are not buying her masquerade. Thus she is starting to see the light, getting ready to face the music—she can even hear what they're going to say about her in the future—she is recalling more and more exactly what did happen on a past Christmas, particularly the last one.

When we all fully and plainly see what Patsy did on that infamous day, she is going to be missed every day from then on. In fact the old Patsy Ramsey has been missing since the day she killed her daughter. Stop for a moment and ask yourself which of the two stories we're hearing is the most accurate—the attempted cover-up the Christmas letter overtly presents or the hidden story from her deeper mind. The deeper story continues.

CELEBRATION: PATSY'S MANIC DEFENSE

Patsy Ramsey tries to handle her pain by celebration. In psychiatry we call it a "manic defense." Act one way when you feel another. That, in fact, is how we conceptualize manic-depressive illness. When someone is manic, they are secretly trying to cover over their painful depression by being "high" and invulnerable. This is exactly what we saw Patsy do in her manic 1995 Christmas letter (see Chapter 14) when she was facing the twin terrors of cancer and the empty nest syndrome. In this letter Patsy moves toward her religious faith as a way of celebrating and covering her pain.

This avenue of "overt goodness" was not available to her in the ransom note because she was playing the part of the terrorist. There she tried to handle her fear and vulnerability by being tough and aggressive—another form of mania.

Patsy has been using a "manic defense" much of her life, coping with her inadequacies by celebrating externals, often on stages designed for externals. We see the same thing particularly in the last part of this letter with her emphasis on "celebration" and "joy" but if we pay attention we will continue to see the pain that she is battling with the celebration and joy interspersed.

This second sentence contains the somewhat unusual expression "miss JonBenét's presence among us." Obviously there's the idea of someone being gone from the group, but a much more natural way of saying it would be "we really miss JonBenét." Patsy substitutes "JonBenét's presence" for at least two reasons.

First it's very formal and less personal—perhaps Patsy found it hard to say that it was JonBenét she missed and preferred to think of her as just a presence. Patsy preferred to minimize her deed. Her familiar use of "We" does the same thing. It's "we the family" miss JonBenét, something she repeats in the very next sentence.

But "presence" also has another particularly special meaning for Patsy. *Presence is what beauty-pageant contestants constantly strive for* and pride themselves on. Isn't this another *confession* that, in part, she was just *using JonBenét to secretly live out her own fantasies on stage,* and that it really wasn't JonBenét that she missed but "JonBenét the stage presence, the performer, the alter ego"—JonBenét the object.

Presence is also what Patsy Ramsey is trying to maintain during this enormous cover-up. But look at what she is telling us—the presence is gone. Is this a premonition that she is not far from collapsing based, of course, on her unbelievable ability to accurately perceive herself deep down? Surely pairing this idea with the ideas that follow of "seeing the light" and "hearing (facing) the music" seems to be a story within a story—and yet another hint of an impending collapse.

MORE OMINOUS THOUGHTS

"On the one hand, we feel like Christmas should be canceled. Where is there joy? Our Christmas is forever tainted with the tragedy of her death."

Christmas ceasing to exist, the absence of joy, and tragedy of death certainly are along the same lines of impending doom we have seen in both the ransom note and this letter. It illustrates the sterling characteristic of the deeper mind to continually repeat itself to convey how it views reality.

Here also is one of the clearest places in the letter for seeing that Patsy Ramsey and the writer of the ransom note are one and the same. Notice the unusual idea that "Christmas should be canceled." To cancel Christmas would be phenomenal. It would be tampering with Christmas, marking it off the calendar as if it didn't exist. This fits with Patsy Ramsey in so many ways.

First of all it *echoes the ransom note wording of tampering with something (the money), of something being marked and set aside.* And doesn't a tainted Christmas fit even better? *Tainted—tampered with—marked. Unusual and sophisticated words.* And of all things Patsy Ramsey was afraid of, it was that she had been so marked and tainted (by cancer) that all her Christmases from here on would be canceled. And it would be a severe tainting, a *"forever* tainting." "Forever tainted with the tragedy of her death" sums up Patsy's deepest issue and tells us why she tainted JonBenét.

THE KEY SENTENCE

"And yet the message rings clear. Had there been no birth of Christ, there would be no hope of eternal life, and hence, no hope of ever being with our loved ones again."

The obvious refrain continues: "No hope" is repeated twice, the second time linked to the permanent loss of loved ones. Again and again Patsy returns to loss and death. By making JonBenét the carrier of death, Patsy lives.

Earlier concerning the ransom note (see Chapters 8 and 10), I speculated that perhaps Patsy (and John to a degree) saw JonBenét as a Christ figure, as someone who would die in her place. This line of thinking seems confirmed here as Patsy links the death of JonBenét to Christ who as a sacrifice is the giver of eternal life and without whom there is no hope.

Sadly this tells us that at the time of the murder, a part of Patsy deep down had no other hope apart from killing JonBenét, apart from someone else temporarily experiencing the suffocating pressure of death that she experienced. In her 1997 Christmas letter Patsy is still dealing with her misperception, at least for the moment, that she is dying. That is one of the central messages, but we must look at this sentence in another light. Other commentators on the letter have noticed the obvious similarity between the ransom note and this letter in the blatant use of the unusual word *"hence."* It suggests two purposes.

First the word is so striking that it is a clear confession that the ransom note and this letter are connected. The way Patsy repeats words over and over is another of her striking characteristics. In this sentence alone she uses the word "no" three times and "no hope" twice.

Beyond this trademark is also something else in the use of "hence": Patsy is drawing our attention back to the entire sentence in the ransom note, the second most crucial sentence in the ransom note. The one sentence where she tells us when she lost control and why. I think Patsy wants us to know that in one sense it was all an accident.

There is yet an even bigger message in the use of "hence": *Hence means "here comes the conclusion." In the ransom note Patsy used "hence" to tell us how the events the night of JonBenét's death ended in such a devastating conclusion, and she is doing the same thing again.*

A CLEAR MESSAGE: BIRTH AND DELIVERY

Twice in the letter Patsy tells us to pay particular attention. *"The message rings clear"* is a distinct clue that she is about to give a very clear hidden message. Later in the letter she uses the expression "the reason" to tell us to pay extremely close attention. *"Clear message" and "the reason" are* **message markers**—*red flags, flashing lights that say "here it is."*

"Hence" does the same thing, and that combined with "clear message" pointing toward one sentence means pay **triple attention** to that sentence, which is the clearest link with the ransom note. In this sentence Patsy reveals why she killed JonBenét, and it strongly hints at the identical motive she revealed in her ransom note.

This sentence is the single most revealing and important one in the Christmas letter. **Patsy** *italicizes* **the entire sentence, unmistakably setting it apart herself.** In multiple ways she is telling us that this is *the central point.* (And just as in the ransom note, at first glance, this key sentence appears rather ordinary.)

After the attention getting "the message rings clear" comes the idea of "no birth" (of Christ) leading to "no hope of (eternal) life" and "no hope of ever being with our loved ones." But what does "birth" remind us of? To be born did not Christ or anyone else have to go through a delivery? Birth and delivery are inseparable ideas.

In the Christmas letter Patsy uses "birth" (or birthday) four times, just as she used "delivery" four times in her ransom note. (This is her unmistakable way of linking the note and this letter, telling us that in case we missed the emphasis on "delivery" in the ransom note, she will make it

plainer in this letter by explicitly and repeatedly referring to "birth.")
Christmas is all about the birth of a baby. On Christmas Day the boy
child Christ and his mother Mary are center stage. The father Joseph is
in the background.

Look at the ideas and not the particulars. The idea is that without
the ability to deliver a child or birth a child (in this case Christ) there is
absolutely no hope of life and there will be a permanent separation from
loved ones. Patsy Ramsey is telling us that because of the loss of her
ability to give birth—caused by her cancer—that the conclusion she
had come to in the back of her mind was that she was about to die,
about to be permanently separated from her loved ones. *In short, she is
telling us the secret code in her mind (when she is looking at herself):
"delivery" means "birth" means "life" means "core feminine identity"
means "Christmas."* **And thus "no birth" means "no mother" means
"no Christmases" means "no Patsy Ramsey."**

In the ransom note the word "delivery" was crossed out shortly
after "hence" to convey the devastation caused by Patsy's cancer, which
destroyed not only her ovaries and her feminine identity, but, as she
saw it, was also about to destroy her life. These consistent ideas are like
"mind prints" unique to Patsy Ramsey at this particular moment, ideas
that she continues to dwell on over and over again in the depths of her
mind. As we would expect from the deeper mind which repeats messages in order to be heard, there's much more of the same.

**As the day of the <u>birth</u> of our Lord and Savior approaches, we
thank all across the nation and around the world for your continued
prayers of concern and support. It is those prayers that sustain us.
We ask that as you gather with your families and loved ones this
Christmas, be joyful in the celebration of the <u>birthday</u> of Christ,
knowing that this is truly the reason for the season. We must continue
to celebrate the <u>birth</u> of Christ for our hope of life together ever after.**

Once more Patsy Ramsey's mind goes to the idea of birth to confirm
that this is the big idea on her mind. But there is also another central
idea here—the day is approaching, the time draws near, something her
deeper mind has strongly emphasized by saying it twice. The day of
delivery approaches whereby Patsy Ramsey will come to the end of her
immediate fate—her guilt will be known—but she is not going out
without a show. Repeating herself in characteristic ways, for the second
and third times she used "celebration" (or celebrate) along with an
emphasis on "Joy" to try and overcome her pain and her fear.

I am not in any way downplaying the crucial importance of Patsy's
religious faith. Surely she will need every last ounce of faith and forgiveness that she can find. But a Christian above all must tell the truth,
and Patsy's soul is speaking volumes to us.

She is showing us how she tends to become showy and look for center stage to ease her pain. She continues to seek, as she has from the beginning, the stage of "all across the nation and around the world." It's not we thank "you"—whoever has been involved—but she thanks "all" as if the entire world is revolving around her.

RECEIVING PRAYERS, GATHERING, AND BIRTH

Then she thinks about "prayers" twice in order to comfort herself, repeating her ideas yet once again. "Prayers" in this context must be read deep down as "attention," "being center stage" because surely more people are praying for justice and truth than for Patsy Ramsey's cover-up. This attention that she is receiving, taking in, that sustains her for the moment.

Patsy follows this with the idea of *gathering* families and loved ones together. Receiving and gathering are feminine symbols at moments, and "family," which she uses twice, is closely connected to the same idea of togetherness and nurture.

Just to confirm that femininity—and trying to repair it—is on her mind, she returns to the familiar idea of birth and delivery. "... be joyful in the celebration of the birthday of Christ, knowing this is truly the reason for the season." Once more as she draws our attention to "the reason" she tells us it has everything to do with birth and by implication "delivery." Forget about Christ for just a moment here because deep down Patsy is preoccupied with the idea of birth as the only means of giving her hope.

Yes, if she is a Christian her hope is in Christ and his birth. But she is also fixated on the idea of birth to undo her constant terror of having no hope and of dying because she can't give birth. Repeated images of receiving, gathering, families, and giving birth as well as "life together ever after" all communicate her understandable and intense need to live, to be a woman once more in her mind.

As if to convince us Patsy quickly repeats "birth of Christ (for our hope of life together ever after)" on the other side of "the *reason* for the season." *Here at the second specific place in the letter where we see Patsy Ramsey's deeper mind telling us to pay particular attention, the central idea is once again that birth is necessary for the hope of life.* The first time it was "no birth means no hope." This time it is "birth means hope." Isn't this striking emphasis on birth and femininity—or the lack of it—a perfect fit with exactly the same key ideas we saw in the ransom note?

CHRISTMAS MEANS BIRTH

Of all the words Patsy repeats in this letter, she repeats "Christmas" or "Christ" more than any other. It is the greatest of her obsessions in this letter, and it is inextricably linked with feminine identity. "Birth (or birthday) of Christ" is used four times. Deep down for Patsy Ramsey, Christ and Christmas mean life, birth, an ability to deliver children, hope—that's the code. And when she sees her femininity damaged by cancer it's a canceled Christmas, a tainted one.

We can see why Patsy clings so desperately to the Christmas story. She is also obsessed with the birth of Christ because she must think of birth when she is so preoccupied with death, symbolized by her inability to have children. Someone who can birth a child brings cause for great celebration.

Patsy is talking on two levels: The birth of Christ is truly the reason for the season, but the deeper message explains her pain—the reason for this season of grief that she told us about at the very first part of the letter again has to do with her inability to have children, the code word for her cancer.

To sum it all up, when we see how many ideas pertain to femininity (with "Christ/Christmas" and "birth" particularly standing out), the sheer number is overwhelming. Patsy Ramsey's obsession leaps from the pages of this second letter, just as it did from the ransom note, and she is telling us this to let us (and herself) know why she took JonBenét's life.

DEFICIENCY

Patsy's 1997 Christmas letter contains references to a related idea: deficiency or loss. Having no Christmas (canceling it), missing JonBenét's presence, missing her today, missing her every day that has gone by, no joy, no birth, no hope of life, no hope of being with loved ones, tainted Christmas, Christmases past (gone forever), and tragedy of death—is the same deep sense of damage or loss connected to her femininity that she revealed in her ransom note.

TIME

Notice how many references Patsy makes to time in this Christmas letter. The Christmas season upon us, anniversary, Christmases past, every day, today, canceling Christmas (Day), eternal life, day (of birth) approaches, birthday, ever after, Holiday, and New Year. In the ransom note she said: (want her to) see 1997, between 8 and 10 a.m., and "early" repeated four times.

Cancer patients are acutely sensitive to time. They wonder "How much time is left?"

REPEATED WORDS

Sometimes an overview gives us an additional perspective, and just to look at the repetitive words tells us what is on Patsy's mind. The simple fact that so many words are repeated in the ransom note and this Christmas letter reveals the writer is an obsessive sort of personality which strikingly points to one primary writer for both. The repeated words in the Christmas letter are: "Christmas" or "Christ" eight times, "birth" four times, "approaching" two times, "family" (including "loved ones") three times, "miss" two times, "death" twice, "day" twice, "no" three times, "joy" three times, "celebrate" three times, "hope" three times, "love" or "loved ones" three times, "prayer" three times, "mean" twice, and "John" twice.

The repeated words in the ransom note are "early" four times, "delivery" four times, "your daughter" six times, "she dies" four times (along with "if want her to see 1997," "unharmed," "99% chance killing your daughter," "her remains," "beheaded," and "don't think killing difficult,"), "bills" two times, "I advise" twice, and "John" three times.

JOY AND A DRAMATIC ENDING

"With blessing and prayer for a Joyful Holiday and the Grace of God's ever present love for the New Year, "
John, Patsy, John Andrew, Melinda, and Burke

Joy is inextricably related to celebration. Patsy refers to celebration three times and to joy three times, letting us know just how much it is on her mind as she battles her demons. From the very beginning of the letter, she plainly tells us just how much joy she is missing. "Where is there *joy*?"—the very first time we see the word—conveys the depths of her pain.

But in the second half of the letter, "joy" appears to be a real possibility, characteristically connected to birth once more ("be *joyful* in the celebration of the birthday of Christ...the reason for the season"). The last time is in the very last sentence ("... and prayer for a *Joyful* Holiday and God's Grace ..."). We continue to see Patsy is desperately battling to keep her head above water, desperately resorting to her manic ways.

She ends the letter with a flurry of capital letters (six)—in her typical dramatic fashion just as she ended the ransom note with the last two words ("John" and "Victory") and the alleged terrorist organization (S.B.T.C.) being capitalized along with two exclamation points. (Just like JonBenét's showy name with two capitals and a striking accent.) Isn't this how beauty queens exit the stage? Both the ransom note and this letter were Patsy's stage. No matter how difficult things get, beauty queens keep on smiling.

A New Year

Perhaps Patsy Ramsey's Christian faith, as distorted and manipulative as it is, is the only thing that has kept her from utter madness. We see this repeated in the last sentence as she capitalizes "Joyful Holiday" and "Grace of God's (ever-present love for the New Year)." Patsy Ramsey desperately longs for a "New Year" with capital longings. She cries out secretly for a new start in so many ways. In a strange way I think she will be relieved when the charade is over so she can get on with whatever is left of her life.

Perhaps there is also another meaning for Patsy Ramsey to "the day of the birth of our Lord and Savior approaches." Notice she capitalizes "Lord" and "Savior." She is suggesting that she is still wrestling with God and knows that the day is coming when Christ will really be born in her heart and she must confess—only then will truth be her Lord.

1997 Christmas Message Secretly Matches Ransom Note in the Following Ways:

• Cancer images prevail (death approaching, forever tainted with tragedy of death, no hope of life, no hope of being with loved ones ever again, etc.)

• A significant focus on Patsy's (damaged) femininity—"birth" used 4 times, just as "delivery" used 4 times in the ransom note.

• "Hence" in both letters is a hidden confession connecting them.

• "Hence" meaning "conclusion" used in one key sentence in both to explain motive for murder .

• "Tainted" (Christmas) is very similar to "tampered with" or "marked" in the ransom note—unusual words.

• Continued themes of deficiency/loss and the pressure of time.

• Additionally, Patsy reveals she is getting close to confessing: hearing the music, seeing the light, and the day approaches.

Chapter Twenty
The Cover-up

A s different as John and Patsy outwardly appear, if we look below the surface we find they're very much alike. Nowhere is this more true than in their efforts to cover up their sordid deed. We would expect them to continue to wear the same masks they've worn all along: nice, upstanding, church-going people, people without a shadow side or any deep flaw.

We would expect Patsy to continue her fairy tale, just as she described her experience of winning the Miss West Virginia title as "getting to be Cinderella for a year." We would expect John to portray himself as Cinderella's prince in the night. But we would also anticipate seeing chinks in their armor—as two extremely controlling, determined people who don't miss a trick. People who can hold a pose at every turn or carefully stage losing control of their emotions at exactly the most sympathy-eliciting moment.

They would know when and how to play the martyr role to the hilt, and we would expect them to use it repeatedly: such as telling the police that Patsy is so beside herself she can't possibly be interviewed for days. And when at last she *does* agree to be interviewed, the Ramseys specify that it must be through written questions or in their own home. Patsy and John are calling all the shots, and as a result months go by before they're interviewed.

They ask their friends not to talk to the police. They refuse to take a polygraph, which could have served to immediately eliminate them from suspicion. If they truly were innocent, they could easily have had polygraphs done privately, as O.J. Simpson did, and use them only if they passed. (Perhaps they did.)

MEDIA WARFARE

Instead, with their backgrounds in advertising and marketing, as well as their years of experience selling their own image, they began an all-out public relations campaign. (How ironic that even Patsy Ramsey's initials fit so perfectly with "p.r." And just as ironic John Ramsey's initials fit with "J.R."—the quintessential conniving person.) Think about it: How many people do you know of who've responded to the loss of a child by hiring a public relations firm?

And they didn't stop there. Next they hired a former top ex-FBI profiler (John Douglas) and charmed him into determining that since they don't fit any typical pattern of a murderer, they can't possibly be guilty.

(No mention is made of whether Douglas's objectivity might be at all compromised—*at least unconsciously*—because he's on their payroll.)

And they don't stop there either. They come up with an actual list of "suspects" and are not afraid to cast aspersions wherever they can, no matter who they hurt. Someone in Shreveport, Louisiana, mails an anonymous letter to the Boulder police informing them about Bill McReynolds, the 67-year-old Santa Claus, who was deemed a good target because he had a daughter kidnaped on the day after Christmas—the same day as JonBenét—22 years earlier. Of course the "lead" amounted to nothing.

But *who* went to the trouble to arrange for the letter to be mailed? Since the only people who would benefit by the harassing and investigation of Bill McReynolds were the Ramseys, we'd be very naive indeed not to suspect that they had something to do with it.

And what about Stephen Miles, a nearby neighbor who the Ramseys have allegedly pointed to as the murderer because of a reported history of being a sex offender? The truth appears to be that Miles, a photographer, was once arrested and charged with sexual exploitation of a child—who turned out to be a 17-year-old boy—and the charges were dropped. Miles is gay with no interest in females, and he's weak from a chronic liver condition, Hepatitis B and C, and too sick to work. Additionally, he insists that he was with his mother the night of the murder and pleads with the Ramseys to leave him alone.

How credible is it that a physically ill male homosexual, with no interest in girls and no history of violence, could be a murdering pedophile? Reportedly the Ramseys provided the police with a list of up to fifty people in the area who could be possible murderers—people who had been in their home or people nearby with police records, etc. The Ramseys still control the purse strings and thus the public relations strategy.

At this point John Ramsey is surviving by channeling his energy into a battle with the authorities. Patsy, who doesn't have the same outlets John does—travel and his business interests—is reportedly struggling. And though her determination to see this thing through might be greater than John's, she doesn't have his ability to compartmentalize things and is more emotionally vulnerable.

Patsy does have an extraordinary ability to create her own reality at times, just as she created her inner fantasy world for so many years. Witness her call to the *Larry King Show*, still trying to get all the mileage she could out of sympathy—entitling her to proclaim JonBenét "America's princess" on a par with Princess Diana. And her constant misperception about how the public views her.

If the Ramseys are guilty, they now have become quite vicious—people who will stop at nothing to save their skins. They don't hesitate to crucify another human being, letting him take the rap at their expense. Once the monster in a person is turned loose, it can grow more terrible than anyone ever expected.

John and Patsy Ramsey have become caricatures of their former selves. In the end they've destroyed their own lives and their own reputations.

However crafty and determined the Ramseys are, however many different strategies their money will buy them, one thing is for certain: They will not escape. Patsy Ramsey's deeper mind has told us so, over and over again, in her ransom note—and so has John. In working with the deeper mind for more than twenty-three years, I've never seen it be wrong.

CONCLUSION

The evidence appears strong that the Ramseys murdered their daughter. The evidence from the deeper mind is more than compelling, offering us a look at the psyche of the killer and her partner in crime that in a cohesive way explains the motive and links it to the crucial pressures in Patsy's life—and John's as well.

The killer has to be someone who faces pressures identical to the ones Patsy does and who has an identical emotional investment in JonBenét. The conclusion, from the picture the killer's deeper mind presents, is that only one person could have written this note: a woman who has experienced a life-threatening illness that might come back at any moment. An illness that has challenged the killer's feminine identity to its core.

Our understanding of the mind, and particularly the devious potential of our deeper mind, shows us that the pressure of emotional pain as severe as both Patsy and John Ramsey went through in the last few years can lead to horrendous deeds. We see from the headlines that people murder their own children. Murder their own sister (a recent case). Murder their beautiful ex-wife (O.J.). Set off a bomb and blow up babies and adults in Oklahoma City. Send fatal or crippling mail bombs to people around the country.

PATSY'S NOTE IN REVIEW

And when the particular trauma that could—and did—consume the Ramseys is described in a "story" in the ransom note (see Chapter 6), it offers its own evidence. What could say more about the amazing ability of the right brain than a story about a scanner picking up a microscopic defect in a person, about constantly being monitored with life or death hanging in the balance, about survival percentages given, about being under constant scrutiny? In every detail it represents Patsy's terrifying bout with cancer—cancer she was told was incurable. The "don't make one false move or you'll die" tone of the entire note shouts cancer at us. She feels blackmailed by the cancer.

Add to this the story of an "exhausting delivery," and it fits even more closely. Add to this bodily anxiety such images as a woman who is beheaded, the bodily remains of a deceased woman, someone trying to grow a brain (to make up for a deficiency), repeated references to delivery of a child (which clearly suggests the body, pregnancy, and bodily damage—one of the most overlooked aspects of pregnancy), a daughter whose body is un-harmed.

The references to a potentially damaged body are far more numerous than we would have expected even in a real ransom note. Culminating in the staccato reminder "She dies, she dies, she dies" to make clear that it's a woman's life that is at stake.

Add to this the sentence "You stand a 99% chance of killing your daughter," which is striking on its own and also as an example of the constant tone of desperate control. Add to this Patsy's repeated put-downs of her husband from beginning to end (reflecting envy), contrasted with symbolic feminine references (containers or nests—bank, attaché, brown paper bag) on a downhill slide along with throwing in a negative image like a stray dog, and we have a very clear picture of a woman who feels deficient and is trying to cope.

The killer is trying to paint a picture of her own vulnerability, to explain and justify why the murder took place. All of this certainly coalesces into a picture of Patsy Ramsey. That is what the deeper mind does: It makes all the roads lead to the payoff.

The deeper mind of the killer is so capable that it goes even further and strongly suggests what happened that night—the immediate trigger attached to the main underlying motive. The most blatant point of chaos in the note links a sexual event where JonBenét is treated like a "pick-up" with Patsy's loss of control and JonBenét's death.

REVIEWING PATSY'S 1997 CHRISTMAS LETTER

Patsy writes a second letter that unmistakably links her with the ransom note as the same underlying themes predominate. The explicit preoccupation with "birth" in her 1997 Christmas letter (see Chapter 19) matches perfectly her ransom note's emphasis on "delivery." Also, death images prevail, repeatedly connected to damaged femininity—an inability to give birth.

By obsessively focusing on the "birth of Christ" along with "joy" and "celebration," Patsy attempts to ward off her deep pain. Nonetheless behind her mask lurk the same central motive—the loss of her femininity soon to be followed in her mind by certain death. Once more she tells us that she had inflicted this insurmountable despair on JonBenét to momentarily escape her terror.

JOHN'S LETTER: DOVETAILING

If we put John Ramsey's letter (see Chapter 12) next to the ransom note (see Chapter 2 through 8) particularly, we see that they dovetail. In her ransom note Patsy hints that John's sexual misconduct with JonBenét played a big part in their daughter's death.

John's letter itself offers impressive collaboration: Quickly linking himself to his wife and to JonBenét's death ("we had a loss," suggesting "we" did it), then hammering away at someone over a false portrayal—an idea from his mind. Then revealing his hypersensitivity to the subject of sexual indiscretions with his daughter when he should have been more vulnerable to being called a murderer (which many people were) strongly suggests guilt.

Most of all we see John's deeper mind operate in characteristic ways just like Patsy's. He repeats ideas to make sure we know a cover-up is going on—"portrayal," "normal," along with more direct references ("small part" of JonBenét and "much more to her") and finally mentioning the "beach," which washes away everything. He gives us one of those key markers "school" to indicate a key message. Then he provides the subtle sexual imagery and describes the dynamics of JonBenét's competition with her mother.

The pattern in John's letter of referring to JonBenét as a thing, an object, and describing her in such impersonal terms along with connecting her to beauty pageants and the beach reveals what kind of object she was for him—a sexual object. He is preoccupied also with someone harming a "young" person, hinting at the magic buzz word of sex offenders ("young"). John Ramsey implies the same thing Patsy did in her ransom note—that she lost control that night when she found herself replaced by a competitive JonBenét.

In the end John reminds us that someone hasn't taken responsibility for their actions, and he hints also that this person is not communicating about their hurtful deed. Finally he reminds us that he and Patsy would never likely find joy again, suggesting just how guilt ridden they are.

When we look at the major ideas on John's mind and the sequence his mind arranges them, he strongly suggests that his letter is meant to be a confession letter, elaborating on his wife's note and more clearly defining his participation. His letter also serves as a reminder that there is another confession note out there (Patsy's), and that his is the matching bookend.

PATSY'S 1995 AND 1996 CHRISTMAS LETTERS

If we look closely we can see the tension building in Patsy Ramsey. In 1995 we see an extremely manic Christmas letter (see Chapter 14) designed to ward off her tremendous vulnerability coming from three sources: her health, her children growing up, and the Ramseys' financial success. But she moves so fast—her code word is "busy"—and so dramatically (seventeen exclamation points) that Patsy indicates she wants us to overlook her stress like she does. As she tells us, her god is "energy"—because energy is the opposite of death, which haunts her. She also shows us how being busy is crucial to her feminine identity as "Supermom."

But in Patsy's 1996 Christmas letter (see Chapter 15), we see a distinct change: Her energy level is down (to only nine exclamation points), and the overall manic tone is significantly less. Still having to read between the lines, her empty nest syndrome is coming into focus much more clearly. Burke is losing all his baby teeth, and JonBenét is now in "real school." You can feel the growing pressure that it won't be long before they're all gone—as says at the beginning of the letter, John's two older children who are either off at school or graduating.

Additionally, Patsy is turning forty. To her already overburdened mind, she sees it as an official kiss of death.

Eerily Patsy seems to foresee the future—and tells us one last reason why. She has apparently picked up on John's involvement with JonBenét—John's real love is a new "old looking boat" (young JonBenét) in place of his old boat, *Miss America* (Patsy). At a phenomenally vulnerable time Patsy predicts her "outrage" and "birthday bash" where she ends the life of JonBenét. As a result she sees national magazines and television in the forecast—another momentary compensation for her damaged psyche.

John Ramsey's Profile of the Killers

Unknowingly John Ramsey accurately profiles his wife as one killer when, as a public-relations ploy, he releases a psychological profile of the killer (see Chapter 18). At the same time he provides an invaluable clue as to his part in the death of JonBenét. In the awkward phraseology *"prevented from **stopping** the life of another,"* he strongly suggests that *he was the one who had to stop JonBenét from breathing*—as she lay unconscious from her head injury inflicted by Patsy.

Other Confirmation

Besides the ransom note, the two revealing Christmas letters and John's profile of the killing, there are spontaneous communications from Patsy and John. All the stories from Patsy's right brain: her major tip-off that two people were involved, her idea that the killer could be a woman as well as a man, impulsively on *Larry King Live* connecting JonBenét's murder to the guilt someone should be confronted with over causing the death of a beautiful young princess (Diana), likewise being so guilt ridden that she fears that her cancer will return, her stories about loving JonBenét too much, her stories connected directly to JonBenét about things being upside down and holding that pose for an incredible length of time, clues that the key to catching the murderer lies in discovering the secret profile of the killer.

In addition we have John Ramsey's magnificent slip on national television ("JonBen-I") and his providing the police with the practice ransom note. And we have the incredible behavior of the two, constantly communicating through actions that they have a ton to hide. An employee of John Ramsey's observed that privately he would rage about the injustice of the media and police incompetence, *but he never commented on the killer.*

Lastly the evidence taken as a whole leads strongly to the conclusion that John Ramsey was sexually abusing his daughter. The evidence at the crime scene with two different vaginal injury findings at autopsy, the highly sexualized JonBenét, Patsy Ramsey's major slip in the ransom note ("pick-up") to go with John's major slip, John's hypersensitivity to accusations, his major clues in his public letter to the artist (see Chapter 12) and his public profile (see Chapter 18), his participation in the cover-up, his bizarre childlike behavior right before the murder, and JonBenét referring to her father as a "guy."

There's one last subtle clue: If you look at the Ramsey family picture taken at Christmas 1993 (see following page), you see John sitting behind a standing JonBenét. He is in the background far more than anyone in the picture, and he and JonBenét are clearly merged, far more so than Patsy and Burke (who is standing next to his mother on her other side and who is the tallest person in the picture). John appears as just a face between Patsy (also seated but more toward the front and taller than he is) and JonBenét. He is the only person whose shoulders and virtually entire body is hidden with JonBenét standing between his legs, which seem to disappear.

We could certainly read this as John is on the same level with JonBenét and that Patsy has pushed him into the background. It also suggests that in the background a special secret merging is going on between John and JonBenét. *But most striking of all is where John's hands are.* His right hand is around JonBenét's waist ever so slightly too low, and covering her entire midsection. But his left hand is over the front of her left thigh, slightly too high up, and if you look closely his left index and middle fingers angle in right over her clothed vaginal area. There is little distance between his two hands, and together they frame JonBenét's pubic area.

The picture points to something secret going on between the two of them as Patsy sits in front of them, oblivious to what is going on behind her back. The whole thing is, of course, quite subtle and possibly innocent. However, *in light of all that has gone on, this is a very significant picture—*

in many ways a prophecy. And we do know that family pictures often tell a powerful story.

Her name, JonBenét, also must have created a special bond between father and daughter, a sense that they were especially close. When the season of trouble with Patsy's diagnosis of cancer came, perhaps this encouraged John to reach out in the wrong direction for comfort, which is exactly what is behind sexual abuse.

Christmas 1993 (Zuma)

A FINAL NOTE

Both John and Patsy Ramsey have had devastating traumas and suffered incredible emotional pain. They've both seen death up close and are terrified by it. **Both of them have had more than enough overwhelming emotional pain from death and dying to inflict that same pain on another human being—even their own daughter.**

There are many hidden but powerful emotional reasons JonBenét would have been the perfect target for them—and for them alone. We arrive at this conclusion based on what we now know of the mind and of human nature: appreciating the hidden power of death experiences and the astounding levels of pain we can carry around inside while still wearing a smile on our faces.

When all is said and done, there's one clear and compelling answer to the question on all our minds, "How could something like this happen?" The answer is: "How could it not?" Anybody under the right tidal wave of circumstances can break, particularly if there are major, hidden defects in their character. For Patsy and John Ramsey that tidal wave came at a time they least expected it, but also at a time when they were the most vulnerable. Consciously, they had no idea that they were both time bombs waiting to go off, no idea that there was a lot about themselves that they had never admitted to before December 26, 1996. What you don't know about yourself can hurt you and everybody you love.

PATSY'S AND JOHN'S COMMUNICATIONS SECRETLY REVEAL:

- **All of Patsy's communications match ransom note.**

- **John's and Patsy's communications verify the same story.**

- **John and Patsy are constantly confessing.**

Chapter Twenty-One
The Experts

Comparison fuels growth and insight, and studying the various profiles that have been offered will enable us to see *the invaluable contribution of the profile from the killer's own mind.*

THE CRIMINOLOGISTS

Criminologist Dr. Jack Levin of Northeastern University noted that the crime was most likely committed by a woman who is a family member close to JonBenét. Most murderers are men, but when a daughter is victim, the killer is more often the mother than the father— men tend to murder the whole family. *Levin finds that a woman who kills is most often depressed and may have a medical illness as well. Additionally, in mother-daughter murders there is a good deal of sexual hostility in the mother, and she is highly competitive with the daughter.*

Although Levin has no particular skill in decoding communication, it is fascinating to see how close his general profile is to the one the killer's own deeper intelligence offers in her ransom note. Certainly the note offers a much more specific profile. The ransom note reveals Patsy Ramsey is depressed from her medical illness, highly competitive, and filled with sexual hostility. She is angry over being a woman and angry at men, in general, and one in particular. Additional information about Patsy Ramsey has confirmed this same picture.

Former profiler John Douglas took issue with this profile because he looked at the clues superficially. Unquestionably violating his own standards, Douglas came to the striking conclusion that this was a revenge crime by someone who was acquainted with John Ramsey in business and knew a great deal about him.

But Douglas failed to look below the surface and completely bought into the ransom note strategy that someone outside the Ramseys was angry at John. Douglas surmised that the angry party was a disgruntled employee and not a terrorist. After spending time with the Ramseys, Douglas came away convinced of their innocence, which only shows that a profiler can be greatly misled unless they have a good working knowledge of the deeper mind.

In his profiling Douglas neglected several basic principles. He failed to separate the Ramseys to see if he could find discrepancies in their stories, and he misinterpreted several messages from the killer.

Revenge killings are meant to shock. The killer would have blatantly left the body out to cause John Ramsey as much pain as he could in as cruel a way as possible. Additionally, killing a child to get back at a father is extremely rare. The most egregious error Douglas made was to fall victim to the Ramseys' charm by buying into their conscious words.

This tells us at least two things: Indeed the Ramseys are charming (Douglas felt their grief was genuine and they are "tremendous liars" if guilty), and that something else was going on to affect Douglas's judgment. Many might think it was being on the Ramseys' payroll. Certainly the second he began working for them his judgment would have been somewhat colored, but I think the major culprit here was Douglas's own success and fame.

He was on the verge of a major book tour promoting his then soon-to-be released fourth book, *Journey Into Darkness*. In short, he was in the midst of significant success and success colors judgment, as we have already seen with John and Patsy Ramsey. All too often after people succeed they have an inordinate need to bring themselves down a notch. Here we can see Douglas undoing a lot of his previous work in building his reputation.

Recently Douglas partially recanted his original comments. He acknowledged that he had not really interviewed Patsy, that John did virtually all of the talking. As of last report, Douglas is not ruling out Patsy, even suggesting that someone who knew the child well committed the murder. But he continues to be fooled by John, insisting that he finds no evidence in him of the tremendous anger expressed in the use of the garrote.

Here Douglas again reveals his limitations. Despite his remarkable sensitivity in being able to "crawl into the skin" of a serial killer, his training is not in psychology and he fails to understand the varied forms of anger—continuing to buy into John's consciously convincing sales job. John has shown many subtle forms of anger including extramarital affairs, excessive control, domination, and a hidden dark side and split in his personality. Like Patsy, John has suffered extraordinary pain in recent years and has powerful reasons to be furious—something he had never expressed directly, again remarkably like his wife.

Robert Ressler, another former FBI profiler, strongly disagreed with Douglas's conclusions and felt that the ransom note, the garrote, and the rope were staged to cover up an accidental murder by somebody who knew JonBenét well. Ressler believed that the staging of the note was the best evidence in the case *and thought that analyzing "psycholinguistic" tendencies would strongly suggest the probable killers*. We see how close Ressler really was and how well his instincts served him: The note provides invaluable clues.

However, both Douglas and Ressler were restricted because they had no opportunity to examine the crime scene. Douglas did have a chance to talk with the principal witnesses, Patsy and John, but simply had to go on his impression of them and admittedly didn't have enough information to make a psychological profile of the killer. The best both of these profilers could do was guess, and with their primary investigation tool (the crime scene) taken from them, their opinions lacked their usual clout and made it more difficult than usual to resolve differences.

Still, Ressler's thinking was clearer, and he pointed us back toward the note as our most valuable evidence. He did us a giant service when he made plain that *under circumstances where the evidence has been tainted, the ransom note assumes tremendous importance.* Ressler didn't know anything about the breakthrough in psychiatry that takes psycholinguistics to an entirely different level, but his own deeper intelligence, honed by experience, knew that the key was in the note.

Another former FBI agent, Alan Hunt, was impressed that the Ramseys had hired a public-relations firm. It was so strikingly unusual that it strongly suggested guilt to him.

MORE ON THE FBI

Newsweek elicited the input of two former FBI experts. First was handwriting analyst Gerald Richards, former head of the FBI's Document Operations/Research Unit. The second was Clinton Van Zandt, who previously had worked at the FBI Behavioral Sciences Unit.

Richards mostly commented on the specifics of the handwriting itself and how it revealed efforts at a cover-up. He occasionally made general observations such as how "attaché" reflected an educated writer with a business background or about the length of the note being unusual.

Van Zandt made some helpful observations about the writer sounding soft and feminine and about seeing no linguistic evidence to point to a foreign entity. He thought the expression "If we catch you talking to a stray dog, she dies" sounded contrived and possibly borrowed from a Clint Eastwood movie. But he overlooked the fact that the use of the expression "stray dog" was very revealing and fit a disguised pattern in the note—whether it was contrived or not. I have not seen Van Zandt's entire analysis, but from what I have seen it is strikingly apparent that he could benefit from understanding the latest developments regarding in-depth decoding of verbatim communication.

THE CORONER

Coroner Cyril Wecht concluded that a "sex game gone wrong" was the primary cause of death, and he viewed John Ramsey as the killer. Certainly Wecht has had a lot of experience but never a case quite like this one—as Ressler noted, "it is highly, highly unusual." And while there was evidence of sexual abuse, all the other factors point toward a rage killing.

THE PROFESSOR

Dr. Donald W. Foster, a professor of dramatic literature at Vassar College, has developed an attributional method for profiling letters of criminals. This follows his work in literature where he has looked at stylistic mannerisms to determine the real author of older writings. In one case he determined that Shakespeare wrote a funeral elegy that other scholars had overlooked. As a result Foster was able to accurately predict the author of the anonymous *Primary Colors*. Because of his expertise, the FBI has involved Foster in teaching agents his techniques for unmasking authors. He has volunteered his efforts in the Unabomber case and now in the Ramsey case.

Recently part of his analysis of the ransom note was revealed in *The New York Times*. While he makes some helpful suggestions about themes in the note, he overlooks most of the hidden clues. For example, his comment on the revealing misspelling "bussiness" is that it was "probably deliberate." Again in fairness, I have not seen Foster's complete analysis, but what I have seen reveals clearly that he is not trained in listening to the deeper intelligence. Nonetheless he made some excellent observations, pointed us in the right direction, and his work is to be applauded.

THE BIBLE EXPERT

Another interesting viewpoint came from Dale Yeager, the president of a small organization that studies religious crime (Seraph Consulting and Training in Berwyn, Pennsylvania), who declared that Patsy Ramsey killed her daughter in a deranged pseudo-spiritual state. He based his conclusions on the fact that when the police arrived the Ramsey family Bible was open to the 118th Psalm—Patsy's favorite— and this seemed to link to the crime and the ransom note with its request for $118,000. Yeager focused on one particular verse (118:27), "God is the Lord, which hath showed us light; bind the sacrifice with cords, even unto the horns of the altar." Having been told of two cases where mothers killed their children and wrote 'Psalm 118' in blood on the wall, Yeager felt that all of this was enough evidence to point to Patsy killing JonBenét in a bizarre sacrifice.

While I have already suggested that JonBenét was a sacrifice in many ways for both Patsy and John Ramsey, there is simply not enough evidence here to make Yeager's case. He appears to be guessing and really has taken only one idea specifically from the note—the number 118.

If Patsy Ramsey did consciously view JonBenét as a sacrifice and incorporate the 118th Psalm in some bizarre way into the ransom note, it was following an unplanned assault along the lines I have suggested (see Chapter 8). However, Yeager could possibly be closer to the truth if he took into account the potential Patsy Ramsey had for "unconscious planning"—concocting a plan in the back of her mind.

THE PSYCHIATRISTS AND PSYCHOLOGISTS

Dr. Jamie Turndorf, a New York psychologist, observed a recent interview with Patsy on Geraldo's show and noted her inappropriately happy state in light of her trauma. While there was clearly evidence of some denial, the investigator on the scene, Jennifer Kay, insisted that Patsy at other moments did reveal grief.

More importantly Turndorf made the mistake of listening to Patsy only on a conscious level and missed the crucial messages from her deeper mind. For example, he reportedly labeled Patsy as near psychotic—when she simply told the story of JonBenét asking her how much Patsy loved her, and then correcting her for loving her too much (more than Jesus), and now being in heaven with Jesus. There is nothing whatsoever psychotic about this story—it's a secret confession from Patsy Ramsey about a central problem in her relationship with JonBenét: She was overly attached to JonBenét.

Yet another psychologist, Dr. Sheenah Hankin, made the same error. As an expert witness for the defense in a mock trial of the Ramseys on Geraldo's show, Hankin testified how normal Patsy and John are as parents. She accepted at face value the description of the Ramseys from their friends, insisting along with many others that they were nice people who couldn't have done it.

Hankin made virtually no comment about the deeper mind except briefly in passing and "accidently." At one point she did comment on the possibility that Patsy may have loved JonBenét too much, but she brushed off the idea as soon as she mentioned it. Hankin's deeper intelligence was picking up on a central problem, but she didn't slow down long enough to hear it.

Earlier Hankin had commented on John Ramsey possibly fitting the profile of a child molester, but she denied there was any connection between child molestation and murder.

Another psychologist on Geraldo's show, Dr. Ann Viviano, commented on her personal reaction to Patsy and John Ramsey's television interview—she felt they were lying. She was also struck by the coincidences in the note regarding the alleged killers having such personal information about John Ramsey.

Others have made efforts to look below the surface. Counselor Carolyn Bushong was struck by John Ramsey's excessive need to present himself in such an ideal fashion, which suggested to her that he was hiding a dirty secret. Bushong also elicited some interesting information from a friend of Patsy Ramsey about Patsy's defective self-image following her cancer.

Psychiatrist Carole Lieberman commented on some of the deeper issues in Patsy's relationship with JonBenét that was strongly suggested both from involving JonBenét in beauty pageants and from the eerie photographs showing JonBenét in the same showgirl outfit her mother wore as a seductive nineteen-year-old. Lieberman noted how Patsy could have pushed JonBenét to win competitions and yet have envied her at the same time.

On another occasion Turndorf commented on the subconscious dimension to JonBenét's relationship with her mother, suggesting Patsy was reenacting a childhood sexual trauma on JonBenét—and living through her daughter.

Patsy's Profile of the Killer: From Her Deeper Mind

All of these various viewpoints offer some insights, but contrast them with hearing the deeper story and seeing the deeper profile from Patsy's own mind. Compare all of these analysts' comments to Patsy's right brain, which tells us about three distinct motives, about the scanner and her abject terror, about her self-perception of being a damaged woman, about a premature execution (a beheading), about her envy of John and her blackmailing him, about how they will be caught, about being so overcome with guilt over causing JonBenét's death that she has to publicly call Larry King, about the hole in her heart when it came to loving JonBenét, about being overly attached to JonBenét and JonBenét trying to correct her, about turning the investigation upside down and holding a pose, and about the Halloween monster of death and deceit lurking behind her Miss America mask.

It's apparent that no one is commenting on the specific messages from Patsy Ramsey's deeper mind—they are overlooking the recent breakthrough in psychiatry. But once we start decoding the messages from Patsy's deeper mind, we find the most incredible profile of the killer. This confirms ex-FBI profiler Robert Ressler's hunch that the ransom note is the single most valuable clue the police have to solving the murder.

Using Psycholinguistics to Profile the Killer

Experienced profiler John Douglas was criticized for overlooking the cardinal principle that behavior speaks louder than words. He ignored the Ramseys' behavior and bought into their words.

By applying the breakthrough to subliminal perception and communication to profiling suspects, we can add a new principle: **"There** are words, and there are words." *The superficial message contains the deeper message. If the killer talks, the killer can't hide.* Even concocting a simple ransom note is revealing, but if the killer goes on in the note beyond the barest minimum, there will be hidden revelations galore from the deeper mind.

In the JonBenét ransom note, the very moment the Ramseys conceived the most deceptive note they could imagine, simultaneously they revealed their identity. **The appreciation of this new paradigm will come down to one issue: The human mind constantly perceives and communicates on a deeper level of awareness (in ways far superior to our conscious mind).** If we're not looking for the hidden messages—or don't know how to—we will not see them.

By comparing the ransom note with Patsy's three Christmas letters and examining two written communications from John Ramsey—along with public comments from both—we have learned a phenomenal amount about how the deeper mind functions in a criminal matter. We have seen Patsy's and John's deeper intelligence manifest themselves in similar ways: repetitive messages, key linkages, verbal markers, an unbelievably strong need to confess, and even predicting the future.

The Ramsey case makes it plain that there is a valuable new tool for profiling killers utilizing verbatim communication when it is available. This breakthrough also offers exciting potential for the interrogation of criminals everywhere.

We have seen Patsy's own mind secretly point to her in her ransom note. We have learned that one of the greatest allies we have in solving the JonBenét case is the deeper mind of the killer—Patsy Ramsey.

Summary

- Former F.B.I. profiler Robert Ressler states that psycholinguistics—decoding the ransom note—is one of the major keys to the case.

- The breakthrough to the deeper intelligence—subliminal perception and communication—represents a paradigm shift in psycholinguistics and profiling. Criminals now profile themselves.

- Criminals can now be interrogated in new ways.

- To solve the JonBenét murder, we must listen to the deeper mind of the killer revealed in the ransom note.

Afterword

In working on this project, I have met many helpful people including several reporters who are quite knowledgeable about the case and who generously shared their insights. I have been exposed to a multitude of different opinions. One thing stands out clearly: Everyone who has an opinion is emotionally invested in his or her opinion. I am certain I am no different with one exception—I have tried to listen to the specific messages from the killer's deeper mind.

In first learning how to listen to the deeper mind, I was most impressed with its ability to predict the future. But to hear the deeper intelligence, I had to give up my biases about what I thought and listen in a new and deeper way—*basically submit to a more perceptive mind.* This is one of the things I think it will take to solve the murder of JonBenét Ramsey—we must all submit to the deeper mind of the killer.

In that light, taking disguised communications in the ransom note, the other Ramsey communications, and the crime scene as a whole I believe something like the following scenario will occur if the authorities know how to pressure Patsy Ramsey (if they don't it's still possible Patsy will confess later—perhaps only if her cancer reoccurs): Patsy Ramsey will emerge as the primary killer and eventually tell us that the head injury came first. She will tell us that she lost control the last night of JonBenét's life in a rage killing caused by finding John Ramsey sexually abusing JonBenét. She will claim the killing was accidental and that she was really angry with John. She will not be able to tell us directly that her fear of cancer was her deepest motive, but she will elaborate that she had been more stressed by her cancer than she admitted (and already has to a degree).

Patsy Ramsey will confess soon and is close to breaking. She will tell us that her Christian faith had a lot to do with her confession—that she wants to see JonBenét and wants to go to heaven. Her faith will keep her from committing suicide.

John Ramsey will continue to try to cover-up his part in the crime and present a ruthless denial. If he ever confesses, he will have only the slightest awareness that he was under stress prior to the murder. Patsy and John Ramsey will most likely divorce, and will not stand by each other during the confession stage.

Praise for "A Mother Gone Bad"

"This is a story of jealousy, envy, terror, revenge, love and hate. The participants try to cover an event that is the stuff of classic drama, and of our own unthinkable unconscious minds. Provocative, original, richly detailed, and hard to refute. Dr. Hodges argument is compelling."
—*James O. Raney, M.D., Clinical Associate Professor in Psychiatry, University of Washington School of Medicine, Seattle*

"Step by tantalizing step, Hodges leads us into the subliminal mind of the ransom note's author, exposing a graphic picture of the killer's identity, the killer's motivation, and the manner in which the crime was most likely committed."
—*Parham H. Williams, Jr., Dean of the School of Law, Chapman University, Anaheim, California*

"A great read, not only for those who love a good mystery, but for those who love the workings of the human mind. The breakthrough to the deeper intelligence is like the discovery of DNA."
—*Irving Weisberg, Ph.D., psychologist and faculty member Adelphi University*

"Dr. Hodges demonstrates Freud's wisdom that we cannot keep secrets, our unconscious mind speaks volumes."
—*Marc Kessler, Ph.D., Associate Professor of Psychology, University of Vermont*

"A remarkable application of a new psychological technique to the decoding of the JonBenet Ramsey ransom case."
—*Marc Lubin, Ph.D., Illinois Graduate School of Psychology, Chicago*

"A delightful validation of cutting edge awareness in hidden communication. A book for the mystery reader and therapist alike."
—*Duncan J.J. Magoon, M.D., Clinical Instructor in Psychiatry, Wayne State University Medical School, Detroit*